R, Geyer

BEYOND THE CROSS TIMBERS

The Travels of Randolph B. Marcy, 1812–1887

BEYOND THE CROSS TIMBERS

The Travels of Randolph B. Marcy, 1812–1887

By W. EUGENE HOLLON

UNIVERSITY OF OKLAHOMA PRESS

NORMAN

By W. Eugene Hollon

Beyond the Cross Timbers: The Travels of Randolph B. Marcy, 1812–1887 (Norman, 1955)

The Lost Pathfinder: Zebulon Montgomery Pike (Norman, 1949)

Library of Congress Catalog Card Number: 55-6357

Copyright 1955 by the University of Oklahoma Press, Publishing Division of the University. Composed and printed at Norman, Oklahoma, U.S.A., by the University of Oklahoma Press. First edition.

To my MOTHER *and* DAD
and my friend and colleague
the late Horace C. Peterson

Preface

IN 1806, Zebulon Montgomery Pike set out to trace the Red River from its source to its mouth, but he didn't even find the river. Fourteen years later Major Stephen H. Long led another expedition over most of the same region, but discovered that he had mistaken the Canadian for the Red. Surprisingly, the Red River, one of the largest rivers in the Southwest, was not traced and accurately mapped until 1852, by Captain Randolph B. Marcy, an American army officer—although his surveyor, young Captain George B. McClellan, fixed the 100th meridian fifty miles too far east, thus contributing to the prolonged dispute between the United States and Texas concerning the boundary between Indian Territory (now Oklahoma) and Texas.

Despite his achievement in the Red River expedition and four subsequent expeditions which accomplished many worthwhile results for the United States, Marcy has not attained the fame of a Pike or Long. Acclaimed in his own time when his journals and his books were published, he has too long languished in obscurity.

I have tried in this book to bring Marcy into his own again—to show why he was one of the important soldier-explorers of the nineteenth century and to place him in his proper relation to others of this era. In doing so, I have purposely condensed the account of his Civil War services.

Lewis and Clark, Pike, Long, and Frémont are all better known, but none traveled more extensively than Marcy, who was not only an explorer, but a map maker, geographer, trail blazer, authority on the Indians, and prolific writer as well. He and his kind of work passed with the frontier, but our heritage, particularly in the Southwest, is immensely richer for his having lived.

In the spring of 1950, the American Philosophical Society advanced me a generous grant-in-aid to make a study of Marcy's life and travels. I have lived with him ever since. Several months of research in the National Archives and the Library of Congress provided me an almost overwhelming load of materials. Thousands of personal letters and official documents written by, to, or about Marcy were found. Months of copying, sorting, studying, eliminating, digesting, and reading followed, and soon a full year had passed. By that time I felt I could piece together Marcy's varied activities into a biographical account with a minimum of blank chapters. One who spent fifty years in the army, as Marcy did, is difficult to lose long at a time.

Another year rolled around before the first draft of the manuscript was finished, and a fourth has now gone, but the last finishing touches have been applied. During these past four years I have been so close to the Marcy family as to feel that I literally belong to them—or perhaps they to me. One cannot read thousands of intimate family letters and official documents without learning his subject's inmost secrets; in time the characters take on a personal relationship to the author and their problems become his own.

Although Marcy sometimes appears a bit stuffy, particularly when he writes to his older daughter on the importance of choosing a husband of wealth and social position, I cannot but imagine that in some ways we are very much alike, for I have always felt myself a frustrated explorer who, had I lived a century ago, would have pushed back new frontiers and opened wilderness roads in the manner of the men chosen for my heroes.

W. EUGENE HOLLON

Norman, Oklahoma
January 10, 1955

Acknowledgments

ANYONE who writes a book knows that it is virtually impossible to accomplish the task alone. There are many to whom I am indebted: First, there is my wife, who bore with me in my travels and researches; and there are the many helpful friends who have read this work but who are not responsible for it. Then, there are those who suggested leads, assisted in locating materials, or entrusted me with personal documents.

The manuscript was read in its rough state by Professor Foster Harris of the University of Oklahoma Journalism School, Professor William R. Hogan, Tulane University, and Professor Albert Parker, University of Wichita. Their many suggestions were given careful consideration and in almost every case improved the readability and scholarship of the manuscript. Others who read individual chapters were Mrs. Florence Peckham, LeRoy Olson, Professor Donnell M. Owings, and Professor E. E. Dale.

I am especially indebted to Mr. Arthur G. Nichols, attorney for the George B. McClellan estate, Washington, D. C., for his co-operation and assistance in allowing me to search for Marcy materials in the McClellan home. Accordingly, a number of photographs and letters were borrowed from the McClellan private library. Also, General Marcy's only living granddaughter, Mrs. M. J. Kernan, Clinton, New York, was most generous in entrusting many Marcy family letters and the General's own scrapbook to me for unrestricted use. The latter item was practically indispensable.

Among others to whom I owe thanks are the following: Elizabeth Drewry, Richard G. Wood, and Mrs. Sarah Dunlap Jackson,

War Records Division, National Archives; Mr. Herman Friis, assistant chief, Cartographic Branch, National Archives; the staffs in the Manuscripts and Newspaper Divisions, Library of Congress; LeRoy Hafen, Colorado Historical Society, H. Bailey Carroll, Texas Historical Society, Robert Dott, formerly director of the Oklahoma Geological Survey, and C. C. Rister, my former colleague at the University of Oklahoma. The Department of History, University of Oklahoma, absorbed part of my teaching load during 1951, in order that I could devote more time to the research project. My thanks go to Miss Meredith Jeary, who typed the preliminary draft of the manuscript, and to Mrs. Horace C. Peterson, who typed the final draft. David Carlson assisted in the preparation of the index. The author assumes full responsibility for all errors found herein.

Contents

Illustrations

BEYOND THE CROSS TIMBERS

The Travels of Randolph B. Marcy, 1812–1887

I

"My Son . . . thinks he shall be pleased with a military life"

1812–1833

It was a bitter cold day in January, 1828, as Leban Marcy sat in his law office in Greenwich, Massachusetts, his quill pen poised over a clean sheet of writing paper. He was a man who always made decisions for his family, but not without careful consideration. For several weeks he had pondered the question of his eldest son's education and subsequent career, and at last his mind was made up. "My son is about sixteen years of age with promising talents," he wrote to the Secretary of War, James Barbour. "He thinks he shall be pleased with a military life."[1]

Lawyer Marcy may have been a reflective man, but it would have been a prophet indeed who could have predicted that the son referred to, Randolph Barnes Marcy, would devote his next fifty-three years to the United States Army. And they were to be fruitful years. Every schoolboy knows the names of Lee, Grant, McClellan, Johnston, Hill, Sherman, and Jackson—officers nurtured in the first half of the nineteenth century and some of the best fighting men America has produced—but it must be remembered that there were other soldiers who also rendered valiant service to their country, although their fame does not rest upon deeds performed on the field of battle. Randolph Barnes Marcy was such a soldier.

[1] The original letter (dated January 25, 1828) is found in the Records of the Adjutant General's Office, National Archives, Washington, D. C. (hereafter cited as A. G. O.), Letters Received, File No. 72.

The Republic was on the move in 1828. It had passed its adolescent stage. Optimism was rampant, and the possibilities of the West had caught the imagination of men. The original thirteen states had grown to twenty-two, and the increase in land area was more than fivefold. The garrison army of six or seven hundred troops of 1800 could no longer protect the boundless frontier of 1828. Indeed, few countries in the world possessed a greater uninhabited area, and a large military force was needed now to man the dozens of military posts, escort the never ending flow of emigrants, subdue the Indians, protect the land surveyors, and cut new roads through the wilderness.

The task of the army was clear, and Marcy's career personifies in experience, spirit, and unswerving devotion to duty the professional soldier of the nineteenth century when the army consisted of a few dozen frontier battalions. Long years of separation from his family, frequent marches across uncharted wilderness, exposure to uncontrollable elements of nature, starvation diets, and brackish water were then a regular part of the soldier's existence. Too frequently he was rewarded by failure to receive promotion and adequate pay. To men like him we owe a debt of gratitude, for it was he and his kind who helped push back the frontier and keep alive our military tradition.

There was also little that Marcy could draw from his youth to prepare him for his future career. Greenwich in 1828 was a typical Massachusetts village which adhered to the traditions of the past. There were "old-timers" still living who could recall forty-two years before when fifty determined Greenwich citizens marched to near-by Springfield to participate in the ill-fated Shays' Rebellion. But to the average Greenwich boy the boldly marked sky line on the ridges of hills that shut in the valley under its blue roof was the boundary of the known world. Strangers must have looked upon the little village with compassion, but young Randolph knew no other. There was school for six months in the year at the old Masonic Hall and sermons twice every Sunday—"Sahbaday" in the vernacular—at the dingy sulphur-colored meeting house.

The hill that rose south of the village was covered with great oaks and chestnuts which had sheltered Indian hunters. The red men called the hill Great Quabbin, and the name belonged to

4

the district as well. To the north rose a lesser hill, Ram Mountain, a somewhat irregular but beautiful cone of granite, jagged here and there with projecting edges of rock and thinly covered with soil. To the east was a third hill, Little Quabbin, but it was too far away to have much part in the landscape. However, it did its best to delay the morning sun. The hills, standing at different angles, shut in the village which nestled under shade trees along the banks of the twisting Swift River.

Greenwich needed only to have been celebrated in song and made famous in story. It did not become famous. Today it rests at the bottom of the Great Quabbin water reservoir, with nothing to remind the world of its once placid existence except the three hills that formerly stood guard over it.

The Marcy family did not come to Greenwich until 1810, but it was descended from the soundest sort of American stock and goes back into Old World history. The name "Marcy" or "De Marcy" is of French origin, apparently having come into Normandy with Rollo (A.D. 912) and thence to England with William the Conqueror (1066), where it attained its present common usage. Mention is made of one "Radus de Marcy" in the patents of King John in 1208.[2]

The date of the first Marcy's arrival in America is unknown, but the records of Elliot's Church in Roxbury, Massachusetts, show that one John Marcy took the covenant on March 7, 1685. Apparently he was the first, since his father was high sheriff of Limerick, Ireland, and did not emigrate to America. Other scattered references to John Marcy have been preserved and show that in 1686 he and thirteen other settlers took possession of Quatosett, now Woodstock, Connecticut. Some time later John married Sarah Hadlock, and the Marcy family, besides being among the original settlers of Woodstock, became prominent landholders and public officials.

John Marcy died on December 23, 1724, at the age of sixty-two, but Sarah lived for another nineteen years. Both died in Woodstock, but they left a brood of eleven children.[3] Their great-

[2] Oliver Marcy, *Records of the Marcy Family* (Evanston, Illinois, 1875).
[3] Among the better-known descendants of John and Sarah, in addition to General Randolph B. Marcy, are William Learned Marcy and Dr. Erastus E. Marcy. William Learned Marcy was a cousin to Randolph Barnes Marcy. He had a long and distinguished political career; among other offices he held

5

great-grandson was Leban Marcy, Randolph's father, who was born at Woodstock on March 7, 1780.

Leban attended Woodstock Academy and later decided to study law, whereupon he moved to Tolland, Connecticut, and read with one Judge Barnes, a prominent jurist of that area. He apparently was not satisfied here as he practiced law for only a brief time at Woodstock before moving to Amherst, Massachusetts. There he read law for another six months as a further requisite for admission to the more complex Massachusetts bar. This latter study was under the Honorable Edward Dickinson, a member of the Massachusetts Assembly, and the two men developed a mutual admiration, remaining lifelong friends.

In 1810, Leban, now thirty years of age, established his office in the small village of Greenwich, Massachusetts, and for the next fifty-one years led an active life as an attorney in Hampshire County. There, despite his affiliation with the Democratic party in a state that still remained steadfastly bound to the principles of the Federalists, Leban represented the county for twenty-one years in the General Assembly. In 1820 and again in 1853 he served as a delegate to the constitutional conventions in Boston, helping to draft new state constitutions, but his many attempts to obtain a seat in the state senate always met with defeat.

The exact circumstances under which Leban met the woman he married are unknown. Family records merely state that he married Fanny Horne, of Sturbridge, "a woman of fine personal appearance and of vigorous intellect."[4] This union produced six children, the oldest being Randolph Barnes (named in honor of the father's former law tutor and personal friend), who was born on April 9, 1812. Practically no records or documents relative to Randolph's early boyhood have survived, although it is known that his first sixteen years were spent in Greenwich. In later life he wrote several books, largely reminiscences of his many adventures on the frontier, hundreds of newspaper and magazine articles, and thousands of official and personal letters, all of which have been

were those of United States senator, governor of New York, secretary of war, and secretary of state. He died in 1857. Dr. Erastus E. Marcy was a younger brother of the officer's who achieved considerable renown as a homeopathic doctor in Hartford, Connecticut, later moving to New York City to practice and to edit *The North American Homeopathic Journal.*

4 Marcy, *Records of the Marcy Family.*

preserved. None of the writings, however, contain a single word about his boyhood days in Greenwich.

As a youth Randolph was lean, wiry, and rawboned. His nose was large and thin, but in keeping with his other facial features. With a strong chin, small neck, broad forehead, high cheekbones, and a mass of black hair, his was an appearance not easily forgotten. At maturity his height exceeded six feet, but he never weighed more than 160 pounds except in the closing years of his long and strenuous life.

For a boy such as Randolph, whose father did succeed in obtaining for him an appointment, the United States Military Academy offered much. Since all who attended that institution did not expect to make a career of the army, it was a convenient way to obtain a liberal education with no strain on the family budget. Cadets in 1828 received sixteen dollars a month in pay and two rations a day, a tidy sum for a sixteen-year-old youth whose New England background had taught him the value of a dollar.

In 1828, when young Randolph entered West Point, the Academy was twenty-six years old. For several years after 1802, it had had a precarious existence. The War of 1812, however, demonstrated the need for competently trained professional officers and troops instead of politicians and inefficient militia. Congress from time to time responded with legislation to enlarge the Academy and to increase appropriations for the growing army. From 1801–10 approximately $1,632,000 was expended annually to maintain the small army of less than one thousand men. By 1820 this figure had been increased to $2,600,000, and by 1833 to $6,700,000. Meanwhile, the number of regular troops had risen to seven thousand,[5] and an appointment to West Point in 1828 afforded an ambitious young man some security and prestige.

Young Marcy's earliest West Point correspondence, found among his military records in the National Archives, is dated May 1, 1828, and informs the Secretary of War that he would "arrive at the Academy for examination between June 1 and June 20." He was duly mustered in, and for the remainder of his life, with the exception of the brief period following his retirement, Marcy wore the uniform of the United States Army.

[5] *Dictionary of American History* (New York, 1942), II, 126.

The plebe class at the Academy in 1828 numbered seventy cadets, ten of whom did not complete the first twelve months' work.[6] The faculty was staffed with twenty-eight civilian and military instructors, but the first-year men were taught only mathematics and French.[7] In both of these subjects young Marcy did poorly, but his standing (in his initial year he ranked fifty-third of the sixty cadets who finished) might have been due to insufficient previous schooling. His final examination score in mathematics was 103 out of a possible 200, and in French he fared even worse—35 out of 100. His being allowed to remain in the Academy at all was doubtless a reflection on the institution's standards in 1829.

During the second year Marcy did a little better, advancing to thirty-third in a class of fifty-three. The curriculum for that year included drawing, French, and mathematics. Natural philosophy, chemistry, and drawing constituted the courses during the third year, and at the end young Marcy ranked thirty-first. In his senior year he took engineering, mineralogy, rhetoric, manual philosophy, tactics, and artillery, in addition to the above-mentioned courses. Mathematics was still his nemesis, however, and he actually showed little improvement in other subjects. Indeed, his scores on the various final examinations averaged little more than 50 per cent.

Forty-five cadets graduated in the West Point class of 1832 and were commissioned brevet second lieutenants in the army of the United States. Marcy's final ranking in relation to his classmates was twenty-ninth. In conduct he stood 147th in the total cadet corps of 211.[8] The class could hardly be considered a great one as far as future generals were concerned. Marcy himself would obtain more renown as a military figure than any of his classmates, for of the top ten graduates only one, Erasmus D. Keys, remained in the army beyond the required three years. Keys served thirty-two years before resigning in 1864 to become president of a gold-mining concern in California. The other nine

[6] George W. Cullum, *Biographical Register of the Officers and Graduates of the U. S. Military Academy* (New York, 1856), II, 411.

[7] A brief summary of the system of instruction and discipline at the Military Academy during Marcy's years there is found in the *American State Papers, Military Affairs*, XX, 350–51.

[8] Merit Rolls, U. S. Military Academy, A. G. O., File No. 230.

eventually became businessmen, excepting Benjamin S. Ewell, president of William and Mary College, and George Watson, a Methodist minister. Sixteen of the class fought in the Civil War, ten for the Union and six for the Confederacy.

One of Marcy's classmates at the Academy was Henderson K. Yoakum, whose name is familiar to most Texans as the author of a history of Texas.[9] Young Yoakum's arrival at the Academy fresh from the Texas frontier created a sensation that soon became legendary. Marcy still remembered the incident nearly forty years later and tells the following story in one of his books:

"Now his [Yoakum's] letter of appointment required him to report in person to the superintendent, Colonel Thayer, who was a very refined, courteous, and dignified gentleman, but, at the same time, was exceedingly rigid in enforcing the strictest discipline, and the highest respect for rank and military authority. My young friend, after ascertaining where the colonel's quarters were situated, shouldered his trunk (he was then about six feet high, and powerfully developed), and staggered under its weight up the steep hill to the superintendent's house, put down his trunk upon the steps, and was at once admitted into the colonel's presence.

"Unlike most of the cadets on their first introduction to this dignitary he was not in the slightest degree abashed, but felt entirely self-possessed, and taking a chair close to the colonel, and looking him attentively in the face, said, 'Old man, are you Colonel, or Captain, or whatever-you-call-um Thayer?' To which the old gentleman very gravely replied, 'I am Colonel Thayer, sir.' 'Wall, now look-a-yere, Kern,' said the youth, 'this yere hill o' yourn am a breather; if it ain't, damn me.'

"The colonel soon comprehended what kind of a specimen of humanity he had before him, and directed his orderly to show him to the barracks, where he was inducted into the mysteries of wholesome discipline."[10]

Of course, few of Marcy's classmates were as unforgettable as young Yoakum. When Marcy received his commission in June,

[9] Henderson K. Yoakum, *History of Texas from 1685 to 1846, from Its First to Its Annexation to the United States* (New York, 1856).

[10] Randolph B. Marcy, *Thirty Years of Army Life on the Border* (New York, 1866).

9

1832, he would not dwell on old memories, as his military life was before him. Despite the many hardships and inconveniences of this army career, his future could not be regarded as dismal. The profession frequently afforded an opportunity to obtain fame as an Indian fighter, traveler, or explorer. Furthermore, the pay, although never high, was always sufficient to allow a young officer and his wife to live with some small degree of comfort and respectability. A few were fortunate enough to have families with property which they eventually inherited, thereby supplementing their modest military pay. By 1832, a large percentage of army officers were graduates of West Point, and family military traditions were already being established. Invariably the Academy graduates constituted a tight little clique at each military post where they were stationed, frequently avoiding the troops except for strictly duty purposes. Since they were generally sent to frontier posts, they took their families with them and endeavored to establish a semblance of culture that heretofore had not existed in the West.

It was to the West that young officers such as Marcy were being sent. When he graduated, the Black Hawk War was being fought. This struggle between the United States and the Indians of the Northwest was one in a long series of frontier wars following the Revolution. In fact, it was part of President Andrew Jackson's vigorous policy of moving the Indians westward. The war was waged in present Wisconsin and Illinois and involved the Sac and Fox tribes and part of the Winnebagoes, all led by Chief Black Hawk. It started, as usual, over land.

In 1804, various Indian chiefs of the region had agreed to give the federal government fifty million acres of land, comprising the northwestern half of Illinois and much of southwestern Wisconsin and eastern Missouri. Trouble between the whites and the red men followed. In 1827, the Winnebagoes took to the warpath, but were thoroughly routed and frustrated in their efforts to drive out the pioneers. This action showed that the Indians had little intention of giving up the land and were going to resist further encroachment by the whites.

Chief among the resistance leaders was Black Hawk. This chief organized a large portion of the Sac and Fox into a confederation, and in 1831, when squatters threatened to seize the site of his village near Rock Island, Illinois, he refused to vacate .

the land and gave every indication that he would retaliate any seizure. To combat this threat and enforce the treaty of 1804, regulars and militia were rushed to the scene, and Black Hawk was forced to withdraw and cross the Mississippi River into Iowa.

By April, 1832, however, the Chief had reassembled his forces and had moved back to the east bank of the river. His announced intentions were to join the friendly Winnebagoes and raise a crop of corn, but General Atkinson ordered him to return to Iowa at once. Black Hawk refused, and war was on. As he moved northeastwardly across Illinois and Wisconsin, excitement mounted, and troops were assembled in the area to shadow his movements. Meanwhile, regulars from the East were ordered to the Wisconsin region to reinforce General Atkinson's troops.

The relief force was under the command of General Winfield Scott, who planned to leave New York by early summer of 1832. While the General was gathering his troops, Lieutenant Marcy was at his home in Greenwich on his graduation furlough. News that a regiment was being sent to the frontier and that several of his former classmates were going caused him to volunteer without waiting for the expiration of his furlough and the receipt of orders for permanent assignment. Therefore, we find him with General Scott's force in Buffalo, New York, waiting to take boats to Detroit. Just prior to embarking from Buffalo, however, Marcy became ill and was forced to secure a private room there. The detachment sailed without him.

The belief that he would be able to follow on the next sailing allayed his disappointment temporarily, but Marcy's health did not improve, and a physician advised him to return to Greenwich until fully recovered. Marcy followed that advice, but the journey back by stage was slow and painful. At Syracuse, on the old Genesee Turnpike, 150 miles from Buffalo, he was forced to stop and again secure a private room. This was to be a consequential delay in young Marcy's life, for while recuperating in this New York village, he met the girl who was to become his bride.

Marcy was taken into the home of the late General Jonas Mann, the town's leading merchant before his death the previous year. General Mann was survived by a wife, one son, and two pretty and talented daughters. The youngest was Mary Mann, who only recently had returned from a finishing school in Troy,

New York. The pretty seventeen-year-old girl attracted the eye of the twenty-year-old West Pointer, and his sojourn, pleasant in spite of his illness, came to an end only when Marcy's need for money necessitated that he resume his journey to Greenwich. Before leaving the Mann household, however, he made a sincere promise to return at the first opportunity.

By the time Marcy reached Greenwich in August, he was so exhausted that several months passed before he recovered his strength. But the attentions of his mother and the memories of pretty, black-eyed Mary Mann doubtless soothed his convalescence and hastened his recovery. He was also anxious to rejoin his comrades in the excitement that he imagined they were experiencing on the frontier and anxious to test his mettle and ability on the field of battle. He was to be disappointed, however, and destined to miss completely what was probably the greatest army action between the War of 1812 and the Mexican War.

This Indian uprising in Wisconsin had been speedily quelled. Black Hawk could not convince his adversaries that his motives were peaceful, eventually being forced to turn back toward Iowa, whence he had come. The regulars "dogged" his every step and were rarely out of his sight despite repeated declarations by the Indians that they wished to have peace. Finally, Black Hawk and his six hundred braves reached the mouth of the Bad Axe River, where they were pounced upon by the army on August 3, 1832, and practically annihilated.[11]

Black Hawk was taken prisoner and sent to Jefferson Barracks, Missouri; then, on September 21, 1832, General Scott forced the Indians to sign a treaty at Fort Armstrong. The Winnebagoes now ceded their land in Wisconsin, and the Sac and Fox gave up their claim to eastern Iowa as reparation for going to war. However, the latter tribe was compensated for its land by the government. The "Black Hawk Purchase," as the former Indian land was called, was all the more important because valuable lead mines were contained in the territory.

Despite the apparent settlement of the problem, it was obvious that more forts and troops would be needed to stand guard on the northwestern frontier. Already vast numbers of new settlers

---

[11] A recent account of the Black Hawk War is found in Oliver L. Spaulding's *The United States Army in War and Peace* (New York, 1937).

were showing their eagerness to move in, and the army was needed to protect these pioneers against future uprisings. Accordingly, Marcy was soon ordered to join Company I, Fifth Infantry, then stationed at Fort Howard, Green Bay, Wisconsin.

Since Marcy's recovery was not yet complete, he wrote the Secretary of War on October 20, 1832, that he was "at present reduced very low and not as well as within a few weeks past as I have been." Enclosed with this correspondence was a letter from his physician stating that the Lieutenant's "health is such that in my opinion he will not be able to join his post in the army under some months."[12] The nature of Marcy's illness was never specified in the various letters to the Secretary of War, but throughout most of his life he was troubled with frequent recurrences of the ailment. One suspects that he suffered from an asthmatic affliction, yet he led a vigorous life in spite of physical infirmity.

By December, 1832, young Marcy had regained his strength and was ready to leave Greenwich. He planned to journey to Albany by stage, thence to continue along the Genesee Road to Buffalo. At Syracuse he fulfilled his promise to visit the Mann family at which time he renewed his acquaintance with Mary, whom he had written regularly during his illness. Perhaps the two had already reached an understanding.

Soon after he arrived at Syracuse, he learned, without disappointment, that ice on the Great Lakes would prevent steamers from sailing until spring. An alternative route—overland by way of Cleveland, Toledo, and Chicago—was possible but extremely hazardous. Regular land travel from Chicago to Green Bay, Wisconsin, was also not feasible during the winter months. Accordingly, Marcy wrote the Adjutant General at Washington to explain the situation, requesting that he be allowed to remain in Syracuse until the first steamer left Buffalo in the spring.

Apparently the request was granted, for we find Marcy there throughout the winter. His four months' visit was pleasantly carefree, and except for a recurrence of his illness, there is no reason to suppose that he did not thoroughly enjoy himself. He and Mary were together frequently, and, as the time of departure neared, he found the prospect of bidding her farewell bitter. At last, with youthful recklessnes, he asked her to marry him and share the

12 A. G. O., File No. 16M–1833.

hardships of frontier life. It was a much more reckless proposal than either imagined, for the frontier then was indeed a wild place. Still, the idea of going West could not have been new to the eighteen-year-old Mary. For years she had witnessed the daily passage of Yankee emigrants along the near-by Genesee Road. Her adventurous spirit, coupled with her love for the dashing young officer, prompted her to accept. Neither could properly visualize what lay ahead, for Mary was accustomed to cultured surroundings, and Lieutenant Marcy had not yet tasted army life at its rawest.

On May 5, 1833, Randolph and Mary were married at her mother's house in Syracuse. Because of Marcy's orders they had to depart for Buffalo immediately after the ceremony. The 150-mile journey to that city was long and tiresome. The coach was crowded and uncomfortable, and in places the road scarcely deserved the name. Eventually they reached Buffalo, and before the breakup of the ice, Marcy secured passage on the first small steamer destined for Detroit. In spite of their status as "newlyweds" the young couple were obliged to share a cabin with twenty-five other persons making the passage. However, with fares less than ten dollars each, first-class accommodations could hardly be expected. The company proved pleasant; vivacious, young, and beautiful Mary quickly captivated her fellow passengers—two of whom were governors with their wives, and two United States judges.[13]

Two weeks from the date of sailing the crowded ship reached Detroit. Despite its long history as an outpost for both the French and the British, this settlement was still frontier. It had not really felt the impact of western immigration until 1831, when the first lake steamer had arrived from Buffalo with pioneers bound for the Michigan and Illinois frontier. By this time it was, in spite of its rawness, a bustling port city, and the Marcys stopped over for ten days while awaiting passage by boat to Green Bay.

The last lap of the journey took another two weeks before they arrived at Fort Howard, Wisconsin, their home for the next

---

[13] The references to the Marcy's early experiences are found in a privately published "Memorial of Mrs. Mary A. Marcy" (1878), by George B. McClellan, a copy of which is now in the George B. McClellan home in Washington, D. C.

four years. Fort Howard was more primitive than they had imagined, and they found themselves ill equipped to make their new home. They did not possess even basic furnishings, having yielded to the advice of friends in Buffalo that these items could be obtained in Green Bay. All they had brought was a piano and a straw carpet. This piano, probably the first such instrument in what is now the state of Wisconsin, and the carpet may have been symbolic of a change taking place on the frontier, but for a residence of four years at an army post they were wholly inadequate.

II

"A life-long complaint"

1833–1842

IN 1833, as now, Wisconsin was a beautiful land of rugged hills, deeply eroded streams, and dense forests. But in 1833 it was also on the extreme edge of the uncivilized and lusty American frontier. Originally a part of the Old Northwest, it had formerly been attached to Indiana and later to Michigan Territory. The American regime had not begun here until after the War of 1812, at which time two forts had been constructed along the Fox-Wisconsin waterway.

Fort Howard was the first post built by the United States to safeguard the route from the Great Lakes to the Mississippi. The Fox flows from the southwest into Lake Michigan near present Green Bay, Wisconsin. Here Fort Howard was located in 1816. Near the source of the Fox River the Wisconsin River passes within one and one-half miles before turning toward the southwest and eventually emptying into the Mississippi at the former French settlement of Prairie du Chien. Here Fort Crawford was also constructed in 1816. Twelve years later a third fort was built to complete the line of fortifications. The latter was situated at the portage between the two streams and named Fort Winnebago, now Portage City. For the next several years these frontier posts stood guard over the rebellious Indians.

During the wet seasons the Fox and Wisconsin frequently merged into one stream, and small boats traveled across Wisconsin without difficulty. But during dry months boats and goods had to be portaged over the strip of land between the two rivers. It was a route, wet and dry, that had been used by the Indians since ancient times; in 1673 it had been traversed by the French explorers Louis Joliet and Jacques Marquette. Both the French and the British traveled it for many decades, and when the United States later acquired the region, she also realized the importance of the waterway to western immigration, continuing to use it as the main artery of transportation from the Great Lakes to the Mississippi.

The Americans would not settle Wisconsin for fifty years after acquiring the territory, partly because of the abundance and accessibility of land elsewhere and partly due to the presence of hostile Indians in the region. But after the Black Hawk War pioneers in large numbers overflowed southeastern Wisconsin and settled below the Fox-Wisconsin line. Within three years after the Treaty of Fort Armstrong (1832) approximately 12,000 people had already swarmed into the area. The country did not offer many agricultural possibilities at first, but lying beneath the thin soil were rich veins of lead and other minerals. Most of the early immigrants, accordingly, were miners rather than farmers.

When the Marcys arrived at Green Bay on May 28, 1833, they found a neat, small post occupied by 201 troops and officers. The trim whitewashed walls of the buildings, surrounded by a picket enclosure, gave the post a clean and quaint appearance. Although built on low ground, the fort was situated on a handsome grassy plain on the north bank of the Fox River, not far from Green Bay. Small patches of cultivation could be seen near by, none large enough to be called a farm. No wagon roads led in any direction from Fort Howard except the one to a small settlement near the mouth of the river. Water was the only means by which supplies could be brought from Chicago, Detroit, or Milwaukee. During the winter when ice covered the bay, mail was delivered irregularly from Chicago by horseback if the Indian trails were not erased by snow.

Fort Howard in 1833 was commanded by Colonel George M. Brooke, an officer who later gained fame in the Mexican War. A complement of three companies of the Fifth Regiment constituted the military force at the time of Marcy's arrival, but regimental headquarters were at near-by Fort Crawford with the balance of the regiment. Marcy was second in command of Company I at Fort Howard, the other two companies being K and H.

The military post was typical of its place and time, with its barracks, officers' quarters, and lesser buildings forming a quadrangle, which was surrounded by a log palisade thirty feet in height. A visitor at Fort Howard in 1824 described it succinctly: "It looked strong, but it had a lonely appearance; all that gave it life was the handsome large garden, which lay to the north. This, however, was the external appearance. There was life enough about it, no doubt; a military life is always lively."[1]

Normally, Fort Howard could comfortably house one hundred troops and officers; but in 1833, with the increase in personnel, living conditions had become extremely crowded, especially since several of the buildings had fallen into decay. Some of the newly arrived officers and their families at first had to be housed in the barracks or crowded in with two or three other families in the dilapidated officers' quarters until extensive repairs could be made.

Two near-by small settlements, Astor and Navirino, had sprung up several years previous to 1820 when descendants of French and British subjects still lived there, engaging in fur trading and lead mining. In 1820, John Jacob Astor put up a warehouse, and in 1837 the settlements were united in the town of Green Bay, Wisconsin. For many years Fort Howard served as the community social and religious center, furnishing a market to the civilians for the disposal of their crops. Outside the palisade a sutler's store, operated by a civilian concessionaire, served as a canteen for the officers and their families. But luxuries were few and prices high. The sutler's store was an adjunct to every frontier post until 1889, when the present post-exchange system was established.

The hospital building also was located outside the picket enclosure, and an army surgeon administered to the settlement as well as the garrison. Some years before the Marcys arrived at Fort Howard, a school building had been erected on the post grounds, and both army and civilian children attended whenever a teacher was available. Thus the military personnel and the citizens of Green Bay were brought closer together.

As soon as quarters were available, Lieutenant and Mrs.

[1] Louise Phelps Kellogg, "Old Fort Howard," *The Wisconsin Magazine of History*, Vol. XVIII, 132.

General Randolph B. Marcy

Marcy moved into their separate dwelling. Mary Marcy's attempt to manage a household quickly became the amusing subject of conversation at the post. Indeed, for the remainder of her life whenever she met old friends of the Fifth Regiment, they invariably reminded her of the singular results of her first efforts. But she soon acquired the art of directing a household, and with the aid of a twelve-year-old servant boy, who helped with cooking and cleaning, Mary managed very well. Although a second lieutenant drew only twenty-five dollars a month and four rations a day in 1833, he was allowed additional compensation for one servant.[2]

Despite the closeness of living quarters and the lack of privacy, the various families quickly became united by ties of mutual respect and confidence. Several friendships formed at Fort Howard by the Marcys were to last a lifetime. Their quarters, while not extensive, were comfortable and clean. The walls were plastered and whitewashed, and a large fireplace was situated in one end of each room. Each building was constructed to house two families, and the Marcys' quarters speedily became the center of many social gatherings, especially since Mary Marcy was an accomplished pianist as well as a gracious hostess.

A federal land office was opened at Green Bay in 1834 to sell land in tracts of 160 or 320 acres to the newly arriving immigrants, and Lieutenant Marcy and several of his fellow officers made judicious purchases that were to enrich them in the future. Of the various forts west of Chicago, Fort Howard remained for many years one of the most isolated of the American frontier. Not until 1837 was a federal road opened to Chicago along the Lake via Milwaukee, a distance of about two hundred miles, requiring almost four days to travel. Despite the remoteness of the post, the officers and their families clung to the customs and activities of a more civilized society, thus bringing to the wilderness region bits and pieces of the best American culture.

One of the earliest commanders at Fort Howard was Major Zachary Taylor, later the twelfth president of the United States. During the Taylor regime, 1817–21, a tradition was established for splendid hospitality on the part of the commanding officer and his family. Civilians and officers mingled freely in card games, balls,

[2] *American State Papers, Military Affairs,* XX, 83.

theatrical performances, and dinners. But when General Brooke commanded in 1833, such frivolity was frowned upon by his Methodist wife. Particularly was Madam General opposed to various amusements in the large mess room which had previously served as a community house and recreation center. But apparently Lieutenant Marcy and his fellow officers were not to be denied, for references to dances held in their private quarters occur regularly in Marcy family correspondence. It may be supposed that General Brooke and his wife were conspicuous by their absence on such occasions.

Dinner parties also were frequent, with all the officers and their families invited. Wild deer and turkey abounded in the surrounding forests, and fresh meat could be obtained with almost no effort at all. Vegetables were grown in season in the near-by garden plots, and wild fruits and berries could also be gathered or purchased at small cost. Whatever else the region lacked, it certainly was not food.

In addition to dining and dancing there were concerts presented by the post band, a small but inspired organization which made up in enthusiasm whatever it may have lacked in technique. Church services were conducted whenever a visiting Methodist, Congregational, or an Episcopal minister was present. When weather and time permitted, large parties were organized to enjoy horseback rides or hikes through the woods or along the shore. Now and then a bee tree was found and its honey divided among the various families. Small game such as coons and squirrels or birds was sometimes captured alive. Mary Marcy was particularly fond of birds and always kept two or three for pets, which she delighted in feeding and talking to several times each day.

One of the few references Marcy ever made to his experience at Fort Howard was in connection with a fellow officer, Captain Martin Scott, later killed in the Mexican War at the Battle of Molino del Rey.[3] The latter was a renowned hunter and the subject of many of Marcy's anecdotes. When Marcy came to Fort Howard in 1833, he brought with him a rifled pistol which attracted much attention, for it was the first of its kind ever seen by his fellow officers at the post. The barrel was about twelve inches long and could throw a ball fifty yards with as much accuracy as a rifle.

Captain Scott was skeptical about the new weapon's power and constantly bantered the junior officer for a demonstration. Since Marcy would not risk a possible failure in the presence of spectators, one day Scott proposed that they go out alone. The Captain had a reputation for being an exceedingly economical individual who, after considerable haggling, had recently purchased an expensive new penknife from the sutler. With it he cut a piece of paper about four inches square, which he fastened to a board by sticking the blade through the center.

Marcy's first shot at a distance of fifty yards struck the lower part of the paper, but the Captain was not convinced that such a feat of marksmanship was not accidental and insisted upon a second demonstration. The lieutenant warned that he might strike the new penknife, but Scott replied that he would "be responsible for it." The second shot struck the end of the prized instrument and splintered it into a dozen pieces.

The Captain stood speechless for several seconds. He then turned to Marcy without saying a word, "looked daggers" at him, and abruptly left the scene. It was several days before he condescended to notice the junior officer again, and neither spoke to the other of the incident throughout the remainder of their long association.

Lieutenant Marcy's reputation as a marksman was established with solid reason. There were few at Fort Howard or at any post where he was stationed later who could excel him in hunting. A compliment received from a fellow officer in later years was more highly prized than all the honors he would obtain as a traveler and explorer: "I never met with one who could crawl and sneak and squirm up to a deer like Marcy."[4]

During the second year at Fort Howard, on May 17, 1835, a daughter was born to the Marcys. She was named Mary Ellen and eventually became the wife of the Civil War leader, General George B. McClellan. The only nurse to be had in the area was an Indian woman of the Oneida tribe, one Polly Doxater, who carried Mary Ellen on her back Indian fashion for the first few months of her life.

The Regimental Returns for the Fifth Infantry reveal that Lieutenant Marcy was frequently reported on the sick list during

[3] Marcy, *Army Life on the Border,* 434 ff.
[4] *Ibid.,* 435.

1833 and 1834. He was apparently still suffering from asthma.[5] Either illness or routine duties occupied most of his time during his early stay at Fort Howard, for no other reference to him except in this connection is made until September 1, 1834. On that date he was placed in command of a small company and ordered to procure building stones for the post.

Fortunately there was little work to be done outside the post in cold weather, as immigrants rarely arrived during the winter. The Indians were quiet, surveyors were unable to work, and the troops with only routine duties to perform found time heavy on their hands. The officers and their families, never at a loss for entertainment, now had time for much visiting; everyone read everything available, especially the latest novels from the East and England. Whenever a copy of the *North American Review* reached the post, it was devoured with eager relish before being passed on. The latest books, plays, songs, or political news—and usually they were all very late indeed on this frontier—still were good conversational topics. Despite its remoteness, events of the outside world eventually became known at Fort Howard and were duly noted.

At the first hint of spring an atmosphere of activity replaced the comforting leisure of the winter. Immigrants began arriving daily, anxious to begin the arduous work of clearing their new farm land and locating their cabins. Surveyors were busy laying out still more farms and roads; work and long hours became the order of the day for both soldier and civilian. The new settlers looked to the army for guidance and the administration of civil government until the population should warrant an organized society.

The War Department, as early as 1830, had ordered the commanders at Fort Howard, Fort Winnebago, and Fort Crawford to cut a road from Green Bay to Prairie du Chien, along the Fox-Wisconsin waterway, to afford better access to the country west of the Great Lakes. But the actual work of cutting the road was not commenced until 1835, when each post supplied an equal number of troops to construct the section near its respective locality. Various detachments of soldiers took turns working on the road while others performed the regular post duties.

[5] Regimental Returns, Record Group 94, A. G. O.

The work was difficult and monotonous, and the Post Returns for Fort Howard show that desertions were high and courts-martial frequent during this period. Part of the region between Fort Howard and Fort Winnebago was open land, and the task at hand merely necessitated staking the road off from point to point. Immediately southwest of Fort Howard, however, was a hardwood forest approximately twelve miles deep, and this section of the road resembled a crudely cut slash through the dense and rugged wilderness, which was dotted with mudholes and stumps. Here trees had to be cut with axes or whipsaws and dragged aside, while heavy underbrush was cleared away and thrown into low places. Surplus logs were used to bridge the numerous streams or placed crossways on the soft, spongy road-beds. The "finished" road soon became deeply rutted and did not afford pleasant travel in wagons, but comfort was always a rarity on the frontier.

Throughout the latter part of 1835 and most of 1836, Lieutenant Marcy's duties caused frequent separations from his family. During these months he commanded Company I, having been promoted with no raise in pay from brevet to second lieutenant on November 25, 1835.[6] Although the work of cutting a road was arduous and the morale of the troops sank to new depths, there was compensation. Wild game was plentiful, and the men who liked to hunt could supply food for the camp. Bear, turkey, deer, and lesser game could frequently be killed within sight of the new road. Camping in the open at night was a change from the dull routine of garrison, and life was made slightly more zestful by the possibility of Indian attacks.

The Wisconsin nights were not always pleasant. When the weather was warm, the air swarmed with mosquitoes and sleep was difficult. When in the spring and late fall the temperature sometimes approached freezing, life for those without tents and sleeping bags could be miserable. The men usually slept rolled up in a blanket, propped against the base of a tree facing the fire. The officers fared much better, since they usually possessed such camping paraphernalia as tents, sleeping bags, and mosquito nets.

[6] A statement relative to Marcy's pay from October 1, 1833, to September 30, 1834, is found in *American State Papers, Military Affairs*, VI, 347. The amount for the above period totaled $778.40, including subsistence and allowance for one servant.

Sickness was a constant menace. The coarse food, plus sudden, violent changes in the weather, caused pneumonia and dysentery, which frequently halted the work.

Two years went into the work on the highway before wagons could travel across Wisconsin from Green Bay to Prairie du Chien. Meanwhile, Lieutenant Marcy was occasionally relieved of the unpleasant road work by being ordered to Chicago to receive and escort new recruits to their respective stations. These journeys, which required most of two weeks' time, usually could be made by boat in warm weather. Upon his return from each sojourn Marcy invariably had presents for his wife and young daughter.

Chicago did not experience rapid growth until a few years after the Black Hawk wars, although Fort Dearborn was first erected there as early as 1803. In 1833 its civilian population was only 150, but four years later this figure had risen to 4,071. Most of the immigrants moving from New England into northern Illinois or southern Wisconsin came through Chicago, many choosing later to return to the bustling new settlement. Milwaukee and Green Bay to the north were also important ports of entry, but they were never able to keep pace with Chicago after 1833.

At the same time that the road parallel to the Fox-Wisconsin waterway was being cut, other highways were under construction west and north of Chicago to the military posts along the periphery of the frontier. Soon after the Lake cities had acquired a semblance of permanency, civilization inevitably followed in the wake of the pioneers pushing into southern Wisconsin. Settlements, protected against the Indians by the frontier military establishments, dotted the wilderness roads. After 1837 travel ceased to be the hazardous adventure that it had been, and inns and trading posts assured one of lodging at the end of the day's journey.

On January 1, 1837, Marcy received a ten-day leave, the first since his arrival in Wisconsin four years previously. Taking full advantage of the opportunity, despite the cold weather, the Lieutenant and his wife left Mary Ellen with friends at the post and departed in a rented hack for a brief visit to Chicago. After four days of hard driving and much suffering, the weary travelers reached their destination.

Chicago still lacked much in the way of urban refinements. Since 1835 the city had experienced a boom similar to the one previously enjoyed by Detroit. Its streets were choked with wagons loaded with household furniture and farming implements and with droves of pigs, cows, and sheep. Some of the pilgrims carried their worldly possessions on their back, and they were always coming or leaving in large numbers. Stores and dwelling houses were under construction on every available space, while the ring of hammers and the rasp of saws echoed throughout the day and night.

Already Chicago boasted a theater and several hotels. In 1836 more than four hundred boats had entered the port, discharging large numbers of immigrants and thousands of tons of goods. During their brief visit the Marcys purchased an ample supply of clothing, shoes, buttons, thread, bonnets, and other items. Each evening they went to the new opera house to see professional actors perform before overflowing, enthusiastic crowds. Indeed, time passed so rapidly that the visitors overstayed their leave, only with considerable effort tearing themselves away from the scene of excitement.

In June, 1838, Marcy was promoted to first lieutenant and temporarily attached to Company K. His pay was now increased to thirty dollars, and his duties for the next few months consisted chiefly of escorting small detachments of new recruits to Fort Crawford, Fort Snelling, Fort Gratiot, and Fort Winnebago. Also, during this year, the various companies of Marcy's regiment were being transferred to different stations, the personnel at Fort Howard going to Fort Gratiot, Michigan. The Marcys now faced the unpleasant task of bidding their friends farewell. For them, as for all regular army families, such farewells would be a lifelong experience, over which they could exercise no control.

Meanwhile, Lieutenant Marcy moved his family to Fort Winnebago, where he was attached permanently to Company D. Routine duties once again became part of a day-to-day existence: cutting roads through the wilderness and escorting newly arrived farmers to their homes. In addition, Marcy served as acting commissary of subsistence and acting assistant quartermaster at the post. The last two positions brought an increase in monthly pay of ten and twenty dollars each. The duties of the post quartermaster were to procure and provide transportation for troops and sometimes to purchase military stores and supplies. The commissary of subsistence was responsible for the purchase of food for the entire post.

Fort Winnebago was closer to Chicago than Fort Howard, and the weekly mail came more regularly, so that Marcy and his family no longer felt as isolated as at Fort Howard. They, like all others, eagerly awaited letters from relatives and friends to break the monotony of their small world.

In October, 1838, Marcy was relieved of frontier duty and assigned to two months' recruiting service at Milwaukee. Thus again he and his family were afforded a brief glimpse of town life. Milwaukee lay on a direct route between Green Bay and Chicago and already possessed a newspaper and a school, signs indicative of a progressive settlement. Within a brief period it would construct its first brewery and during the forties would receive thousands of thrifty German immigrants who would swarm into the port city from the "Old Country."

Returning to Fort Winnebago in December, the Marcys remained two full years without extended separations. Fort Winnebago was only ten years old in 1838, but its appearance already was somewhat shabby. Most of the quarters for officers were stone buildings with clapboard roofs that leaked badly and cellars that were unsuited for use because of constant dampness. Blizzards frequently banked the sides of the dwellings in winter, thus making entrance impossible until tons of snow and ice were removed. Huge fireplaces consumed cords of wood in their ceaseless struggle against the chill air, while the occupants shivered on one side and burned on the other.

Approximately one hundred officers and troops occupied the fort during 1838 and 1840. Garrison life could be dull, but shining leather, cutting firewood, polishing buttons, doing guard duty, and drilling with musket and saber kept the soldiers and officers busy. Discipline, although considerably relaxed since the War of 1812, was still rigidly enforced, and punishment was harsh. Desertions were frequent, and Lieutenant Marcy was sometimes ordered to track down the renegades, a task he disliked but one in which he proved very apt.

On June 10, 1840, the officer received the welcome news that he would soon be transferred to the East on recruiting service. This assignment would afford him and his family a pleasant change from frontier life and enable him to place his daughter in a school somewhat superior to the one at Fort Winnebago. He secured passage on a boat for Buffalo, thence by stage to Syracuse, where Mary Marcy visited briefly with her mother and sisters for the first time in seven years. From Syracuse they journeyed to Greenwich, Massachusetts, where former friends and eager relatives assembled to greet the Lieutenant, his wife, and their five-year-old daughter.

Marcy arrived at his new station, Hartford, Connecticut, in August, 1840. Obtaining lodging, he and Mary took up a happy existence in the charming and friendly surroundings of the New England town. For the next two years they enjoyed a way of life they had never before experienced together. Friendships with the leading families of Hartford were established quickly and frontier hardships were soon forgotten, what with the rush of receptions, teas, balls, and theatrical performances. Later they would look back upon this period as the happiest of their lives, and at every opportunity they would return to Hartford for brief visits.

Recruiting service in 1840 did not demand much of one's time. Most of the army recruits were newly arrived Irish or German immigrants between sixteen and nineteen years old. The officer in charge of each recruiting station was responsible for rations for the new men until a group of six to ten were assembled and assigned to permanent stations. Periodically these small detachments were escorted to regimental headquarters by a junior officer attached to the recruiting office.

The trimonthly reports which Marcy sent regularly to the Adjutant General's Office reveal that he was fairly successful as a recruiter, enlisting about twenty-five or thirty men each month. Privates in the army at this time received only five dollars a month and one ration a day in pay.[7] The only physical requirement was that they be not "less than five feet six inches high, and not less than eighteen and not more than twenty-five years of age." The term of enlistment was for five years, with each recruit receiving a bounty of twelve dollars, while the recruiting officer was paid two dollars for each enlistee. Most of the recruits were from the so-called "lower classes" and, needless to say, did not take readily to army discipline. Many were illiterate.

[7] *American State Papers, Military Affairs*, XX, 83.

Two letters written during Marcy's tour of duty at Hartford shed some light upon the sundry activities of a recruiting officer: "I have the honor to report the apprehension of a deserter (Victor Holcomb)," he reported to the superintendent of recruiting service at New York, "who deserted from this rendezvous on the 19th day of August, 1842. After his apprehension, as I have reason to believe, he maimed himself by cutting off two of his small toes upon the left foot, and in consequence of it, is in such a state that it would not be prudent to remove him at present. . . . I would ask if it would be advisable to obtain his immediate discharge from the service."[8]

"A very respectable citizen at this place desired me to inquire," he wrote on another occasion, "if a man who enlisted at New Haven some time in the year 1839 and went to Florida is still in the service. His name is Benjamin Montross; his relatives are anxious to know what has become of him."

The answer to the latter inquiry must have proved slightly embarrassing. "B. Montross," it read, "a private of Company 'K' of the 5th Regiment, Infantry, enlisted May 1, 1839. Present in confinement at Fort Howard, 31 December, 1840, for desertion."[9]

On the whole, however, life as a recruiting officer was pleasant, too pleasant to last long. Since by July, 1842, most of the Indians living east of the Mississippi had been removed to Arkansas Territory and the Seminole War in Florida appeared ended, the army ordered its recruiting office at Hartford closed. Although Marcy was much chagrined at the thought of returning with his family to another frontier post after having tasted the pleasures of "civilized society," he had no alternative but to accept his new assignment as an inevitable consequence of military life. As it turned out, it was not too horrible; the new post, Fort Gratiot, near Detroit, was a far more satisfactory place than either Fort Howard or Fort Winnebago, and Marcy could once again engage in his favorite sport of hunting.

8 Marcy to Colonel N. S. Clarke, Fifth Infantry, Supt. Recruiting Service, New York, May 25, 1842; File No. 189M–42, A. G. O.

9 Marcy to General R. Jones, February 25, 1841, endorsement; File No. 42M–42, A. G. O.

III

"Miserable and ignorant wretches"

1842–1846

W<small>HEN</small> M<small>ARCY</small> <small>RETURNED</small> to frontier duty in 1842, he was thirty years old and had already served the army for fourteen years. Now a competent and experienced officer, he would have been content to remain in military service for the rest of his life had it not been for the hardships his family was forced to endure. Fortunately, Mary Marcy seldom complained of the frequent moves and long separations, for doubtless she and the Lieutenant realized the difficulties he would encounter in beginning a different career.

For the next three years the Marcys remained at Fort Gratiot. Near-by Detroit was an old settlement, predating Chicago by 137 years. Established by the French and later occupied by the British, it was not taken over by the United States until 1796.[1] For many years its growth had been slow because of its location, but the opening of the Erie Canal in 1825 made it an extremely important port of entry for immigrants coming into the Old Northwest. After 1831 lake steamers, jammed with immigrants at three dollars a head, began to arrive regularly from Buffalo, and within five years the sleepy frontier village had sprung to life, so that it now possessed a permanent population of ten thousand inhabitants.

Additional thousands of persons from New England passed through the port, preferring the voyage to the Northwest to the more hazardous journey along the National Road. Soon the Detroit newspaper could boast of a theater, museum, public garden, li-

---

[1] The British abandoned the post on June 1, 1796, in conformity with the Jay Treaty (1795).

brary, lyceum, historical society, and a water and sewage system. Detroit was one of the few places west of Pittsburgh that possessed a street-lighting system, reputedly so inefficient that "only a few more lights were needed to produce total darkness."[2]

Fort Gratiot was situated about forty miles, as the crow flies, northeast of Detroit. A road and an all-water route made the two settlements readily accessible to each other. Since Mary Marcy's mother had moved from Syracuse to Detroit when the Marcys returned to the West in 1842, the two families undoubtedly saw much of each other with a minimum of inconvenience.

Mary Ellen Marcy, who was eight years old in 1843, attended the post school conducted by the chaplain at Fort Gratiot. A letter from her maternal grandmother concerns her progress at this time: "I had not expected such a perfect composition and good spelling from such a little girl as Nelly Marcy. . . . In your next letter I wish you to tell me what you think of Mrs. Opie's stories about lying. I was much amused and edified by reading them. I hope that you will take these little books I sent you and read each one through. As soon as you have read through Mrs. Opie, write me and tell me what they tell of."[3]

During this period Lieutenant Marcy continued to perform routine duties. He sometimes served as commander of the post and, when not otherwise engaged, again acted as assistant commissary of subsistence and assistant quartermaster. Although he was still officially attached to Company D, the Post Returns indicate that most of his work from October, 1842, to August, 1845, was that of a staff officer, during which time he made frequent trips by boat or wagon to Detroit for garrison supplies.

Fort Gratiot normally housed approximately one hundred troops, or two full companies. The post was located on the St. Clair River, having been constructed there in 1816 as a link in the long chain of forts along the periphery of the Great Lakes. It protected against possible attack one of the routes from Canada by Lake Huron and stood as a bulwark against potential Indian uprisings in the Michigan area. Life for the Marcys here in the 1840's was much less primitive than it had been a decade before in Wisconsin.

[2] Ray Allen Billington, *Westward Expansion* (New York, 1949), 304.
[3] Mrs. Mary Mann to Mary Ellen Marcy, December 5, 1843, George B. McClellan Papers, Manuscript Division, Library of Congress, 2nd Series, I.

A small settlement of some seven hundred inhabitants known as Port Huron was situated only one and one-half miles southeast of the military establishment. Its civilian population and near-by military personnel appear to have maintained a fraternal relationship, and visits with the town ladies made frequent diversion for those at the garrison.

The original draft of the plans for the Michigan post, now in the Cartographic Division of the National Archives, reveals that Fort Gratiot possessed one large barracks building, two stories high and 130 feet in length, and four smaller structures for officers' homes, each built to accommodate two families. All of the above buildings, together with separate structures for the quartermaster's office, hospital, arms and ammunition supplies, and commissary stores, were arranged in a quadrangle around a parade ground. The building which housed the arms and ammunition supplies, commonly called the magazine, was stoutly erected of stone and brick; the remainder were constructed of logs and hewn timber. Surrounding the quadrangle was a solid log palisade which extended about 12 feet above the ground and enclosed a space approximately 300 feet in length and 200 feet in width. Blockhouses were constructed at each corner of the palisade, thus making it difficult for an enemy to storm the walls.

Outside the post grounds was a large garden plot where vegetables and fruits were raised for the soldiers' mess and where officers' families tended their separate patches. Except for some imported staple foods and military supplies, the garrison was largely self-sustaining. Fort Gratiot was situated about three hundred yards from the banks of the St. Clair River. It was connected by an adjoining road to a wharf which extended several feet into the river. Surrounding the post was a six-hundred-acre reservation, but, unfortunately, most of the land within the reservation was low and swampy, so that during the spring and summer months malaria was always a menace. The Regimental Returns show that five persons at Fort Gratiot died of this disease during the summer of 1845.

Despite a variety of duties between 1842 and 1845, Lieutenant Marcy somehow managed to find time to hunt and fish. Michigan had grown from territory to statehood by 1837, and deer and turkey had long since disappeared from the Fort Gratiot region. But geese and ducks were still plentiful, the numerous streams contained a bountiful variety of fish, and it was rare indeed that Marcy returned empty-handed from an outing.

Travel in eastern Michigan in the 1840's offered many interesting diversions for the military families, and small parties were organized regularly for horseback rides across the level countryside or to the shores of Lake Huron at the mouth of the St. Clair River a few miles from the post. The forests still abounded with large and beautiful trees, and the absence of underbrush made it possible to ride in almost any direction with ease.

The three years at Fort Gratiot passed pleasantly enough for the Marcys, doubtless helped by the occasional visits of their relatives from the East. The Indians had ceased to be a menace in eastern Michigan, and with the Webster-Ashburton Treaty in 1842 there was little reason to expect trouble with Canada. Except for its strategic location in respect to illicit traffic on the lakes, Fort Gratiot perhaps would have been abandoned by the army before this time.

During the spring of 1845, Mary Marcy returned to the East by boat to visit friends and relatives, Mary Ellen being left under the care of her grandmother in Detroit, where she attended a private school. Among the family correspondence for this period is a letter which Marcy wrote from Fort Gratiot to his young daughter on July 8, 1845, in which he refers to his wife's trip: "Mother will visit Greenwich this month, then return to Hartford, finish her visit there and from there she will go to Albany to visit Governor Marcy [William L. Marcy]. After that she will return home. I shall go as far as Buffalo to meet her," he concluded, "and if you are a good girl you can go with me."[4]

Before Marcy could undertake the voyage to Buffalo, trouble broke out between the United States and Mexico. On March 1, 1845, three days before leaving office, President Tyler signed the joint resolution for the annexation of the Republic of Texas to the Union. Mexico served warning immediately thereafter that she would declare war if and when her former province, whose independence she had not recognized, became a part of the United States. But the Texans, never wavering in their enthusiasm to join the Union, in June, 1845, voted overwhelmingly for annex-

[4] *Ibid.*

ation. Mexico showed signs of fulfilling her threats of retaliation.

The rumbling sounds of war along the lower Río Grande were clearly audible in faraway Washington. James K. Polk, now president of the United States and elected on a platform which called for the "re-annexation of Texas," quickly dispelled any doubt about acquiring Texas. He ordered the concentration of military troops at Corpus Christi during the late summer of 1845 "to protect, what in event of annexation, will be our western boundary." General Zachary Taylor was given command of the "Army of Occupation," whose initial force included more than half the regiments scattered along the far-flung frontier.

The Fifth Regiment was among those ordered to Texas in August, 1845, and Lieutenant Marcy's request for a month's leave of absence to meet his wife at Buffalo came too late. On August 19, Companies D and F left Fort Gratiot for Detroit. There they were joined by Companies C, E, and H to constitute the First Regimental Battalion under the command of General Brooke, Marcy's former superior at Fort Howard. From Detroit the troops marched immediately to Cincinnati and took passage on the steamer *Plymouth,* reaching St. Louis on August 30.

Meanwhile, Mary had arrived back at Fort Gratiot. She and Mary Ellen then had no alternative but to return to the East, where they were to remain until joined by Lieutenant Marcy a year later.

From St. Louis the *Plymouth* and its cargo of approximately 250 officers and men continued under full steam to New Orleans. Ocean steamers in 1845, unlike river steamers, were rare, and the only available passage from New Orleans to Corpus Christi was by sailing vessel. By October, 1845, troop transports and supply ships began to arrive at Shell Island, sixteen or eighteen miles offshore from present Corpus Christi. This long, narrow strip of land that extends along the Texas Gulf coast was then separated from the mainland by a water channel only three feet deep, and small steamers plied back and forth for several days, transferring the troops, stores, and camp and garrison equipage ashore. Until the channel eventually was deepened to allow more rapid debarkation, each shuttle boat could make but one trip a day, thus causing debarkation to be long and laborious.

When the "Army of Occupation" arrived at Corpus Christi in 1845, it found a small Mexican hamlet of approximately one hundred inhabitants. For many years the port settlement had been the center of operation for Mexican smugglers who dealt in illicit tobacco, violating Mexican law which attempted to reserve this trade as a government monopoly. Almost every male and female native above the age of ten in the settlement smoked cigarettes made of leaf tobacco and rolled in cornhusks, a custom Marcy observed with much surprise. The miserable Mexican hovels were equally shocking to the American soldiers.

The region west of Corpus Christi was a broad, flat prairie, most of which was thickly covered with chaparral. Travel was extremely hazardous except by way of a wagon road that connected Corpus Christi with Matamoros, 150 miles to the south near the mouth of the Río Grande. Another 150 miles to the northwest was the old Spanish town of San Antonio, with which contact was irregularly maintained by a crude trail that had been traveled for more than a century. Corpus Christi was situated near the mouth of the Nueces River and few people lived closer than Matamoros to the south and San Antonio to the west, the main center of Texas' population at the time being in the Brazos and Colorado "river bottoms."

Although Mexico had served repeated warnings that she would resist with military force any encroachment by United States troops on Texas soil, she now appeared reluctant to interfere with Taylor's army at Corpus Christi. It soon became apparent that the war would have to be "carried" to the Mexicans; therefore, President Polk placidly ordered the army to make preparations to move from the Nueces to some point on the Río Grande opposite Matamoros. By the end of 1845, Taylor had begun carrying out these orders, although several months were required before the troops were actually ready to move.

The task of transporting an army of three thousand men and its equipment overland from Corpus Christi to the Río Grande was not easy. Some wagons and horses had been brought from the United States, but their number was inadequate for the large quantities of baggage, rations, grain, and camp and garrison supplies. It was therefore necessary to hire mules, horses, and additional wagons from the near-by American traders and Mexican smugglers, all more than eager to profit from the enterprise.

Large herds of mustangs, or wild horses, roamed the prairies

34

along the Texas Gulf coast in 1845, and the Mexicans were very adept at capturing them and selling them to the army for thirty-six dollars a dozen. Good mounts brought as much as six or eight dollars each, and most of the officers soon acquired two or three for their personal use. The problem of feeding a mustang was negligible since it could subsist altogether on grass, and its endurance was remarkable.

As soon as the wild horses were brought into camp, they were hobbled and branded. Then the amusing job of breaking them to harness began. Most of the American soldiers at this time were foreigners, or boys from large cities who had never before driven in a wagon train. Before long, however, they became competent teamsters and learned how to break the fiery little animals and train them to pull the heavily laden supply wagons. Meanwhile, General Taylor saw no need for haste while the President was endeavoring to negotiate with the Mexican government.

Apparently, Lieutenant Marcy's duties at Corpus Christi were light. The Regimental Returns of the Fifth Infantry for this period reveal that he did detached service now and then, mostly procuring timber for the construction of living quarters.[5] There was time for hunting, the officers frequently organizing small expeditions which remained away from camp for three or four days. . . . Game was so abundant that on one occasion Marcy and three of his fellows "bagged twenty-seven deer, seventy-three wild turkeys, four tiger-cats, and several dozen wild geese and ducks," all on a four-day hunt.[6]

It was sometimes necessary for small military trains to leave Corpus Christi with supplies and money for the troops at San Antonio and Austin, and General Taylor encouraged his officers to accompany the expeditions to gain some knowledge of the country. Marcy made the four-hundred-mile journey at least once, discovering that the land was a desolate, brushy prairie, practically void of inhabitants, with the exception of a few settlers living in hovels near San Antonio. As a protection against the Indians, the people here lived underground in miserable quarters and eked out a wretched existence by hunting and by raising a few scrawny cattle.

[5] Regimental Returns, October, 1845; A. G. O., Record Group 94.
[6] Marcy, *Thirty Years of Army Life on the Border,* 435.

35

At San Antonio he found a settlement of approximately three thousand Anglo-Americans and Mexicans, but everywhere signs of stagnation were evident. The Alamo still showed the effects of the siege of a decade earlier, and in many respects seemed to typify the general deterioration of the old Spanish town. (Ten years hence Marcy would return to San Antonio to discover a bustling and prosperous city, hardly recognizable as the shabby place he had seen in 1846.) Between San Antonio and Austin the company traveled through the small hamlet of New Braunfels on the Guadalupe River. This settlement consisted of no more than a few crude huts recently erected by a colony of German immigrants, whose descendants constitute the majority of the present-day town's population. From New Braunfels the military train trudged on to the new capital of the youngest state in the Union, though in 1846 Austin could boast of no more than five hundred citizens.

Apparently Marcy was unimpressed by the town, for he makes no mention of its appearance in any of his subsequent writings. But from what he had seen of Texas in general in 1846, he formed an opinion that was to prejudice him against the state for several years. During future visits he would refer to Texans as "miserable and ignorant wretches who can not be trusted," and on one occasion in a letter to his daughter he used the phrase "detestable Texas."

Back at Corpus Christi awaiting the transfer of the army to the Río Grande, Marcy found time to write to his wife and daughter in Greenwich: "We have warm weather and all vegetables are growing," he remarked to Mary on February 15, 1846. "We have lettuce and radishes and shall soon have green peas; flowers also are in blossom. We shall leave here in a few days for the Rio del Norte, which you will find upon the map. It means in English the Grand River of the North and is one of the longest in the United States. It is navigable for small steamers about three hundred miles above its mouth.

"We shall see a great number of Mexicans when we get there and I shall try to get you a pretty Mexican blanket shawl. The Mexicans are very dark people, and live in homes made of posts set into the ground and covered with clay. They have no floors but live upon the ground. They are very fond of dancing and have

36

balls which they call 'fandangoes' every night. Anybody can go without an invitation and dance as much as they please, but every time a gentleman dances with a lady, he must take her to the bar and give her some cakes or beer or whatever else she might like. She takes the cakes and carries them home with her and feasts upon them until the next fandango. . . . Do not believe any of the reports you may see in the papers about the Mexicans, as they are about all false. The people here have started several reports which they know to be false for the purpose of keeping the army here. They have settled here and are dependent upon us for support. When we leave, their business suffers, and of course they hesitate at nothing to keep us here. But we shall disappoint them."[7]

In an earlier letter to Mary Ellen, whom he affectionately called "Nellie," he observed that there were few children at Corpus Christi except those belonging to the soldiers. "Some of the people of the village have children but there are no schools. We have preaching today for the second time and you can tell your mother that I shall go and hear a Presbyterian clergyman. He preaches in the theater."[8]

Mary Ellen, now eleven years of age, was attending a private school in Greenwich. Her father never neglected to express a profound interest in her studies, constantly urging her to devote particular attention to French. "I shall expect you to beat your mother in French when I see you," he invariably remarked.

The order to advance to the Río Grande was issued by General Taylor on March 8, 1846, after weeks of preparation. Most of the troops were to travel overland, although many were still suffering from the effects of dysentery, which had already resulted in several deaths. The sick, numbering almost five hundred, were to be transferred by boat from Corpus Christi to Point Isabel, near the mouth of the Río Grande. The boats likewise were to transport heavy siege guns and various supplies and equipment not portable by wagons.

The main force of approximately 2,500 troops was divided into four columns, separated from each other by a day's march. Many officers and a few enlisted men had either brought horses with them from the North or had purchased mustangs from the

[7] McClellan Papers.
[8] January 26, 1846, in *ibid.*

37

Mexicans, but the vast majority of Taylor's army was forced to walk the 150 miles to the Río Grande. Each column was strung out for several miles along the trail, averaging only about twenty miles a day, but the spring climate and occasional open stretches of prairie made the journey less difficult. Not a single inhabitant was encountered between Corpus Christi and Matamoros, but deer and antelope were almost always in evidence.

A few days' march from the mouth of the Nueces brought the travelers in sight of a vast herd of mustangs. "As far as the eye could reach to our right, the herd extended," wrote U. S. Grant in his *Memoirs* several years later. "To the left it extended equally. There is no estimating the number of animals in it; I have no idea that they could all have been corralled in the State of Rhode Island, or Delaware, at one time. If they had been, they would have been so thick that the pasturage would have given out the first day."[9]

Further excitement was afforded later by the rumor that Mexican troops planned to ambush the Americans upon their entering a mesquite thicket some distance ahead. Dragoons were quickly sent forward to rout the enemy, but the Mexicans had already taken flight. Consequently, the army marched on to the Río Grande without serious mishap, arriving there seven or eight days after its departure. General Taylor promptly ordered the engineers to lay out a fort on the north bank of the river across from Matamoros.

The immediate task, then, was to construct a stout fortification so that the additional troops and supplies could be brought up from Point Isabel. All men were given specific jobs. Lieutenant Marcy at first was assigned to a company and ordered to procure timber; later he was made responsible for his regiment's supplies. Meanwhile, the Mexicans anxiously watched the proceedings, not daring to attack the main body of American troops, although experience soon proved that small groups of Anglo-Americans venturing far from the encampment risked ambush.

As the fortification neared completion, the rations and supplies brought overland from Corpus Christi were almost exhausted. The ominous possibility of a superior Mexican force's surrounding Taylor's troops and starving them into surrender showed

[9] *Personal Memoirs of U. S. Grant* (New York, 1885), I, 87.

38

on the anxious faces of every American private. The work continued at a furious pace from daylight to dark until the latter part of April, when the fort was ready for occupancy. Major Jacob Brown thereupon took command, with the Seventh Regiment designated by Taylor to hold the place against possible attack until fresh supplies could be obtained. The few pieces of light artillery brought from Corpus Christi were dragged inside the walls and placed at strategic positions.

On the morning of May 1, General Taylor marched forth with approximately two thousand troops. The day's journey to Point Isabel, about twenty-five miles, was made without incident, but no sooner had the troops reached the mouth of the river and were in sight of their supply ships than they heard the distant booming of cannon. They realized instantly that their post was under attack and the war was on! Few men slept soundly that night, despite great fatigue from the arduous march, and for the first time in several weeks silence prevailed where grumbling had been the order of the day.

The supply ships were anchored some miles offshore, and a full week was required to unload them. At three o'clock in the afternoon on May 7, General Taylor and his army turned back to the west, prepared for the inevitable attack. Fortunately the road to Matamoros was over open country, and obviously the Mexicans would not make a stand on the prairies. Reinforcements at Point Isabel had increased Taylor's strength to approximately three thousand troops, and once his men were in motion, an atmosphere of confidence seemed to replace the serious tenseness.

On May 8, Taylor approached a place known as Palo Alto, six miles from the beleaguered fort. Here in plain sight stood a Mexican army prepared for battle. Taylor called a quick halt and arranged his men in a horizontal line, three deep; then, as the Mexicans opened fire with their cannons, he gave the order to advance.

The effect of the Mexican artillery would have been ludicrous had the occasion been less serious. The solid shots from the enemy guns fell far short, hitting the ground and bouncing like large rubber balls before starting to roll through the tall grass. The lines of men opened here and there to allow the balls to pass harmlessly by. Quickly the American artillery was rushed forward in advance of the infantry, which by now had halted, each man resting on his musket.

The guns brought by the supply ships consisted of a few twelve- and eighteen-pound howitzers which threw shell instead of solid ball and had tremendous range in comparison with the lighter Mexican artillery. When they opened fire, the Americans perceived that their shots were taking effect and that the Mexicans were giving way. Taylor's infantry then plunged forward to exchange musket fire with the retreating forces, whose former position soon was taken. The first battle of the Mexican War ended quickly with complete victory and the loss of only nine men.

The fighting was renewed with more vigor the following day, May 9, 1846. At a place called Resaca de la Palma the enemy was again encountered in large numbers and routed. That same afternoon the Americans reached the fort, bringing safely inside all their troops and equipment. They now learned that Major Brown was dead, but that otherwise the garrison had withstood the siege in good order. The fort was subsequently named in honor of its fallen commander, and later the settlement called Brownsville sprang up near by, which today numbers more than 25,000 inhabitants.

Shortly after May 9, news arrived that Congress had officially declared war on Mexico, and Taylor began immediate plans to cross the Río Grande to carry the fighting to Mexican soil. By May 18, Matamoros was safely in American hands, and the enemy had retreated up the south bank of the river.

The thirty-four-year-old Lieutenant Marcy had participated in each of the major engagements, but to what extent he performed is not known since he was never one to boast of his military exploits in subsequent writing. Official records make little or no mention of individual performances during the two engagements. Marcy's own brief references to the fighting of May 8–9 relate mostly to the injury sustained by his good friend and fellow officer, Lieutenant Colonel James S. McIntosh, for whom the post at Laredo, Texas, was named. The latter officer was one of twenty-nine soldiers of the Fifth Regiment severely wounded at Palo Alto and Resaca de la Palma, while twelve others were killed. Colonel McIntosh soon recovered, only to meet death a short time later at Molino del Rey.

While the army remained at Matamoros for several weeks awaiting reinforcements, several officers were ordered to the East on temporary recruiting duty. Marcy, who had been promoted to captain on May 18, 1846, was among those selected by their regimental commanders for the special duty, his ill health at the time undoubtedly furthering his selection.

On June 4 he secured passage at Point Isabel on a vessel bound for Philadelphia, and reached Harrisburg, Pennsylvania on July 15, after having first gone to Greenwich to see his family. He had been separated from them for one year, during which a second daughter, Fanny Marcy, had been born, on February 10, 1846. The reunion must have been a happy one.

This was the sum total of Marcy's fighting experiences prior to the Civil War. Although the conflict with Mexico continued for two years more, Captain Marcy remained on recruiting duty. By the time he rejoined his regiment the war had drawn to a close, and a new phase of life was to begin.

IV

"Respect and esteem"

1846–1849

Pᴿᴇꜱɪᴅᴇɴᴛ Pᴏʟᴋ was much chagrined at the Mexicans' failure to capitulate after Taylor's victories on the Río Grande. It became increasingly evident that the southern republic was anxious to avenge past wrongs at the hands of the United States and actually was confident of victory. Indeed, her army, at least on paper, was five times as large as the regular United States force, and her people were united in hatred of their northern neighbor.

Soon after the Congress of the United States officially declared war on May 13, 1846, it inaugurated plans for raising 50,000 troops, and in spite of warning to the contrary, the President elected to mobilize by the volunteer system. The slogans "Come all ye gallant volunteers" and "Ho, for the halls of Montezuma" suddenly rang throughout the country. But in many sections, particularly in the East, the war was not popular, making the task of obtaining young men for foreign service difficult. At first, recruits were enlisted for six months, but later the minimum period was raised to one year. As an added inducement volunteers were promised $124 bonus for enlisting and 320 acres of government land when honorably discharged.

Captain Marcy's recruiting staff at Harrisburg consisted of six noncommissioned officers, one musician, and one civilian physician who agreed to examine the new recruits for twenty dollars a month. Marcy already had developed a faculty for influencing people, and apparently he performed his recruiting duties well. Several letters of commendation to him from Adjutant General R. Jones are found in the War Records Office of the National

Archives, and an article which appeared in the Harrisburg newspaper in June, 1847, reported that Marcy had recruited 340 troops in eleven months.[1] Considering the contributions made by the entire Northeast, which furnished fewer than 8,000 of the 70,000 volunteers for the Mexican War, this was a good showing for one recruiting officer.

In addition to four rations a day and forty dollars a month basic pay, Marcy also received a bonus of two dollars for each new recruit—small enough, but it enabled his family to live with some degree of comfort. The Marcys boarded at a hotel, since furnished houses or apartments were not common a century ago. Military people found living away from an army post rather expensive, but certainly less drab. As Mary Marcy had a servant girl to care for Fanny, she found both time and opportunity for local society. As always, she quickly acquired a number of friends in Harrisburg, for indeed the military was now "all the vogue," with the Captain possessing the added prestige of having already participated in two victorious battles in the young war.

During the months that the Marcys remained in Harrisburg, Mary Ellen continued school at Greenwich. "You seem quite hurt that we did not bring you on to Harrisburg," her mother wrote on August 30, 1846. "I assure you that we should both be most happy to have you with us, but you must feel that it is entirely for your own good that we consent to be separated from you, as there is no good school in Harrisburg."[2] Though Mary did not know it then, it would be a rare event when her entire family would be together again during the succeeding decades.

By regular correspondence and infrequent trips to Greenwich the anxious parents kept in close touch with Mary Ellen's progress, admonishing her to study her French, practice on the piano, and "take plenty of exercise." Nor was the spiritual aspect neglected: "Your father and I attended the Episcopalian Church and heard a most remarkable sermon," Mary wrote on September 24, 1846. "It

[1] No exact date is given with the article, nor does the name of the newspaper appear. The story was clipped from a local newspaper by Marcy, and along with hundreds of other clippings was pasted in his personal scrapbook. The scrapbook is now in the possession of Marcy's granddaughter, Mrs. M. J. Kernan, Clinton, New York. It will hereafter be referred to as Marcy's Scrapbook.

[2] McClellan Papers.

43

was very solemn; the clergyman announced the death of one of the most beautiful ladies in Harrisburg. She died so suddenly and without the least preparation. Oh, the horrors of putting off penance till too late. Do not forget, dear Ellen, that you have a soul to save. You are not too young to think seriously of these things. I trust you read a chapter in the Bible each day. I also trust that you attend Sunday school."[3]

In June, 1847, the War Department ordered Marcy to rejoin his old regiment in Mexico. The Fifth Infantry had been actively engaged for more than a year, participating in all the major battles of the war, and its ten companies already had suffered heavy casualties. A short time later, at the battle of Molino del Rey, more than 30 per cent of the regiment were killed or wounded. Included among the dead in this engagement were Marcy's old hunting companions, Lieutenant Colonel Martin Scott and Brevet Colonel James McIntosh. The Regimental Returns also show that all but four of the officers in the entire regiment had been either killed or wounded by the end of 1847.

Before Captain Marcy's expected departure, a tribute to him appeared in the Harrisburg paper on June 14: "[He] has won the respect and esteem of our citizens by his courteous, gentlemanly and dignified deportment . . . and he has rendered the army such services as but few officers can boast of."[4]

On the same day that the above tribute appeared, Marcy received instructions from Washington to remain in Harrisburg. "I regret to learn," remarked the Adjutant General, "that the state of your health will not justify your joining the Army in Mexico at this time. And as the chronic complaint under which you have been laboring may render it necessary for you to remain at the North during the hot weather, you will continue on the recruiting service until further orders. Your reports show that you have been very successful, and I trust you will continue to enlist as many men as possible."[5]

Another year passed with the Marcys remaining in Harrisburg. Meanwhile, the Mexican War was rapidly being brought to a victorious end. On February 2, 1848, the Treaty of Guadalupe Hidalgo was signed, the defeat of Mexico became a reality, and

[3] *Ibid.* [4] Marcy's Scrapbook.
[5] Letters Sent, V; A. G. O., File No. 349M–47.

44

the War Department no longer wanted one-year volunteers. Instead, it now needed five-year recruits to build up the regular army of ten thousand men, but patriotic fervor cooled quickly with the ending of the war; enticing men into military service at seven dollars a month proved a difficult matter in peacetime. Captain Marcy soon found his duties dull and boresome, and when he received orders on August 14, 1848, to report to Camp Jefferson Davis, East Pascagoula, Mississippi, he was more than ready. Immediate plans were made to send Mary and Fanny to Greenwich temporarily.

During the rush of last-minute preparations for the long journey to the South, Marcy received an expression of appreciation, signed by thirty-five leading citizens of Harrisburg, praising his "character, position, and service." "We beg leave to tender you a public dinner at such time and place as will suit your convenience before you leave for a distant and perhaps perilous camp,"[6] the commendation added.

But the invitation was refused graciously because of lack of time. "I assure you, gentlemen, that I shall always look back to the two years spent in your hospitable town with the utmost pleasure, and I shall cherish the remembrances of your kind and disinterested friendship with feelings of the most profound gratitude, respect, and affection."[7]

Three days later Captain Marcy and 352 recruits reached Fort Columbus, New York, where passage was immediately secured on an ocean steamer for East Pascagoula. Arriving at Camp Jefferson Davis on September 24, 1848, they found that the Fifth Infantry had recently landed from Mexico and was now demobilizing and reorganizing. Of the 600 troops in the regiment at the close of the war, the Regimental Returns show that 113 deserted soon after the Treaty of Guadalupe Hidalgo, while more than 40 others later died of wounds or sickness. The remainder, approximately 440 men, were honorably discharged upon reaching Mississippi. Twenty-two of the latter group re-enlisted, and soon after Marcy's arrival the total strength of the Fifth was brought up to 317 men.[8] The average number of men in each of the ten

[6] Marcy's Scrapbook.   [7] *Ibid.*

[8] "Annual Returns of Alterations and Casualties incident to the Fifth Regiment, 1847"—Regimental Returns; A. G. O., Record Group 94.

companies, therefore, was slightly more than 30. Meanwhile, Congress had authorized a standing army of 10,000, an increase of more than 2,000 above the prewar figure, and the Fifth was eventually brought up to full strength.

Captain Marcy's one-month voyage from New York to East Pascagoula came off without incident except for the death of two recruits and the desertion of another en route. Soon after reaching Camp Jefferson Davis, Marcy was ordered to proceed by steamer to Little Rock, Arkansas, in advance of several companies that would follow in his wake to frontier forts in present Oklahoma. At Little Rock he contracted for several river steamboats to transport the troops from there to Fort Smith on the Arkansas River. Companies D, K, H, and A arrived at Little Rock on October 21, 1848, and in two more days completed their journey to Fort Smith, where General Arbuckle, commander of the Seventh Military District, took charge.

Ultimately, Companies D and K were attached to Marcy's command and ordered to Fort Towson, 120 miles to the southwest in the Choctaw Nation, while Companies A and H were subsequently stationed at Fort Washita, immediately west of Fort Towson in the Chickasaw Nation. Marcy's journey with heavily laden military wagons to Fort Towson, five miles north of Red River, took six days, the rutted road constantly impeding his progress.

The Fort Towson Post Returns show that the military party arrived on November 3, 1848. "He [Marcy] assumed command of the post, relieving Lieutenant Davis, Sixth Infantry, who with a detachment of sixteen men of the Sixth left for Fort Washita on the 6th of November, 1848."[9] With the arrival of Marcy's command, Fort Towson's garrison was brought up to seventy-eight troops, considerably more than occupied the post during war years. In addition to the commanding officer, there were the five following junior officers on permanent station at Fort Towson: one assistant surgeon, two second lieutenants, one first lieutenant, and one brevet second lieutenant. Several months passed before the arrival of any other women to join the sutler's wife and fourteen-year-old daughter.

9 Post Returns; A. G. O., Record Group 94.

46

Between 1825 and 1840 various Indian tribes still living east of the Mississippi River had been "driven" westward by the United States government in order to establish a "permanent" Indian frontier beyond the ninety-fifth meridian. The story of their removal is long and sordid and needs no further retelling here. But one result, at least from a military point of view, was the establishment of several forts in present Oklahoma. The problem of white and red men living in close proximity had always been vexing for the American nation. After the United States acquired the vast Louisiana Territory from France in 1803, various explorers sent from the East returned with the conviction that Louisiana offered a solution to the racial dilemma: "If all Indians east of the Mississippi were removed to the 'Great American Desert' their valuable lands would be open to settlement, friction between the two races removed, and natives protected from the sins and diseases of the white men."[10] Thus the answer to the age-old problem seemed assured at last.

By 1825, the plan first began to take shape in the removal of the Plains Indians from the vicinity west of the ninety-fifth meridian. At the same time negotiations were begun with the Choctaws and Cherokees to surrender their Arkansas lands for tracts immediately east of the proposed frontier line. The Choctaws received a reservation between the Red and Canadian rivers in the southeastern corner of what is now Oklahoma, while the Cherokees were given a similar region to the north. For the next fifteen or twenty years the task of moving all the eastern tribes continued, the northern groups generally being transferred into present Kansas, while the Five Civilized Tribes in the South were "escorted" to present Oklahoma. This last group included, in addition to some remaining Cherokees and Choctaws, the Chickasaws, Seminoles, and Creeks.

The policy that appeared so simple in theory did not work well in practice. The Plains Indians looked upon the eastern tribes as intruders, and keeping peace between the new settlers and the nomadic Comanches and Kiowas and sedentary Wichitas was almost as difficult as between the whites and the Indians. Obviously new forts were needed in the area along the ninety-fifth

[10] Billington, *Westward Expansion,* 469.

47

meridian, strong points permanently manned by United States troops. Accordingly, in 1824, Fort Towson was built in the Choctaw Nation and Fort Gibson established in the Cherokee Nation. As the need arose for still more forts, new ones were built, Fort Washita being located approximately eighty miles west of Fort Towson and Camp Holmes some sixty miles north of Fort Washita.

For several years after 1827 these and subsequent log and mud outposts stood guard over the various Indian tribes in Oklahoma, filling the need of constant vigilance to prevent perpetual civil war. Few, if any, of the Indians were satisfied with the new arrangement, but fear of federal troops kept the hostile forces apart for a time. It was, for them, a tense and miserable predicament.

Captain Marcy's arrival in present Oklahoma in 1848 began a new phase of his military career. By now, the immediate dangers of civil war on the Indian frontier had been checked, and fate was to cast the thirty-six-year-old officer in the new character of adventurer and explorer. It was a role that fitted his talents and past experiences well, eventually bringing him much renown.

During the early months that Marcy was commander at Fort Towson, he had ample opportunity to examine the Red River region while leading several small hunting and exploring expeditions. The near-by Choctaws were a peaceful people, not likely to cause trouble unless provoked to it by an invading band of Plains Indians. Consequently, Marcy found life at Fort Towson frequently dull in the absence of his family, and the opportunity to hunt and explore was a welcome diversion for his restless spirit.

In the meantime, Marcy's family remained in the East. Mary Ellen was now enrolled in a private school operated by a Miss Strong at Hartford, Connecticut, and Mary and Fanny had gone to Catskill, New York, to be with Mary's sick mother. As soon as conditions would permit, the Captain expected his wife and daughter to join him, but not until after the cholera, then raging throughout the Southwest, had subsided.

Marcy regularly wrote to his family of his varied experiences in the new country; his letters reveal not only a subtle sense of humor but also a flair for writing which later was demonstrated in his published works.

"Day before yesterday," he wrote to Mary Ellen on January

8, 1849, "I took my gun and crossed Red River, which you will perceive from the map divides Arkansas and the Choctaw Nation from Texas. I went into the woods about twenty miles from the river without any road to guide me except a small path. . . . As I was going along I heard a chicken crow at quite a long distance off from the path. I turned my course towards the direction of the sound, and after going about a mile I came to a log cabin in the woods. I went to the door and found a woman with four small children. She asked me in and as soon as I was seated told the oldest child to go out and bring in a turnip, for the 'stranger must be hungry.' I told her I was much obliged, but (as I did not care about making my supper from a raw turnip) I declared upon pretense of not being hungry.

"I asked her if I could stay all night and she said I could, and that she would be very glad, for she had not seen anyone except her husband for about three months. She told me that her husband worked for the nearest neighbor about eight miles off, and that he only came home on Sundays; the balance of the time she stayed alone with her little children, cut her own wood, fed her cow and a few pigs she had, and in fact did everything about the house. I asked her if she was not afraid to stay so far off in the woods alone. She said no, that she was afraid when she first came there but that she had got used to it. After I had fed my horse I took my gun and went out hunting while the woman was getting supper. I returned in about an hour and brought a fine deer, half of which I made a present to my hostess.

"After supper, which was a cake of corn and some stewed pumpkins, I told her I would go to bed. She pointed to a place in one corner and said I could sleep there. I went to the place and found one of her children on the back of the bed. She said he was to sleep with me, but I was much surprised when getting into the bed to find another one of the children stowed away at the foot, and he set up a tremendous howl as I gave him a good punch with one of my feet. I continued kicking him occasionally, so as to keep him howling, until the mother came after a while and took him to her own bed. I then slept quietly until morning, as I was very tired.

"In the morning I took my horse and came home. This is the manner in which many of the people of Texas and Arkansas live.

They are ignorant and poor and having never known any other kind of life are satisfied and probably happy. I was very sorry for the oldest little girl at the house where I staid; she was quite a nice child. I asked her if she ever saw any sugar plums or raisins; she said 'no sir,' and I presume the nearest thing she ever saw to them was a sweet potato, as she appeared to relish a sweet potato as much as most children do sugar plums. I told her if I came there again I would bring her some."[11]

Early in 1849, Mary Marcy's sixty-four-year-old mother died, and she was free to join her husband in the Southwest. On January 24, 1849, she wrote to Mary Ellen from Trenton, New Jersey: "I will depart for Baltimore tomorrow where I will be joined by Major McPhail, Major Ruggles and family, Captain Whitall and family, and Lieutenant Collidge and wife, who will go the whole distance in company, which will make it very agreeable for me."[12]

Although eager to see her husband again, Mary was not altogether happy to leave the East because of the anticipated long separation from her older child and the fear of cholera in the Southwest. But as frequent moves and absence from friends and loved ones had long since become part of her life, she accepted the inevitable with little complaint. At the last moment she decided to leave behind her Negro servant, Jane (an act she later regretted), since "Randolph talks of purchasing two slaves who keep his mess at Fort Towson and I shall have no employment for more than two slaves."

On January 25, 1849, Mary and Fanny, now three years of age, joined the military company at Baltimore, whence they journeyed by the cars to Philadelphia and on to Pittsburgh. There the small party and 188 recruits being escorted to Fort Smith, Arkansas, obtained passage on "a miserable little steamer." Cincinnati was reached on February 2, where a brief stop was made. Mary's comments about the city, then commonly referred to as "Porkopolis," were far from flattering: "A dirty place, more muddy than Detroit used to be." It must indeed have been bad.

From Cincinnati the crowded steamer reached Napoleon, Arkansas, a small town at the mouth of the Arkansas River, in seven

11 McClellan Papers.
12 Unless otherwise documented, all remaining quotations in the present chapter are from Mrs. Marcy's letters to Mary Ellen, McClellan Papers.

Black Beaver, Marcy's Delaware guide on the Fort
Smith–Santa Fé expedition.

days. Although Mary made no comment on the appearance of this settlement, a young officer passing through it two years later wrote: "This is the sorriest excuse for a town I have ever seen in my life."[13] In regard to the voyage in general Mary observed: "I thought at first I could not stand so much filth, but we got accustomed to it at last and found we could make ourselves very comfortable, notwithstanding dirty bed rooms and greasy food. . . . I have not seen anything that could compare with one of our beautiful towns in the North."

The country along the Mississippi and for some distance up the Arkansas was low and uninteresting to the eastern travelers viewing it from the winding rivers with mingled feelings of revulsion and dismay. The monotonous landscape was broken here and there by cotton plantations, and Negro slaves could be seen working in the near-by fields. On February 11, 1849, the steamer docked at Fort Smith, a small settlement that owed its importance to the fact that it was the farthermost point on the Arkansas that could be reached by water during all seasons of the year. A fort had been built here in 1817, and since that time Fort Smith had served as the headquarters and supply depot for the Seventh Military District. Within a short time a small settlement grew up around the post, which in 1849 was commanded by General Mathew Arbuckle, who informed Mary upon her arrival that her husband was not expecting her until spring. "He will be astonished when I walk in on him," she wrote Mary Ellen.

The officers whom Mary accompanied were journeying to various western posts in the Seventh Military District—none, however, to Fort Towson. Mary had intended to go on with some of them from Fort Smith to Fort Washita, situated on the Washita River in present south-central Oklahoma. This route followed a well-traveled military road and passed by the old trading post then known as Boggy Depot. From Fort Washita one could travel safely by flatboat back down the Red River to within five miles of Fort Towson—a long, out-of-the-way journey, but at first appearance offering the best means of travel, since the 120-mile trip overland from Fort Smith to Fort Towson was not feasible for a woman and a small child alone.

However, General Arbuckle found it necessary to send a

[13] Rodney Glisan, *Journal of Army Life* (San Francisco, 1874), 29.

military train direct to Fort Towson, and Mary was informed that she could accompany it. After four days at Fort Smith, during which time she and Fanny boarded at the local hotel, Mary began the final phase of her long journey. Her happiness at the prospect of rejoining her husband after a separation of more than six months must have been clouded somewhat by the distressing rumor that he might soon be ordered on an expedition to Santa Fé, and she concluded that in such an eventuality she and Fanny would return to Fort Smith to remain with Captain Caleb Sibley's family, old friends from Fort Gratiot days.

The seven-day journey to Fort Towson is described as follows to Mary Ellen: "My establishment consisted of a kind of carriage they call in this country an ambulance, with four mules attached to it. My baggage was all in a separate wagon so that Fanny, myself, and driver were the only occupants, and yet it was quite as much as the poor little mules could do to drag us over this most horrid road.

"We were obliged to sleep in a tent one night. The rest of the time we had Indian houses which were far from being clean or comfortable. Certainly the dirtiest and most horrid places you ever saw. They would not speak a word of English, as they have a terrible aversion to our language, though they understand all that's said to them."

Five days after leaving Fort Smith the escort was met by a tall, bewhiskered officer on horseback whom Mary immediately recognized as her husband. Two days earlier he had learned of his wife's coming and had set out immediately to meet her. "Your father appeared in excellent health and was fatter than I had ever seen him," Mary described the meeting. "The remainder of the trip to Fort Towson was indeed a happy one except for poor little Fanny, who by this time was fatigued to death and cross as a little bear."

The weather became extremely cold during the rest of the journey, a chill north wind making life even more uncomfortable than the rutted road. On the second evening after the Captain had joined the travelers, they reached Spencer Academy, twelve miles east of Fort Towson. This small institution had been opened five years previously and since 1846 had been operated by the Board of Foreign Missions of the Presbyterian church. Several "very pleasant missionary families," in addition to approximately one hundred Choctaw boys, lived there in 1849. At the insistence of the missionaries' wives the Marcys welcomed the opportunity to spend the night; and one of the ladies, a Mrs. Kingsbury, later became Mary's intimate friend. Mary seems to have had an extraordinary talent for forming permanent friendships wherever she went.

Mary's first impression of Fort Towson as she approached it the following day was of a beautiful but lonely place in the midst of a rolling prairie: "The parade is very large and the few people who are on it seem quite lost. The ground is laid opposite in squares and sodded. Great walks running in every direction. There are also many trees within the enclosure, which add much to the beauty of the place. I think that when I get settled that I shall be very contented, although I shall be the only lady within the Fort till Mrs. Abercrombie arrives, which will not probably be before April. There are six young officers here, all very pleasant and they profess to be delighted to see me arrive."

By 1849 the two companies at Fort Towson were at full strength, the Post Records showing 102 enlisted men and 6 lieutenants besides Captain Marcy, the commanding officer. The only other whites in the Choctaw Nation were the near-by missionaries, licensed traders, and the Fort Towson sutler and his family. The Choctaws were industrious farmers, and their well-kept fields and fences impressed and surprised those who traveled through their nation for the first time. The natural beauty and agreeable climate of the country added to the pleasant surroundings.

Fort Towson held the reputation for many years of being the best-built and best-kept military post in the West, and few military establishments could boast a more attractive site.[14] One entered the grounds from the south and immediately was afforded a full and impressive view of the entire grounds. Oak, pecan, and fruit trees were everywhere in abundance, except of course on the parade field. The well-placed post, unlike many of the period, was not obstructed by a palisade. It occupied a mile-square rectangle with buildings placed along three sides and lay at the foot

[14] A detailed description of Fort Towson as it appeared in 1849 is found in W. B. Morrison's *Military Posts and Camps in Oklahoma* (Oklahoma City, 1936), 48–49.

of a one-hundred-foot bluff running east and west. Three lime-
stone story-and-a-half buildings facing south stood on the edge
of the bluff overlooking the parade ground and constituted the
officers' quarters. Below and in front of these structures on opposite sides of the parade ground were two rows of buildings,
quartermaster, mess, magazine, hospital, and four barracks. The
last were built of logs and stones and were conspicuous on account of the tremendous chimneys at each end. Inside were large
fireplaces, "nine feet high, four feet deep, and six feet from stone
floor to arch," capable of roasting an entire beef or ox.

Prior to Mary's arrival, Marcy had lived with the junior officers in one of the buildings on the bluff. Their mess was managed
by two Negro servants, whom the Captain eventually purchased,
but now that Mary and Fanny were with him and he momentarily
expected to leave on detached service, Marcy began preparations
to move into separate quarters. Meanwhile, the Marcy household
furnishings had not arrived from the East; and he and his family
moved into a spare room offered them by the sutler's wife, whose
house was but a short distance from the post grounds.

On March 7, 1849, Mary again wrote to Mary Ellen: "We
have not yet got into our house, as they are painting, whitewash-
ing, and making some additional furniture, but when once in there
we shall be delightfully situated. There are four fine rooms on a
floor, with kitchen below and an attic above for servants' rooms.
There are folding doors between two of the rooms, one of them
I shall use for a parlor and the other for a dining room—fine closets
in all the rooms. On the other side of the hall are two other rooms,
one I occupy for my bedroom and the other I shall keep for company. The porch is very large, it is only built on three sides, the
front entirely open. The garden is filled with fine peach trees,
which are all in blossom."

The next letter found Mary happily settled: "In my front
parlor I have a pretty nice carpet and have had lounges made and
covered them with a crimson and black cloth, with my writing
case, toilet bottles, and your mat, as well as portfolio, which has
been much admired. On the mantle piece are the lamps and other
little articles. My pictures hang upon them also, which is quite an
improvement to the room. In the back parlor is the old yellow
carpet, and other furniture, very comfortable. My room has the

green carpet on it. The furniture has all been made here, and is painted white and looks very neat and comfortable."

The Marcys had just moved into their new home when Lieutenant Colonel John J. Abercrombie arrived at Fort Towson on March 20, 1849, to relieve the Captain of command of the post. Four days later Marcy took leave of his family and departed for Fort Smith to join a detachment of thirty-eight troops which had left Fort Towson two weeks previously. From there the officer soon would launch the first of several expeditions beyond the Cross Timbers and across the Great Plains. According to tentative orders dated February 16, 1849, he was to command a military detachment escorting some two thousand emigrants from all parts of the country as far as Santa Fé, New Mexico. These emigrants, like thousands of others in 1849, were destined for the California "gold fields."

With the exception of the few months in which he had been engaged in the Mexican War, Marcy's life heretofore had been as routine as that of other military men of his time. But now a change was taking place from the monotony of garrison duties to the adventurous life of exploring. For the next decade Randolph B. Marcy would experience more active service, explore more unknown country, and witness more hardships than any other officer in the army. Indeed, immediately before him were the great days, the climax, of his life.

V

"Wagons . . . westward"

1849

No SINGLE EVENT of the nineteenth century had a more dramatic effect upon the American people than the discovery of gold in California in 1848. Whether one joined the forty-niners in search of the new El Dorado or remained at home, still in some degree one's whole life was affected. Captain Marcy was no exception. The Argonauts were digging for gold in California, and in far-off Indian Territory Randolph B. Marcy was being converted into an explorer, a role to bring him fame as the map maker preeminent of the Southwest.

Every schoolboy is familiar with the feverish rush to the West that followed the news that gold had been found on the American River. Transportation west was needed badly—and pronto—as goldseekers by the thousands took passage on steamers and sailing vessels for the long voyage around Cape Horn to the Pacific Coast, and still others went by way of Mexico and Central America. Because it was cheaper, however, the vast majority of California immigrants were forced to suffer privations and often death on the more hazardous, uncharted, and largely unknown road across the plains and mountains. Much has been written of their suffering, death, and adventure.

Even in 1849 a few overland routes were available to the goldseekers who found it expedient to travel in large companies for protection. The most popular road was the California and Oregon Trail along the Platte, through South Pass, and across Nevada by way of the Humboldt. Several trails came together at El Paso, thence continued by way of the Gila River to Lower California, and others collected at Santa Fé before swinging out in divers directions toward the Pacific. On the whole, the few available maps were inaccurate, guides were scarce, and well-marked roads and data about the West were desperately needed to save precious time and to avoid the needless loss of lives.

Fort Smith, Arkansas, headquarters for the Seventh Military District, quickly discovered its importance relative to the California gold fields. In 1849, steamboats from the Mississippi could easily reach the frontier outpost on the Arkansas River some eight hundred miles due east of Santa Fé. It was believed that much time and effort could be saved by eastern pilgrims taking this route to California; moreover, the citizens of Fort Smith and its near-by rival, Van Buren, were not blind to the profits that could be made from outfitting emigrant trains. Accordingly, a frenzied campaign soon was launched to advertise these settlements as the most strategic terminals for a quicker and safer route to California.

The chief disadvantage of Fort Smith as a debarkation center was the absence in 1849 of a well-marked road west of it to Santa Fé. A decade before, Josiah Gregg had blazed a trail to Santa Fé from Van Buren (five miles downstream from Fort Smith), which by-passed the latter settlement situated on the opposite bank of the river, and continued westwardly to the point where the Canadian empties into the Arkansas. There he followed the north bank of the Canadian to the 102nd meridian, crossed over to the south bank, and pushed on across the prairies to Santa Fé. Van Buren residents now were eager to kindle interest in Gregg's old road, and the commercial spirit of Fort Smith businessmen was likewise aroused—they wanted a trail blazed that would be more favorable to their own location.

The commander of the military post at Fort Smith, General Matthew Arbuckle, was an interested spectator to the affray, and his support for a Fort Smith–Santa Fé road was solicited by the local inhabitants. Perhaps, so the wily citizens hoped, sufficient political pressure could be mustered to force the army to construct the proposed road, provided, of course, the General himself could be convinced that the scheme had merit. After careful study of Gregg's published journal[1] and to the delight of the Fort Smith

[1] Josiah Gregg, *Commerce of the Prairies* (2 vols., New York, H. G. Langley, 1844).

settlement, General Arbuckle finally agreed to support the proposal, whereupon a local committee was promptly organized in December, 1848, and adopted a master plan of strategy.

On January 6, 1849, a large group of Fort Smith boosters met with the Arkansas Legislature to solicit support for the project. The legislature responded by drawing up a memorial relative to the desirability of a road which would parallel the Canadian River from Fort Smith to Santa Fé. The *Fort Smith Herald* reported on February 6, 1849, that the memorial was presented to the Secretary of War by Arkansas Senator Solon Borland. Meanwhile, Congress had already given serious consideration to the exploration of the newly acquired Mexican cession, while the War Department was eager to have a national road, or railroad, laid across the continent to link the East with the West. On January 31, 1849, the Senate Committee on Military Affairs recommended to Congress that the route between Fort Smith and Santa Fé be surveyed by army topographical engineers. One month later Congress allocated $50,000 from the army's general appropriation fund to defray the cost of various surveys from the Mississippi River to the Pacific Coast, the Fort Smith project being included along with several others. It was stipulated that the Fort Smith–Santa Fé survey be made in conjunction with a military escort for the various emigrant companies then gathering at Fort Smith.

Approximately two thousand people from various parts of the United States, anticipating favorable news from Washington, were making preparations to leave Fort Smith around April 1, 1849. When word finally came that a military escort would be furnished them as far as Santa Fé,[2] the emigrants were both pleased and disappointed. As far as the troops went, that was fine, but the Argonauts had been led to believe that they would receive military protection all the way to California. Further appeals and petitions to the Secretary of War failed to alter the orders. General Arbuckle went forward with the task of organizing a command of troops to survey the road and escort the emigrants to Santa Fé, and that was all.

Originally the escort was to have consisted of two companies of dragoons, but since so large a number of dragoons could not be spared for the particular task in 1849, General Arbuckle se-

[2] Grant Foreman, *Marcy and the Gold Seekers*, 123ff.

lected Captain Marcy to command a combined detachment of infantry and dragoons. In choosing the young officer, General Arbuckle passed over Captain B. L. E. Bonneville, who had eagerly sought the assignment. Captain Bonneville, the famous hero of Washington Irving's *The Adventures of Captain Bonneville*, was fifty-six years old and in 1849 was no longer in the army, factors which doubtless caused Arbuckle to pass over him. The choice, however unpleasant to Bonneville, proved wise.

When Marcy reached Fort Smith on April 2, after a six-day journey from Fort Towson, he received the following orders: "An escort consisting of one subaltern and thirty men of the 1st regiment of infantry, will leave Fort Smith, Arkansas, on the 5th instant, for Santa Fé, New Mexico, for the purpose of protecting our citizens emigrating to our newly acquired territories."[3] The orders instructed Marcy to employ a civilian physician to accompany him and to draw upon the local quartermaster and commissary department for necessary funds, supplies, medicines, and subsistence for five months.

Additional instructions concerning the route to pursue and the objectives of the expedition were given two days later: "The commanding general directs that you . . . ascertain and establish the best route from this point to New Mexico and California; to extend to such of our citizens as design leaving here in a few days and traversing your route such facilities as circumstance may require, and it is in your power to give, to insure them safe and unmolested passage across the prairies; and to conciliate as far as possible the different tribes of Indians who inhabit the region of country through which you will pass."[4] Marcy was also directed to make an accurate examination of the country, to survey and measure the road traveled, to keep a correct journal of each day's march, to note the distances between good camping places, to note those subjects that would be of interest to the future traveler, and to hold "talks" with the principal chiefs of the Plains Indians.

Dr. Julian Rogers, a civilian physician from Newcastle, Delaware, was employed to accompany the expedition, and the mili-

[3] Acting Assistant Adjutant General F. F. Flint to Captain R. B. Marcy, Fort Smith, Arkansas, April 2, 1849, published with Marcy's report of his route from Fort Smith to Santa Fé, 31 Cong., 1 sess., *Senate Exec. Doc. No. 64* (1850), 169.

[4] *Ibid.*, 169–71.

tary officers in addition to Marcy were as follows: Lieutenant
J. H. Simpson of the topographical engineers, Lieutenant J. Buford, Company F, First Dragoons, and Lieutenants M. P. Harrison and J. Updegraff of the Fifth Infantry. Noncommissioned officers and privates numbered twenty dragoons and fifty infantrymen.
The dragoons and all of the officers were mounted, while the remainder of the detachment manned the eighteen supply wagons,
beef cattle, and surplus work stock. Each military wagon was
drawn by six mules or oxen, the former having recently been
purchased from Mexico and ultimately proving unsuited for the
arduous task. One six-pound iron cannon and a portable forge
were included among the arms and equipment. A surveying chain
and other scientific equipment were likewise procured at Fort
Smith, in addition to food, medicine, camping equipment, ammunition, and corn for the animals.

Previous to Captain Marcy's arrival at Fort Smith, some of his
troops under Lieutenant Updegraff had already departed with a
company commanded by Captain Frederick T. Dent, Fifth Infantry. This party was making a preliminary survey of the heavily
timbered country immediately west of Fort Smith and was to join
the main expedition at a designated point along the march. As
Captain Dent, U. S. Grant's brother-in-law, was acting under separate orders, he was not attached to Marcy's command.

Meanwhile, the goldseekers, who had organized themselves
into various companies, were encamped in the vicinity of the Fort
Smith settlement. Some small companies had already pushed forward in their anxiety to start, traveling Gregg's old road along the
north bank of the Canadian, but the remainder were advised to
delay their departure for one week after Marcy's military train had
started. All emigrants and troops were to rendezvous near the former site of Chouteau's Trading Post, approximately 165 miles west
of Fort Smith and near present Lexington, Oklahoma, on U. S.
Highway 77.

Captain Marcy commenced his journey westward on the evening of April 4, 1849, but the largest company of emigrants, the
so-called Fort Smith Company, did not depart until April 11.
The latter consisted of 479 men, women, and children, and included several merchants with large stocks of goods to be disposed
of en route, or after reaching California. The Fort Smith Company

alone possessed seventy-five wagons and five hundred mules, horses, and oxen, but emigrants, as well as various members of the smaller companies, carried their provisions and equipment on pack-mules and saddle horses.

Heavy rains during February and March, 1849, had turned most of eastern Oklahoma into a sea of mud. Consequently, with the bulging wagons frequently sinking to their axles, the first 150 miles from Fort Smith proved to be such a constant struggle for both men and animals that some of the travelers lost their enthusiasm before they reached the firmer footing of the open prairies which their more persevering companions found beyond the Cross Timbers.

Opposite Edwards' Trading Post, approximately 125 miles west of Fort Smith, Captain Marcy encamped. For many years, James Edwards had conducted a flourishing business here, his house being at the terminus of a well-known Indian trail extending into Texas. This post was situated on the north bank of the Canadian, not far from present Holdenville, Oklahoma, and Marcy's detachment remained for several days while the commander made frequent crossings of the stream to purchase supplies and secure the services of Indian guides. In the meantime, his animals were given an opportunity to rest, and repairs were made on the wagons and harness. Edwards' Trading Post afforded the last opportunity for the travelers to replenish their food larder and to obtain corn and additional work stock before pushing on to Santa Fé.

Emigrants arrived daily, some momentarily stopping at Edwards' store while others crossed the Canadian and camped near the troops to await their forward movement. "There are about two thousand emigrants upon the road from all parts of the United States, so you see that we have a great plenty of company," Marcy wrote to his wife at Fort Towson. "They are generally a very decent class of people, and some of them are intelligent and gentlemanly men. There are some families with them but not many. I have often wished to be with my dear family since I had been out, but I know it is for my benefit to make the trip and I try to console myself, but I am never content away from you."[5]

---

[5] This letter is postmarked "Camp near Edwards' Trading Post." It was eventually carried back to Fort Towson to Mrs. Marcy by Captain Dent, and now is among a collection possessed by Marcy's granddaughter, Mrs. M. J. Kernan, Clinton, New York.

Before renewing his march on May 1, 1849, the commander obtained the services of the famous Indian guide and interpreter, Black Beaver, who since 1834 had performed many services for military and scientific explorers. In 1849 he was principal chief of a band of five hundred Delaware Indians living in the vicinity of the trading post on the Canadian. Because of his knowledge of the language, habits, and character of the Plains Indians, his services to Captain Marcy's expedition would prove invaluable: "He has spent five years in Oregon and California [wrote Marcy]—two among the Crow and Black Feet Indians; has trapped beaver in the Gila, the Columbia, the Rio Grande, and the Pecos; has crossed the Rocky Mountains at many different points, and indeed is one of those men that are seldom met with except in the mountains."[6]

At last, with repairs completed, supplies replenished, and the rains temporarily subsided, the expedition resumed its way. Some of the emigrants preferred to continue along Gregg's route as far as Chouteau's former trading establishment, while others chose to follow the military train along the south bank of the river. The country now being approached was less hilly and was changing gradually to a rolling prairie spotted with numerous small motts of timber. Streams of pure spring water framed with a variety of trees were never beyond a few hours' march. On May 3, the expedition reached the site of Captain Dent's camp, where the detachment of Marcy's command under Lieutenant Updegraff was waiting. A short distance beyond was the principal rendezvous point, where once again the wagons would hold up until all the emigrants had gathered.

Captain Dent, who had surveyed the new road thus far, now turned back toward Fort Smith, while Marcy's immediate course lay over a seven-hundred-mile stretch of uncharted prairie. His confidence about reaching Santa Fé never altered, for his command was at last intact. On May 7, 1849, he observed in his journal: "We are now coming into the vicinity of the Comanche 'range.' I have given orders for cartridges to be issued to the command, and shall take up our line of march from this time in the following order: the dragoons in advance about one mile from the train, the main body of the escort directly in front of the train, the cannon in the centre, and the guard in the rear."

[6] *Senate Exec. Doc. No. 64,* 169–227. Unless otherwise indicated, all

On May 9, the party reached the eastern edge of the Cross Timbers and encamped a short distance from the Canadian River, not far from the present town of Purcell, Oklahoma. The Cross Timbers, extending in 1849 from the Colorado River in Texas north and west for several hundred miles, provided an effective barrier to commerce and were the dread of every traveler. Josiah Gregg penned a graphic description of this dense, thorny brush in his *Commerce of the Prairies*: "The Cross Timbers vary in width from five to thirty miles, and entirely cut off the communication betwixt the interior prairies and those of the great plains. They may be considered as the 'fringe' of the great prairies, being a continuous brushy strip, composed of various kinds of undergrowth; such as black-jacks, post-oaks, and in some places hickory, elm, etc., intermixed with a very diminutive dwarf oak, called by the hunters 'shin-oak.' Most of the timber appears to be kept small by the continual inroads of the 'burning prairies'; for, being killed almost annually, it is constantly replaced by scions of undergrowth; so that it becomes more and more dense every reproduction. In some places, however, the oaks are of considerable size, and able to withstand the conflagrations. The underwood is so matted in many places with grapevines, green-briars, etc., as to form almost impenetrable 'roughs,' which serve as hiding places for wild beasts, as well as wild Indians; and would, in savage warfare, prove almost as formidable as the hammocks of Florida."

Across the stream from Marcy's camp on the edge of the Cross Timbers could be seen the ruins of "Old Fort Holmes," where General Arbuckle had negotiated a treaty with various Plains Indians in 1835, stipulating that the white men be permitted to pass safely through the Indian country. Close by were the remains of Chouteau's Trading Post, built by Colonel A. P. Chouteau in 1836 and abandoned two years later at Chouteau's death. In 1849 it, too, was in ruins. Near here some of the emigrants who had taken the road along the north bank of the Canadian in preference to Marcy's route had already encamped. The Fort Smith Company, however, had been delayed by incessant rains and had not yet reached the rendezvous.

While Marcy waited for the wagons to assemble on the south bank of the stream near his own camp, he availed himself of the citations in the present chapter are taken from the above document.

opportunity to explore the Cross Timbers in the hopes of finding a natural road through them. With Black Beaver and two days' supply of rations, the commander skirted the edge of the thicket for several miles before finding a small stream (Walnut Creek) that seemed to flow from the west. Further investigation revealed that wagons could be taken through the Cross Timbers along a narrow strip of prairie bordering the creek.

When he returned to camp with the news of his discovery, Marcy learned that all but the Fort Smith Company had arrived and were encamped near by; word soon reached him that it would join the main company in three days. Impatient to move on without further delay, Marcy now gave the order to advance. For the next few days the expedition plodded along at a snail's pace of five or six miles between camping sites, slowed by rains, muddy roads, construction of bridges, and the occasional clearing of underbrush. On May 17, the Fort Smith Company overtook the main party, and morale was raised immediately by the realization that "we shall now move on more rapidly."

Before the emigrants stretched a boundless sea of grass. "We are now launched upon the broad Prairie of the West and feel as if we are upon the wide ocean, nothing intercepts the view to the West," Marcy wrote to Mary on June 19. "As far as the eye can extend it is one uninterrupted expanse of prairie, with occasional skirts of small trees along the water courses. We have seen many buffalo tracks lately, but have not come up with the varmints. We are constantly in expectation of seeing them, and at the appearance of the first one I expect to witness some of the finest kind of scampering, for the emigrants will all be certain to make a dash for him, and if they do not run some of their horses to death it will be strange. They behave tolerable well thus far, and I am in hopes will continue to do so. There are a good many families among them and the women are not content unless they are near us. One belle of the prairie (Miss Conway) joined us again this evening after being kept back for two weeks by the bad state of the road. She is in fine spirits and has a crowd of young gentlemen in constant attendance.

"We expect to reach Santa Fé in forty days or perhaps less and shall remain there about a week, then turn our faces homeward. . . . I have not had a razor to my face since I left Fort Smith, and I begin already to look rather barbarous, or rather anti-barbarous. We had a tremendous thunder storm a few nights since, accompanied by a perfect tornado. At the first blast (about 10 o'clock) every one of our tents were laid flat upon the ground, and such a scampering has not been seen for some time. I poked my head out from under my tent which had fallen upon me and by the flashes of lightning I could see officers and men running in all directions. Some following a hat, blanket, or bed, which the gale had seized upon and was hurrying off upon the prairies, others running around trying to find a shelter from the storm; in fact, it was the most perfect scene of confusion for a few minutes I ever saw.

"After the shower was over all the beds were drenched except mine. I had taken the precaution to cover it with my India rubber cloth and I found it perfectly dry, notwithstanding it had been out in all the shower. We have had no sickness among our men and all are in good spirits."[7]

Miss Conway, whom Marcy referred to as "the belle of the prairie," was the eldest daughter of Dr. John R. Conway. The Conways were a prominent Arkansas family, two members having served as governor of the state. Seventeen-year-old Mary Conway was described by Marcy as "charming, vivacious, and possessing a fine education." Mounted on a beautiful black horse, she rode with the grace of a thoroughbred, surrounded by the young unmarried officers and gentlemen of the expedition. She, with her parents and nine brothers and sisters, was a member of the Fort Smith Company, and like thousands of others, looked forward to a new home in California. Mary had several proposals of marriage before the expedition had progressed many weeks, among her suitors being Dr. Julian Rogers, the civilian physician, Lieutenant John Buford, and Lieutenant M. P. Harrison. Harrison and Buford were the chief rivals until Miss Conway eventually chose the former.

Lieutenant Montgomery Pike Harrison, at this time twenty-three years old, also came from a distinguished family: his paternal grandfather, William Henry Harrison, was the ninth president of the United States, and his maternal grandfather was the

---

[7] This letter was brought to Fort Smith by an Indian guide returning from the expedition and is now among the McClellan Papers, 2nd Series, I.

eminent pathfinder, General Zebulon Montgomery Pike. An older brother, Benjamin Harrison, would be elected to the presidency in 1888. The handsome young officer, anxious to seal the engagement by immediate marriage, sought Dr. Conway's permission. The doctor approved the match, but did not want the ceremony to take place until his family had settled safely in California. Accordingly, he informed Harrison that if and when he could secure a leave from his regiment, he would be most welcome to come to Los Angeles and take Mary Conway as his wife.

When the company eventually reached Santa Fé, Harrison again pleaded with Mary's parents that he be allowed to wed his fiancée at once, but permission was denied and the young couple parted tearfully. Lieutenant Harrison vowed that he would follow his sweetheart to California as quickly as possible, but unfortunately he was not able to keep his promise.

Once the caravan of soldiers and emigrants reached the firm prairies, they could move along with greater ease and not infrequently traveled thirty miles in a single day. Captain Marcy and Lieutenant Simpson kept separate logs of the distances between campsites. Mileage was determined by both a viameter[8] and a surveyor's chain, while bearings were taken with a compass each mile, and magnetic variation was noted approximately every two hundred miles. This data, together with general observations and information obtained from the experienced guide, enabled the commander subsequently to construct the first accurate map of the region.

Wood, grass, and water, three essential elements for emigrants crossing the Plains during the mid-nineteenth century, were abundantly supplied by nature for the first weeks beyond the Cross Timbers. "We passed several high round mounds of a very soft sandstone, rising almost perpendicular out of the open table land," wrote Marcy on May 23. The soil now was a gravelly sand, and, except for the high mounds, nothing obstructed one's view but patches of timber bordering the various ravines. These tributaries of the Canadian cut perpendicularly across the expedition's

[8] A viameter was an instrument formerly used to register the revolutions of a wheel. Marcy attached it to a wagon wheel and computed the distances by multiplying the number of revolutions by the circumference of the wheel. This method was less accurate than that of a chain because of the contour of the earth.

path and sometimes caused minor delay. Buffalo, antelope, and turkey appeared more frequently as the wagons approached the heart of the vast prairie ocean and provided fresh meat to satisfy the voracious appetites of toiling men and women.

Near the eastern edge of the Texas Panhandle the party encountered their first Plains Indians when four Kiowas rode into camp dressed in war costume and armed with rifles, bows, lances, and shields. Had they not been few in number, they would have created considerable excitement among the emigrant families, but Marcy greeted them warmly and asked his interpreter, Black Beaver, to invite them to sit down for a brief conference.

The military commander advised the warriors, who professed to be on their way to Chihuahua, Mexico, to steal horses and mules, that their "Great Father" in Washington desired to be on peaceful terms with all his "Red Children." He told them that many more "whites" would follow those now on the road and cautioned that the Great Father expected them to remember their treaty agreement of 1835, which they promised never to forget.

"I was much surprised at the ease and facility with which Beaver communicated with them by pantomime. The grace and rapidity with which this mute conversation was carried on upon a variety of topics relative to our road and their own affairs astonished me beyond measure. I had no idea before that the Indians were such adepts at pantomime; and I have no hesitation in saying that they would compare with the most accomplished performers of our operas."

The route pursued by the expedition continued almost due west and parallel to the Canadian. Occasionally, the stream ranged out of sight on the northern horizon, for it sometimes was expedient to stay well beyond the sandy bottoms in order to find a solid roadbed for the wagons. Except on Sunday when the train stopped to rest, each day became more like the one before—an occasional birth or death bringing excitement or sorrow to interrupt the monotonous routine. On June 8, 1849, twin boys were born to a family of the Fort Smith Company, and the mother named one of them "Marcy" in honor of the commander of the expedition. "If I never see the gold fields myself," the Captain happily rejoined, "I shall have the satisfaction of knowing that my name is represented there."

Marcy too infrequently comments upon the activities of his vast following. Perhaps he felt that such observations were not particularly germane to his report to the Secretary of War, but Lieutenant Simpson's journal[9] furnishes many facets of human interest. The various emigrant companies had their separate captains, officials, treasurer, and regulations, and each traveled as a unit in the general caravan, which extended for a distance of five or six miles. At night each company chose a separate campsite with respect to water, grass, wood, and possible Indian attack, while the guardian shepherd, the military, pitched their tents apart from the others—on high ground when possible, in order to view the vast panorama.

At the end of each day's march each company leader, who had previously ridden ahead to select a suitable camp, spotted his wagons as closely together as possible. Then the mules and oxen were unhitched and turned out to graze, and a guard detailed to watch them. All the wagons were placed in a huge circle with their tongues crossed so as to furnish a corral for the stock at night.

Now came the most exciting time of the day: Simultaneously each family pitched its tents and unrolled its bedding, cut wood, brought water from a near-by stream, and began preparations for the evening meal. The sound of axes and the ring of the blacksmith's hammer rent the air, and children finishing their chores quickly collected in groups to run and play until time to eat. With supper over and twilight approaching, the signal was sounded for the guards to drive the stock into the enclosure and to establish a camp watch for the night.

Before bedtime had arrived, the fiddles, guitars, and flutes were brought forth, and some groups gathered to sing, dance, and frolic about huge bonfires for an hour or so. As sunrise approached next morning, the travelers were aroused by the sound of a bugle. Fires were lighted, animals fed and watered, and breakfast was prepared and eaten hurriedly. Down came the tents, and into the wagons they went once again with the baggage and cooking equipment; a bugle was sounded to bring up the animals, and soon came the command to break camp. Thus the bivouac ended, and the day's march was on.[10]

[9] 31 Cong., 1 sess. (1850), *Senate Doc. No. 12.*
[10] *Ibid.,* 12–13.

Wood was sometimes scarce, and the inexperienced travelers did not at first accept the idea of using "buffalo chips" for fuel, but their qualms were soon dispelled by necessity. Marcy observed in his journal that subsequent emigrants should be advised to carry a few sticks of dry wood at all times for emergencies. "It should be cut short and split into small pieces; then [after] digging a hole in the ground about twelve inches in depth, and of a size suitable for the wood and cooking utensils, all of the heat is preserved, and a very small fire serves to cook a meal."

Few explorers journeying on the great western Plains in the nineteenth century failed to be amazed at the sight of the inevitable "prairie-dog" towns, and Captain Marcy was no exception. Like his predecessors he was puzzled that the interesting little animals were called "dogs instead of squirrels," and he was curious to examine them more closely. When the explorer Zebulon Montgomery Pike came upon a large "town" near the banks of the Arkansas River in 1806, he attempted to capture a live prairie dog by pouring huge quantities of water into its hole, but after more than twenty buckets the effort was abandoned. Marcy tried the same experiment and obtained the same results. His interest likewise was awakened by the domestic arrangement whereby rattlesnakes, owls, and prairie dogs lived together in one hole. When one of his soldiers succeeded in killing a tremendous rattlesnake, an autopsy revealed that it had recently swallowed its unfortunate host, and the question of the relationship between the inhabitants seemed answered.

June 14, 1849, was a day remembered by all, for on this date the expedition arrived at the base of the famous *Llano Estacado*, that phenomenon better known to Anglo-Americans as the Staked Plain—the high, level part of northwestern Texas and eastern New Mexico which lies above the Cap Rock escarpment. In 1541, Coronado led the first expedition of white men across it; later, other Spanish explorers visited the region, so named, perhaps, because a similar expedition had driven stakes at intervals by which to retrace its route.[11]

"When we were upon the high table-land, a view presented itself as boundless as the ocean. Not a tree, shrub, or any other object, either animate or inanimate, relieved the dreary monotony

[11] *The Dictionary of American History* (New York, 1942), V, 154.

of the prospects; it was a vast illimitable expanse of desert prairie
. . . a land where no man, either savage or civilized, permanently
abides; it spreads into a treeless, desolate waste of uninhabited
solitude, which always has been, and must continue, uninhabited
forever," Marcy wrote.

At the latitude where the travelers crossed it in 1849, the
Staked Plain was approximately twenty-eight miles wide. Unlike
the rolling country over which Marcy had previously traveled, it
was an uninterrupted expanse of "dead level" prairie, approximately one thousand feet above the surrounding area. Here the travelers came upon an elusive mirage which sometimes appeared as
a tremendous sheet of water, sometimes as a great cloud of smoke,
or again as a distant shifting forest. As they dropped down from
the western rim of the great plateau, they once again emerged
on a rolling country where the huge cactus in all its rose-like glory
and the sotol plant with its dagger-like blades stood here and
there like proud sentinels.

A few days after the caravan had left the Staked Plain, a band
of twenty or thirty Comanches was encountered. These "nomads
of the plains," as Marcy called them later, were well-mounted on
mustangs and presented a colorful spectacle. Most of them were
"decked-out" in leggings of bright red strouding, blankets ex-
travagantly worked with beads, headgears of vivid feathers, and
large rings in their ears and on their arms, while their sole weapons
consisted of bows slung over their shoulders and a quiver of arrows
attached to each saddle.

The chief of the band, Is-so-Keep (Wolf Shoulder), made
signs of his peaceful intentions and was allowed to come alongside
Captain Marcy, who had ridden forward to meet him. Is-so-Keep
then leaned over in his saddle to demonstrate his affections for
the Americans in general and Marcy in particular. "For the good
of the service, I forced myself to submit," Marcy subtly recorded
in his chronicle. "Seizing me in his brawny arms and laying his
greasy head upon my shoulder, he gave me a most bruin-like
squeeze; after undergoing which I flattered myself that the salu-
tation was completed; but in this I was mistaken, and was doomed
to suffer another similar torture, with the savage's head upon my
other shoulder, and at the same time rubbing his greasy face
against mine, all of which he gave me to understand was to be

70

regarded as a most distinguished and signal mark of affection for the American people (whom he loved so much that it almost broke his heart) and which I as their representative, had the honor to receive."

The convention duly honored, Marcy informed the chief that many more wagons would follow, and that he expected the Comanches to remember their treaties with the whites. He then presented the braves with pipes and tobacco, which they received with an outward display of gratitude.

The following day being Sunday, the emigrants encamped to rest and make repairs, and, as expected, their new friends paid a second social call—this time bringing their wives and children. Is-so-Keep once again sought out the military commander, bestowing upon him the same greeting as before. He then stated that he was ready for "big talk" and gathered his braves about in a large circle. Captain Marcy took his place upon the ground, while a crowd of approximately five hundred emigrants and soldiers gathered to watch the proceedings; then, to the apparent exclusion of the commander, Black Beaver and the Comanche chief immediately became engaged in an argument.

Marcy at last was provoked into interceding and demanded that his interpreter translate the conversation. "He say, Captain, he bring two wife for you," replied Black Beaver. To the commander's surprised horror he beheld two of the most repulsive and unseductive creatures that he had ever laid eyes upon, "covered with filth and dirt, their hair cut close to the head, and features ugly in the extreme." Suppressing an embarrassed smile, Marcy politely requested Black Beaver to inform his most generous guest that he already had one wife at home and was not disposed to marry others when abroad. Black Beaver relayed the message, and after a brief exchange with the puzzled chief he turned again to Marcy: "He say, Captain, you the strangest man he ever see; every man he see before, when he been travelin' long time, the fust thing he want, wife."

The humor of the situation was not lost upon the group of whites gathered around to witness the meeting, but Marcy was anxious to get down to serious business. He then informed the chief that the President of the United States was a friend of his "red children," with whom he desired to live in peace. Is-so-Keep replied stoically that such a statement surprised him since he had been led to believe that the "Big Chief" held his "red children" in small esteem, judging from the few trifling presents he had received the day before.

Marcy somehow managed to conclude the conference soon thereafter.

The farther the travelers went, the greater their speed. Gradually the Canadian River veered toward a north-south course, away from the path that the expedition was taking, and eventually it was lost from sight completely. On June 23, the caravan arrived at a sparkling spring of cold water, approximately one hundred miles southeast of Santa Fé, where the trail forked. One road turned toward the northwest and continued along the east bank of the Pecos River to the town of San Miguel, while the other veered to the southwest toward Anton Chico. Most of the emigrants decided in favor of the San Miguel route on to Santa Fé, but Marcy and his military command took the road to Anton Chico, arriving there at sunset on the same day. The troops encamped near the edge of the town, which was the first settlement they had seen since leaving Edwards' Trading Post several weeks earlier. The grubby inhabitants of Anton Chico, an adobe town of about five hundred population on the west bank of the Pecos River, subsisted principally by farming, but they received the Anglo-Americans with characteristic Mexican cordiality. The next day being St. John's Day, Marcy decided to remain in order that his men could watch the celebration and the animals get a well-earned rest.

Horse racing and cockfighting occupied most of the next morning and afternoon, and in the evening the visitors were treated to a "fandango," which the soldiers entered into with "real hearty good will." "I was much surprised to see with what ease and grace a 'peon,' who is degraded to a condition worse than slavery, and is constantly employed in the lowest kind of menial services, would hand his signorita [sic] to the floor to engage in a gallopade or waltz. They are really graceful," the commander observed.

On June 25, Marcy once again took up the trail. Crossing the Pecos at Anton Chico, where the water was only one hundred feet wide and two feet deep, he and his troops and a few emigrant wagons continued west fifty-eight miles to the small village of Galisteo. At one point along the road, the Captain and Black Beaver left the main party and rode north a short distance to survey the surrounding country, when suddenly and unexpectedly they came upon the crest of a bluff terminating the high plain. The view which unfolded before their eyes was described as the most significant one Marcy had ever witnessed:

"As I stood upon the top of the almost perpendicular cliff bordering the valley of the Pecos, and one thousand feet above it, I could see the valley up and down the river for several miles. It is here about one mile wide, and shut in with immense walls of lime and sandstone. Casting my eyes down from this giddy height, a magnificent carpet of cultivated fields of wheat, corn and other grains was spread out directly beneath me, with a beautiful little river winding quietly and gracefully through the centre; this, together with the Mexicans in their broad-brimmed sombreros and strangely shaped costumes, plodding quietly along behind their ploughs and 'carretas,' and the Sierras Blancas, covered with perpetual snow, and glistening in the distance like burnished silver as the sun shone upon them, formed one of the most beautiful landscapes that it is possible to conceive of."

At Galisteo, twenty-six miles from Santa Fé, the expedition found a large encampment of emigrants recruiting their animals and laying in a supply of provisions before continuing to California. For the most part they had come from Independence, Missouri, having journeyed along the Santa Fé Trail. On June 27, Marcy took a course due north of Galisteo and struck the Independence road (Santa Fé Trail) around noon the following day. The geological formations suddenly changed from a barren plain to granite cliffs and rugged mountains—hard going, but Marcy now was only five miles east of his destination.

Winding through the canyons along a narrow pass, the travelers soon emerged into the green valley of the Río Chiquito, a small tributary of the Río Grande, around four o'clock in the evening, June 28, 1849. Before them lay the end of the trail, the ancient but now bustling city of Santa Fé, situated at the foot of the Sangre de Cristo Range.

The expedition had completed its journey in eighty-five days and had covered a distance of 819.5 miles since leaving Fort Smith. During the sixty-five days of actual travel it had averaged slightly less than thirteen miles a day, but the route Marcy had chosen proved a good one, for his party was without water or wood at only four campsites. His long journey had followed a course practically due west of Fort Smith and approximately along the 35° 30′ N. latitude. "I am, therefore, of the opinion," he wrote the Secretary of War, "that few localities could be found upon the continent which (for as great a distance) would present as few obstacles to the construction of a railroad as upon this route. It is true that, upon the western extremity, there is but little timber except cottonwood; but in many places destitute of timber there are large quantities of lime and sandstone . . . which could easily be . . . used as a substitute for timber. The surface of the ground is generally so perfectly even and level that but little labor would be required to grade the road; and, as there are but few hills or ravines, there would not be much excavation or embankment."

Lieutenant Simpson of the topographical engineers, however, disagreed with Captain Marcy concerning the desirability of constructing a railroad across the country. "To my mind," he wrote in his report, "the time has not yet come when this or any other railroad can be built over this continent . . . contemplate the immense area of uncultivated and untimbered land . . . the absolute poverty of this whole expanse, in respect to . . . a good producing population . . . and the resources which such a population naturally develop."[12] Perhaps Simpson was right, for some twenty-two years elapsed before a railroad was completed across the continent.

Marcy's expedition to Santa Fé in 1849 was not a particularly remarkable one, considering the equipment, personnel, and arms at his disposal. But the success of his first large-scale exploring venture gave him confidence and courage for the more arduous tasks ahead. Indeed, his name thereafter would be famous in the army because of this undertaking, and ultimately the succeeding years would bring even more fame.

[12] *Senate Doc. No. 12*, 22–23.

VI

"All in fine health"

1849

ORIGINALLY, Captain Marcy had anticipated remaining in Santa
Fé for only a week or two before resuming his return march; but
his work stock, particularly the Mexican mules, were in such miserable condition that they could not be used immediately. Accordingly, he ordered a small detachment of troops to take them to
grazing grounds some distance from Santa Fé to be fattened on
corn. Six weeks were needed for the animals to regain their
strength; meanwhile, the commander had to wait.

Santa Fé was a colorful, exciting, and unabashed melting pot
in 1849, with every day a moral holiday. Its normal population of
approximately five thousand Mexicans and Anglo-Americans had
suddenly been doubled by the arrival of California immigrants.
Weary travelers reached the former Spanish outpost after weeks
of suffering, some too dejected and penniless to continue their
journey, and many of them scattered about the country searching
for employment. Usually, however, the gold seekers tarried only
briefly at this continental crossroad to repair their wagons, rest
their stock, and lay in provisions. Meanwhile, Santa Fé, which
had its full share of sin, offered a last and lusty opportunity for
relaxation to those headed for the "promised land."

Captain Marcy was fascinated by the exciting scenes about
him. Although not a participant in the perpetual monte games
at the gambling houses, he was no bluenose puritan either; one
may assume that his free time was not spent in seclusion. "The
damned human race," as Mark Twain called it, is never boring
to persons like Randolph B. Marcy. There was work to do, too.

Both the Navajos and the Apaches were showing signs of unrest, and most of Marcy's detachment joined the regulars from near-by Fort Marcy[1] to quell them. The commander did not accompany the expedition, but utilized the time afforded by the temporary absence of his troops to prepare for the long trek back to Fort Smith.

Since he was interested in examining as much of the country as possible, Marcy decided to follow a different route on the journey home. He therefore made inquiry relative to the practicability of blazing a wagon trail from a point south of Santa Fé due east to the Pecos River and thence to the headwaters of the Red River, but he discovered that all too little was known of the region. The few Mexicans at Santa Fé who professed a knowledge of the Pecos and Red River country were unwilling to serve as guides because the hostile Apaches roamed the area. Ultimately the Captain learned that a Comanche Indian named Manuel, who lived at near-by San Miguel, had been a guide for the famous traveler, Josiah Gregg. When Manuel assured Marcy that he could lead him to the western border of Texas by a southern route, his services were promptly obtained. The choice, for Marcy, proved fortunate.

Before launching on the course now envisioned, Marcy reasoned that it would be wiser first to proceed south for approximately three hundred miles below Santa Fé to Doña Ana, then turn eastward to the Texas border. Doña Ana, containing some three hundred Mexican farmers, was situated on the old Chihuahua Trail about sixty miles north of El Paso. As all emigrants leaving Santa Fé for California were obliged to go down the Río Grande to Doña Ana before intercepting Cooke's California road,[2] Marcy thought that he might render an important service: if a suitable trail could be blazed from Doña Ana east to Fort Smith, the distance from the latter point to southern California could be shortened by several hundred miles.

According to Manuel, the expedition ultimately could reach the headwaters of the Brazos by following a course due east of

[1] Fort Marcy was named in honor of former Secretary of War William L. Marcy.

[2] Colonel Philip St. George Cooke made the first wagon road to California in 1846. His course followed a general direction west of Doña Ana, New Mexico, along the Gila River to San Diego, California. It soon became a link in one of the principal transcontinental trails.

Doña Ana. Marcy knew that once he reached the river, it would be relatively easy for his Delaware guide, Black Beaver, to find his way on to Fort Smith since he knew that country well.

With final plans completed and the mules and oxen in good condition once again, the company was ready to move. The same military personnel that had accompanied Marcy to Santa Fé would now return with him to Indian Territory, with the exception of Lieutenant Buford of the dragoons and four infantry privates. One of the latter was so ill that he had to be left behind, while the other three had deserted soon after the expedition reached Santa Fé. Lieutenant Buford, it will be recalled, with Lieutenant Harrison, had courted Mary Conway. Before Marcy's company was ready to depart, Buford received orders transferring him to California, where he doubtless anticipated renewing his courtship of the "Belle of the Prairies." But if he did harbor this hope, he was to be sadly disappointed, for Mary ultimately married a sea captain.[3] Lieutenant Delos B. Sackett from Fort Marcy (Santa Fé) assumed command of the dragoons, replacing Lieutenant Buford for the return trip.

The expedition left Santa Fé on August 14, 1849, with a feeling of relief at not being encumbered by the miles of emigrant wagons that had followed it westward. A short distance below Santa Fé the travelers came upon the northern edge of the dreary Jornada del Muerto, an eighty-mile stretch of barren desert which could be traversed only at night because of the intense heat. Three days later the desert had been conquered, and the expedition was rolling rapidly toward Doña Ana. On August 29, the party reached the small village on the Río Grande, where Marcy stopped to rest his animals and repair the wagons before swinging eastward toward the Texas border.

Marcy remained at Doña Ana only until September 1, when his party took up the march once again, pursuing a course (N 81 degrees) toward the San Augustine Pass in the Organ Mountains. This unusual range, which had received its name from its similarity to the pipes of an organ, was reached on September 2; and after passing through it, Marcy altered his course more toward the southeast. The flat, sandy valley lying ahead made progress easy; the company arrived at the base of the Waco (Hueco) Moun-

[3] Grant Foreman, *Marcy and the Gold Seekers*, 338.

tains two days later. The Wacos were a north-south range about forty miles east of and parallel to the Organs. Manuel, having been here before, had no trouble leading the company through the mountains to a near-by spring of clear, cool water, where it encamped for the night.

East of the Waco Mountains lay another north-south range, the Guadalupe Mountains of southeastern New Mexico, and between the two ranges ran a valley which was hard, smooth, and luxuriously covered with various grama grasses. According to Marcy's measurements, the Guadalupes were approximately 147 miles east of Doña Ana, the distance having been covered by his party in ten days. In places the range reached a height of two thousand feet and was a much more formidable barrier than the previous mountains. The expedition skirted the western base of the Guadalupes until a narrow gorge flanked by sandstone bluffs was discovered through which a passage could be made. Marcy described the region as wild and rocky, abounding with grizzly bear, bighorn sheep, and black-tailed deer—literally a hunter's paradise. The slopes of the giant peaks were covered with pine, fir, and cedar; the commander correctly prophesied that some day this virgin timber would be used for building purposes.

Once the gorge had been located, the expedition passed through the Guadalupes and soon struck Delaware Creek, which it followed for forty miles before arriving on the west bank of the Pecos River. So far, the journey had been more like a pleasant outing than a monotonous march through an unexplored desert. Quail, plover, deer, and fish were so bountiful along Delaware Creek that the evening encampments frequently took on the spirit of a holiday crowd. Also, during the sixteen days since the travelers had left Doña Ana, they had had mostly mild, clear weather.

The worst part of the journey still lay ahead, and as the expedition stood poised on the western bank of the Pecos, it became increasingly obvious that getting the wagons across would be difficult indeed. "The stream here is about thirty yards wide, very sinuous, rapid, and deep, with high clay banks," the commander wrote. He therefore decided to continue south along the west bank of the river until he found a suitable ford. Not until five days later did he find such a place, but even there the embankment was twenty feet above the water.

"I was obliged to resort to one of those expedients which necessity often forces travelers in this wild country to put in practice," he explained. First the embankment was leveled several degrees to make it possible to roll the wagons down to the edge of the water. Then one of the heavy wagons was unloaded and its bed removed. Six empty barrels were wedged inside the bed and two barrels were lashed to the sides, so that, when the wagon was turned, it became an excellent makeshift raft, capable of carrying a tremendous load. Marcy next selected an experienced swimmer to swim to the opposite bank holding the end of the rope with his teeth. The soldier splashed his way across, and once ashore fastened the rope securely to a well-driven stake some distance upstream. The other end of the line was attached to the raft, which was now packed high with approximately two thousand pounds of freight. When pushed into the swift current, the "ferryboat" swung gently to the opposite bank, where it was unloaded immediately and pulled back for another cargo.

After the baggage and all the supplies had been safely deposited on the eastern side, the mules, oxen, and horses were roped together, arranged in single file, and forced to swim across. At last all of the work stock were hitched together and made to pull the empty wagons through the fifteen-foot-deep current by a long, stout rope. Thus the treacherous Pecos was crossed in one day. The operation completed, a great sigh of relief went up from every man in the party—from the commander to the lowest private.

The expedition now traveled generally northeast, the course it would follow until reaching the Red River several weeks later. The region immediately east of the Pecos was a sandy, barren prairie that extended from eastern New Mexico to the high plains of the *Llano Estacado* (Staked Plain) in western Texas. On September 29, the travelers again came upon this great plateau, only to be faced with a sixty-mile stretch of deep and ever shifting sand, where water was scarce and the sun showed no mercy to man or beast. Marcy now had to employ every animal to pull the heavily laden wagons, but by October 2, 1849, another obstacle had been overcome. Luckily, soon after the party had dropped down from the eastern rim of the Staked Plain, it came upon "a fine spring of water," the present Big Spring, Texas, some six hundred miles from Santa Fé.

Marcy's exhausted men and jaded animals were now near the headwaters of the Colorado River, and the commander felt that several days' rest was badly needed. Since Black Beaver reported that the country from here on to Red River was familiar to him, it was no longer necessary to employ Manuel, who, paid in silver for his excellent services, set out for Santa Fé alone. Although Marcy recognized the Comanche's aid in his official report of the expedition to the War Department, not until many years later did he relate the following anecdote:

[The two Indians, Manuel and Black Beaver, had bivouacked at the same fire during their long journey together in 1849.] "On visiting them one evening according to my usual practice, I found them engaged in a very earnest and apparently not very amicable conversation. On inquiring the cause of this, Beaver answered, 'I've been telling this Comanche what I seen 'mong the white folks.'

"I said, 'Well, what did you tell him?'

" 'I tell him 'bout the steam-boats, and the railroads, and the heap o' houses I seen in St. Louis.'

" 'Well sir, what does he think of that?'

" 'He say I'ze damn fool.

" 'I tell him the world is round, but he keep all e'time say: "Hush, you fool, do you 'pose I'ze child. Haven't I got eyes? Can't I see the prairie? You call him round." '

"I then asked him to explain to the Comanche the magnetic telegraph. He looked at me earnestly, and said, 'What you call that magnetic telegraph?'

"I said, 'You have heard of New York and New Orleans?'

" 'Oh, yes,' he replied.

"Very well: we have a wire connecting these two cities, which are about a thousand miles apart, and it would take a man thirty days to ride it upon a good horse. Now a man stands at one end of the wire in New York, and by touching it a few times he inquires of his friend in New Orleans what he had for breakfast. His friend in New Orleans touches the other end of the wire, and in ten minutes the answer comes back—ham and eggs. Tell him that, Beaver.'

"His countenance assumed a most comical expression, but he made no remark until I again requested him to repeat what I had said to the Comanche, when he observed, 'No, Captain, I not tell him that, for I don't believe that myself.'

"Upon my assuring him that such was the fact, and that I had seen it myself, he said, 'Injun not very smart; sometimes he's big fool, but he holler pretty loud; you hear him maybe half a mile; you say 'Merican man he talk thousand miles. I 'spect you try to fool me now, Captain; maybe so you lie.' "[4]

October 4 found the party once again in motion, traveling through a beautiful timbered valley towards the Colorado. The country now became increasingly interesting, with quail, turkey, and meadowlarks everywhere and mesquite groves and wild chinaberry trees on the banks of the small creeks.

Yet, despite the relative ease of the journey, Marcy had to delay again on October 7, until he could recover from a severe case of dysentery. While recuperating, the commander suggested to Lieutenant Harrison that he make a brief survey of the trail ahead in hope that some time could be saved when the march was renewed. Harrison rode off immediately. Several hours elapsed without his return, and darkness arrived before much thought was given to his prolonged absence. "I think he must have wandered farther than he intended," Marcy recorded. ". . . I have had the cannon fired and if he is within twenty miles of us he will be likely to hear it, as the atmosphere is perfectly still and clear."

The following morning, when a second signal from the cannon still brought no response from young Harrison, Marcy sent Lieutenant Updegraff with Black Beaver to search in the direction taken by the officer, at the same time ordering the dragoons to examine the surrounding country for possible signs of hostile Indians. Within two hours Lieutenant Updegraff and Black Beaver were back in camp to report that they had followed the officer's tracks for about one and one-half miles to a spot where it appeared that he had been intercepted by a small band of Indians and had ridden off with them toward the south.

Lieutenant Sackett and his dragoons were promptly ordered to follow the trail until Harrison was overtaken and rescued; meanwhile, Marcy could only remain in his tent, too ill to stir from his

[4] Marcy, *Army Life on the Border*, 84–85.

bed. Sackett had little difficulty following the trail beyond the point where Harrison had been intercepted, but just two miles away from it, searchers came upon the scalped body of their missing comrade—shot through the head and stripped of his clothing and equipment. Two men were sent back at once to relay the news to Marcy, whose personal fondness for the young officer would make the event even more tragic. Marcy ordered a wagon dispatched to recover the corpse, while Black Beaver and the remainder of Sackett's detachment followed the trail of the murderers until darkness made further search impracticable.

Next day, Sackett renewed the chase for a distance of twenty miles, but was forced to abandon it again on account of the condition of his horses and the realization that the Indians were by now many hours beyond the scene. In their hasty flight across the prairies the renegades had carelessly dropped a pair of moccasins, a lariat, and a saddle which Black Beaver correctly identified as Kiowa.[5] Later, when the dragoons returned to report their failure, gloom enveloped the whole company. Some of the soldiers had served in the Mexican War, and Marcy observed that he had supposed them incapable of emotion, but now they were excited to tears, "knowing that in Harrison's death they had lost a good friend."

Two men fashioned a crude coffin from a wagon bed. Then Harrison's body was covered with a thick coat of tar and placed inside between two layers of charcoal, and the coffin was sealed. In this manner his remains were returned to Fort Smith and buried with full military honors. Because of the victim's distinguished ancestry and the tragic manner of his death, the details of his murder were given wide publicity in newspapers throughout the country, inadvertently bringing dramatic notice to Marcy's expedition.

When Mary Marcy ultimately received the news of young Harrison's death, she was grieved by it no less than her husband, for she had come to know the Lieutenant well during their recent journey from Baltimore to Fort Towson. "He was one of the noblest young men I ever knew," she wrote to Mary Ellen. "His sad fate is a deep and heartfelt affinity to us all. We all mourn for him as for a brother."[6]

[5] W. B. Parker, *Through Unexplored Texas* (Philadelphia, 1854), 30.

Santa Fé, around 1850, a "colorful, exciting, unabashed melting pot."

Resuming the march on October 10, the expedition maintained a steady course over a level plain covered with mesquite and rich grama grass until it struck the Double Mountain Fork of the Brazos River in present Stonewall County, Texas, on October 12. Here the travelers encamped for the night, but neither men nor animals got any sleep, for soon after darkness a bleak Texas norther roared into camp, followed by torrential rains. The change in temperature was so sudden that somehow it caused the death of thirty-three mules. A full day was required to dispose of the dead animals, dry the bedding, and separate the ruined equipment from the salvageable.

A few days after the storm the expedition came upon the first large band of Indians encountered on the return trip, when several hundred Comanches with their women and children suddenly descended upon the train from all directions. Marcy reluctantly permitted them to approach, believing they would commit no depredations in the presence of their families. Then, within minutes, a second band was detected approaching from across the prairies. The latter group, identified by Black Beaver as Kickapoos, consisted of approximately one hundred "fine dashing-looking young fellows, all well-mounted and armed with good rifles." Before continuing the council with the Comanches, Marcy asked the Kickapoos where they were going, for he knew that this was not their usual habitation. They replied that they were on their way to Colorado to find game for the winter months, and after receiving a few paltry gifts, they soon departed.

Turning again to the Comanches, Marcy realized that they were apt to be more of a nuisance than the Kickapoos. Their chief, "a dignified, fine-looking old man" who called himself Senaco, after the usual embracing ceremony, anxiously assured the commander that he was "not a Comanche, but an American." Marcy promptly and graciously responded that he was "soul and body a Comanche, without an ounce of American blood." Senaco then exhibited a number of certificates from different white men whom he had met which he claimed testified to his friendly disposition, and insisted that the Captain read the documents at once. The first certificate examined read: "The bearer of this says he is a Comanche Chief, named Se-na-co; that he is the biggest Indian and best friend the

6 November 21, 1849, McClellan Papers, 2nd Series, I.

whites ever had; in fact, that he is a first-rate fellow; but I believe he is a damn rascal, so look out for him."[7]

Nôt wishing to embarrass his guest, who had kept his eyes fixed upon the commander's face, Marcy suppressed his amusement with difficulty. As soon as he could manage a serious tone, he explained to the chief that "the paper was not as good as it might be," whereupon Senaco destroyed it at once without comment. The remainder of the conference proceeded in typical fashion, and after the usual presentation of gifts and warnings to the Indians to behave themselves, both parties went their separate ways.

Five years later Marcy again saw the old chief near this same spot, when to his surprise Senaco recognized him immediately, pronouncing his name quite distinctly.

The region where Marcy's command had met these Comanches and Kickapoos was near the headwaters of the Double Mountain Fork and the Clear Fork of the Brazos, a beautiful, timbered country flanked by low mountain ranges and abounding with small streams. On October 22, the party came to the banks of the Clear Fork and continued downstream to its confluence with the Brazos, where the water was approximately two hundred yards wide but shallow enough to be forded easily. It occurred to Marcy that here was an excellent site for a military post: in the proximity of the Comanche, Kiowa, Lipan, Tonkawa, Wichita, Caddo, and Waco tribes, a fort situated near the Brazos unquestionably would provide a strong influence toward putting a stop to the depredations which these Indians were accused of committing upon the frontier settlements in Texas. The War Department must have thought well of the idea, too, for two years later it ordered the construction of such a fort (Belknap), which ultimately became one of the most important military establishments on the American frontier—a tribute to Marcy's judgment.

The west fork of the Trinity River was but two days' travel from the Brazos, and once across the fork the expedition climbed to the center of the ridge which divided the Trinity from the Red. A well-marked wagon road, the first sign of civilization east of Doña Ana, followed the ridge in a straight, eastward direction.

[7] Marcy, *Army Life on the Border,* 58.

84

The wagons rolled smoothly over the hard prairie turf, reaching the edge of the Cross Timbers on October 30, where the travelers camped near the site of future Gainesville, Texas. A few miles beyond the western edge of the Cross Timbers the road on the divide intersected the Preston Road. This north-south highway constructed by the Republic of Texas in 1841 ran from Austin to the Red River near present Denison. The small settlement that developed on the Texas side of the river at the terminus of the road was then known as Preston, and soon the road itself took the same name. Today Preston is forgotten, its site lying beneath the waters of the recently constructed Lake Texoma.[8]

Reaching the Preston Road, the expedition turned north on it to Preston, only forty miles below Fort Washita in Indian Territory. Here the travelers encamped on November 4, and Marcy learned from a near-by farmer that Mary was anxiously awaiting him at Fort Washita. Also, according to the Texan, whom Marcy merely identified as "Mr. Butt," a rumor had persisted for the past month that the commander and his entire company had been massacred by the Indians. Although "highly exaggerated," the story was too good to die, and each time Marcy went on a subsequent expedition it would crop up anew—each time adding to the fame of the explorer.

The party crossed the river at Preston on a small ferry operated by B. F. Colbert, a Chickasaw Indian, and arrived without further incident at Fort Washita on November 7, 1849. Eighty-five days had elapsed since the company had left Santa Fé, sixty-eight of them spent in actual travel, and they had averaged more than thirteen miles a day on the thousand-mile journey. The tattered uniforms and unshaven beards of the travelers, plus the dilapidated wagons and animals, undoubtedly presented a pitiful sight, but only the news of Lieutenant Harrison's death clouded an otherwise gay reunion.

Mary Marcy had returned to Fort Towson only three days before the expedition reached Fort Washita, and the Captain's disappointment in not meeting her and little Fanny there must have been acute. "I passed four weeks very pleasantly among my friends

[8] John William Rogers, *The Lusty Texans of Dallas* (New York, 1951), 26–27.

at Washita," she wrote to Mary Ellen a short time later, "and returned home hoping that I would have some intelligence from your dear father, but alas. . . ."[9]

Marcy did not tarry at Fort Washita. The dragoons under Lieutenant Sackett headed for Fort Smith on November 10, via the old military road through Boggy Depot. A few days later Marcy and the rest of his military detachment, consisting of an infantry company, headed for the home post, Fort Towson, some eighty miles due east of Fort Washita.

The commander's arrival home ended an eight months' absence. These months must have been trying for Mary as well as for Marcy. Her letters during this period reveal a sickening uncertainty about her husband's welfare, and she occasionally asked herself in them if she were to be doomed forever to such loneliness. But the Captain's return magically changed her despondency. "I determined to occupy my mind as much as possible so as to keep from borrowing trouble with regard to him," she later wrote to Mary Ellen, "although everybody seemed anxious for his fate. . . . I accordingly commenced housecleaning the next day after my return [from Fort Washita] and on Thursday finished putting everything in first-class order.

"I started out to pay a visit to Mrs. Leon[?], and on my way was met by one of our young officers who said to me, 'Have you heard the good news?' I replied, 'What news?' He then said, 'Captain Marcy and command arrived on Tuesday last, all in fine health at Washita.'

"Only think, three days after I left there—was it not too bad that I could not have met him at that place. You can easily imagine my delight. The first thing I did was to sit down and cry for joy as hard as I could. On Saturday eve as I sat sewing and thinking it strange he did not come, one of the servants ran up calling out, 'Captain Marcy has come, Captain Marcy has come.'

"I rushed out on the back piazza and there I met him face to face, and such a face as his was, covered with beard about six inches long. You can imagine how much he was disguised. It was one of the happiest moments of my life, I assure you, to see him return once more to me in health after such a long absence and

[9] November 21, 1849, McClellan Papers, 2nd Series, I.

such a perilous march of two thousand miles. . . . Have we not great cause to be thankful, my dear Ellen, to our Heavenly Father, that your own dear parent was preserved from all danger and that he did not share the same fate with poor Lieutenant Harrison. We are indeed blessed by our kind Protector. Let us be constantly thankful for what we receive."[10]

Before he could enjoy a well-earned rest, Marcy had to report the results of his recent journey to General Arbuckle at Fort Smith. Accordingly, he left Fort Towson on horseback two days after his arrival there, reaching the Seventh Military District Headquarters on November 19, the same date that the detachment of dragoons arrived via a different route. The next few days were busy; Lieutenant Harrison's body was given a formal burial, at which time all of the military personnel and many citizens of the town paid their respects; letters had to be written to officials in Washington; and matters pertaining to the disposition of the wagons, animals, and surplus supplies had to be attended to. In addition, Marcy had to discuss with the commander of the military district certain matters relating to the completion and ultimate publication of the journal of the expedition.[11] But all this was accomplished quickly, so that the explorer was able to return to his family and friends by November 27.

The details of the Santa Fé expedition in 1849 were made public through Marcy's journal, which was published a few months later, and through the articles which appeared in newspapers throughout the United States. On November 20, 1849, a correspondent, whose article was signed "Crawford," wrote from Fort Smith to the *New York Sun*: "The officers and men, constituting the escort, who have just returned, are in fine health and spirits, but appear rather ragged and rugged in their faces and clothing, having accomplished a journey of 2000 miles, believed to be the longest march ever performed by the United States Infantry. Captain Marcy is a most gentlemanly man and accomplished officer, and it is to be hoped that a narrative of his journal will be pub-

[10] *Ibid.*

[11] Marcy's Journal, previously cited, was not put in final form for several weeks. It was eventually turned over to Lieutenant F. F. Flint, acting assistant adjutant general, Seventh Military Department, who later forwarded it to the Adjutant General's Office in Washington.

lished, for it cannot fail to be deeply interesting. . . . It is now proclaimed and believed here that this [the southern, or return route] will be the principal overland route to California."[12]

In 1849 much of the region beyond the Cross Timbers in present western Oklahoma and Texas was unexplored and relatively unknown, as evidenced by the number of inaccuracies on contemporary maps. Marcy's first extensive expedition was, therefore, important in that it enabled him to correct many topographical errors. It had been generally believed that a tremendous north-south chain of mountains lay somewhere northeast of El Paso which were virtually impassable. Indeed, three parallel ranges were found in this region, but they were by-passed or crossed with small difficulty. Also, most maps of the period showed the Pecos River as a stream some forty miles east of and almost parallel to the Río Grande, whereas the actual distance between the two streams was approximately two hundred miles. The headwaters of the Colorado, Red, and Brazos likewise had been charted inaccurately.

One problem that vexed prospective California immigrants in 1849 was whether to use oxen or mules as beasts of burden in crossing the plains. Marcy, who used both as work stock on his Santa Fé expedition, became convinced that oxen were much more desirable for the following reasons: oxen not only were hardier and less susceptible to disease and the changing weather of the plains, but could subsist almost altogether on grass; they were cheaper to purchase, less apt to stray from camp, not desired by the Indians, and could be killed and eaten in an emergency. Also, and on this point many of the commander's contemporaries disagreed, oxen with a heavy load could travel daily from six to eight miles farther than could mules or horses with the same load. He declared, furthermore, that oxen were better in the mud. Many California immigrants subsequently followed Marcy's advice and used oxen as beasts of burden in preference to mules or horses; others, who perhaps were more skilled in the handling of mules and horses, refused to have anything to do with oxen. In general, however, the commander's opinions proved valid.

Perhaps the most significant result of Marcy's expedition was

[12] Marcy's Scrapbook.

the discovery that the southern route from Doña Ana to Fort Smith not only possessed a year-round supply of wood, grass, and water for travelers, but shortened the distance to the Pacific Coast by some three hundred miles. Furthermore, the commander noted the opportunities that this route offered for a continental railroad: "Throughout this entire distance it would not be necessary to make a single tunnel, or to use a stationary engine. There would be but few heavy excavations or embankments; and for a great portion of the distance, the surface of the earth is so perfectly firm and smooth that it would appear to have been designed by the Great Architect of the Universe for a railroad, and adapted and fitted by nature's handiwork for the reception of the super-structure."

The route about which Marcy wrote speedily became a link in a great highway from East to West, and by the end of 1850, literally thousands of emigrants were moving along the road between Fort Smith and Doña Ana. (Most of them deviated a bit and went via El Paso, thence north to Doña Ana, where they took Cooke's road to California.) In 1858, John Butterfield established his famous Overland Express from St. Louis to San Francisco, his Concord coaches being the first to cross the continent. The distance from one end of the line to the other was 2,795 miles, more than one-third of which overlapped Marcy's 1849 road and touched such points as Preston, present Gainesville, Fort Belknap on the Brazos, Horsehead Crossing on the Pecos (a few miles below the place where Marcy had crossed), and El Paso.[13]

Undoubtedly the railroad which Marcy envisioned along his Doña Ana–Fort Smith road would have been a reality fairly soon had not national politics intervened. Sectional feeling became increasingly bitter between 1850 and 1860 over the location of a transcontinental railroad route. Southerners insisted that the federal government should support a line along either of the roads that Marcy had marked out between Arkansas and New Mexico in 1849. Northerners held out for a course that would be more favorable to them, and the Civil War settled the issue in their favor—the Union Pacific and Central Pacific were completed in 1869. Twenty years after these railroads were chartered, the Texas

[13] Marcy's original wagon road came within thirty miles of El Paso at one point.

and Pacific Railroad, which generally followed the old Overland Express route (Marcy's southern route from New Mexico) across Texas, reached El Paso. There it joined with the Southern Pacific, which generally followed Cooke's old California road. Thus, after thirty-three years, Captain Marcy's vision of a southern transcontinental railroad became a reality.

VII

"People of some consequence"

1849–1850

IT WAS ONLY FOUR WEEKS after Mary's arrival at Fort Towson that Captain Marcy departed for "services on the prairies," leaving his wife and "Little Fanny" at the lonely frontier garrison for eight months. Mary was determined not to complain but to try to remain cheerful, for she had long since accepted frequent family separations as the lot of military people. Having "two good black servants" to take care of the house and meals, she was freed from much menial work that today is made easier by household gadgets. With her wide interests and boundless energy, she had not yet suffered from boredom—whether at a fashionable gathering in the East or alone at an isolated frontier post.

In February, 1849, Mrs. Abercrombie arrived with a brood of small children, but unfortunately her presence added little to local society, for the only other white woman at the post was the sutler's wife. There were, however, four or five missionary ladies at near-by Spencer Academy, and before the end of 1849 the wives of two of the younger officers arrived at Fort Towson. The monotony of life at the garrison was further relieved by the occasional visits of friends from Fort Washita, some eighty miles away. Indeed, these visits were anticipated with much excitement and feverish preparations, followed by an exhausting round of dances and dinner parties.

Other activities claimed Mary's time, too. She usually rode horseback daily along the banks of the Red River or into Texas. She inspected her vegetable and flower gardens, and fed her pet mockingbirds and squirrels. In addition to these recreational pursuits, she had to preserve fruits and vegetables, supervise the servants, make clothes for Fanny, knit socks and sweaters, and write letters to family and friends.

Once a week, except when the roads were impassable, the mail arrived from Fort Smith. Rarely did it fail to bring a belated letter from Mary Ellen and rarely did Mary Marcy fail to answer by return mail. Like any other mother long separated from her teen-age daughter, Mary was constantly concerned about Mary Ellen's progress in school and about her health. Mary Ellen must have grown weary of reading the same admonishments for almost three years—"Be sure you wear your flannels, thick stockings, and India rubber shoes, when the weather is the least bit cold or damp . . . study your French and practice on the piano one hour each day . . . the whole regiment expects to see a very accomplished young lady in you."[1]

Although Mary Marcy strove earnestly to be patient and brave, occasionally a murmur of discontent crept into the loquacious correspondence to her older daughter. Once she complained, "This world is full of disappointments, just think of me—after six months of separation from your dear father, and coming this long journey to be with him one month that he should so soon again be called away. It is a bitter trial for me to bear but yet I know there is no help for it and I must be resigned." Sometimes she said that Fort Towson was "a beautiful spot" and the climate "perfectly delightful," and again that it was a "dull, out-of-the-way place" and the weather "unbearable." "I don't like the South," she also wrote. "Give me the cool bracing climate of the North. . . . I do not like the general character of the people in this region either. They all keep so many slaves they are not compelled to make the least bit of exertion and appear accordingly."

During the long months that Captain Marcy was away on the Santa Fé expedition, Mary's principal comfort was her daughter Fanny, who in 1849 was three years old and already attending the post school. She remarked frequently to Mary Ellen that Fanny was "a very spoiled child," and that "there is no one for her to play with except the young officers. . . . The other day she put on her bonnet and said that she was going out to find Sister Nellie,

---

[1] Unless otherwise indicated, all quotations in this chapter are from the Marcy family correspondence found in the McClellan Papers, 2nd Series, I.

but she came back in tears a short time later and said she could not find her."

Upon completion of his business at Fort Smith relative to his first expedition beyond the Cross Timbers, Captain Marcy returned to Fort Towson on November 27, 1849, hoping to enjoy a long period of uninterrupted domesticity. But first he had to complete and polish his journal and maps before forwarding them to the Adjutant General's Office for study and publication. "He has read me certain portions which are very interesting," Mary remarked. "He will no doubt gain much credit and become well known from the expedition. He cannot have too much praise bestowed upon him in my opinion."

Marcy did not mention in his journal the exact circumstances by which he acquired a twelve-year-old Mexican boy in Santa Fé, but Mary made frequent references to the boy in letters to Mary Ellen. She also explained that "John, the Mexican boy, will be bound to us until he reaches the age of twenty-four." In addition to John, the Marcys owned outright two aged Negro slaves, "Uncle Andrew" and "Aunt Mary." The latter did the laundry and house cleaning and helped care for Fanny, while Uncle Andrew cut the wood for the huge fireplaces and cookstove, looked after the vegetable garden and flower beds, and assisted with the housework. John's duties were to sweep and wash the hearths daily, wait on the table at mealtime, and attend to the fires. "The little Mexican boy is learning to talk fast in English," Mary wrote a few weeks after his arrival. "He goes to the Post school taught by our Chaplain. He is trying to learn [*sic*] Fanny Spanish. You would laugh to see her speak it after him. He improves every day, though he had the worst temper I ever saw, when he came here."

The Marcys and their three servants were by no means lonely, for four young officers without families of their own took their meals with them. The mess was managed by a free Negro and his wife. Whether this was the kind of domestic bliss that the Captain had looked forward to is not known, but his household was certainly not a small one—at least not during mealtime.

Besides the three servants and the Negro couple who kept the mess, another member was added to the household: "I have taken a little orphan girl on trial. She is the daughter of a soldier, both parents are dead. She is thirteen years of age but is very small, almost a dwarf. Fanny is very fond of her. I never knew her to become so attached to any servant. I have not yet concluded what to do. I pity her very much. She is a well-disposed and amiable child, but I feel afraid of a garrison. You know how difficult it is to bring up a girl respectable where there is so much temptation." Mary never explained clearly whether the child was a servant or a protégée.

The first Christmas at Fort Towson resembled any other day for Marcy's family, with the Captain away, as usual. On December 20, he was ordered to Fort Smith for court-martial duty and did not return until January 5, 1850. When he did come home, he at least could look forward to the remainder of the winter months without interference, for his journal and maps had been finished and forwarded to Washington. Almost a year had passed since he had been able to devote much attention to Mary Ellen, but in a series of long letters written during January and February, he described to her in careful detail the high points of his recent adventure. As much of his description of the country, emigrants, and Indians was identical to portions of his official journal, these letters must have made exciting reading for the sixteen-year-old school girl.

In writing to his daughter, however, Marcy spoke more freely concerning his personal reactions to New Mexican customs and religion than he did in his official journal. He made no attempt to conceal his New England prejudices, confessing that he was appalled by "the priests [who] tell them there is no harm in gambling and dancing, and [that] during the services two or three fiddlers always play the liveliest kind of dancing tunes." Nevertheless, he admitted that the Mexican people seemed devout and sincere, observing that his own church (Presbyterian) might well profit by their example in this regard.

The early months of 1850 passed pleasantly for Randolph and Mary Marcy, although the Captain daily expected orders to report to the Secretary of War in Washington to give an oral account of his recent trip to Santa Fé. Unhappily for Marcy, the orders never came; instead, there were constant rumors that the entire military personnel at Fort Towson would soon be transferred. Such a prospect was not pleasant, for moving inevitably meant weeks of travel, uncertainty about new quarters, and always the breaking of friendly ties. Even though the rumors persisted, the Post Returns show that Lieutenant Colonel Abercrombie remained as commander of Company D.

Also, according to the Post Returns, Marcy served as acting assistant quartermaster and acting assistant commissary of subsistence from February to June. The extra compensation must have been welcome, for Mary Ellen's schooling cost from six to eight hundred dollars a year. This obligation, plus the expense of maintaining a houseful of servants, caused Marcy constant financial concern, and he complained that his meager pay and rations were far from adequate. Although the land acquired in Wisconsin several years before had increased in value, as yet he had "realized little from it," and he was forced to borrow money from his father from time to time.

Spring arrived early in Indian Territory in 1850, and Randolph and Mary were eager to see more of the virgin country before they were transferred to a less desirable place. Accordingly, they left Fanny behind with Uncle Andrew and Aunt Mary and struck out on a cross-country tour, with Fort Washita their first objective. Despite "the horrible roads" the travelers made rapid progress across the Choctaw Nation, keeping their camping equipment, baggage, and supplies to a minimum. "A faithful corporal" drove the light four-wheel ambulance with Mary on the high spring seat beside him, while the Captain led the way on horseback. Sometimes Mary cantered alongside of Randolph on her favorite saddle horse, and together they marveled at the green foliage and the profusion of wild flowers. The trio followed the military road which ran west of Fort Towson for about forty miles, until they reached the place where it changed its westward course to veer toward the northwest to Boggy Depot. There they struck out across a trackless prairie straight west to Fort Washita, arriving there on May 6, 1850.

The eighty-mile journey from Fort Towson had taken only two days, and once Randolph and Mary were among friends at the post on the Washita River, they became the center of lively social activity. Two days later they made an early start for Fort Gibson, 160 miles to the northeast, where they planned to see other old friends of the Fifth Regiment. The second lap of their cross-country tour followed the frequently traveled Gibson Road (via Boggy Depot), today the general route of United States Highway 69 and the Katy Railroad. "The country between Fort Washita and Fort Gibson is mostly prairie and very pretty, of course being covered with a variety of flowers," Mary wrote to Mary Ellen. They arrived at Fort Gibson on the evening of the fourth day and went immediately to the quarters of Captain Stevenson, whom they had known in earlier years in Wisconsin.

Fort Gibson, one of the most famous forts in the early days of Indian Territory, had been built in 1824 on the Grand River, not far from its confluence with the Arkansas. Its chief fame, not too happily, came largely from the high death rate among the troops stationed there, and it was frequently referred to as the unhealthiest station on the American frontier. In its early days the officers and enlisted men had acquired bad reputations for gambling, wenching, horse racing, and excessive drinking.[2] Militarily, the site of the fort was strategic; and despite its reputation, Mary Marcy described it as "delightfully situated, the quarters all separate and each family possessing a garden and yard all to themselves—which makes it appear more like a little village than anything else."

Many famous military names have been associated with the history of Fort Gibson: Jefferson Davis, Stephen W. Kearny, Albert Sidney Johnston, Robert E. Lee, Zachary Taylor, George H. Thomas, Kirby Smith, and John B. Hood. In 1850, the commander was General W. G. Belknap, after whom the post in Texas was soon to be named. Mary described him as "a venerable pleasant old gentleman, has a lovely wife and two interesting daughters grown." (In subsequent years during the incredible period of American history known as the "Grant Regime," the once-honored Belknap name would be tarnished by the "Belknap Scandal."[3])

Another Fort Gibson officer whom Mary mentioned to Mary

[2] Morrison, *Military Camps and Posts in Oklahoma*, 28–47.

[3] In the spring of 1876, Secretary of the Treasury Benjamin H. Bristow uncovered irrefutable proof that Secretary of War W. W. Belknap (General W. G. Belknap's son) had collected $24,450 from the post trader at Fort Sill as the price for keeping the office. A House committee brought impeachment charges against Belknap, but President Grant accepted his resignation, which placed the offender outside the jurisdiction of the Senate. John Hicks, *The American Nation*, (New York, 1949), 55.

Ellen and whose name also became infamous during the Grant administration was Captain Frederick Dent, later Grant's brother-in-law. It will be remembered that Dent had cut a wagon road from Fort Smith to the Cross Timbers for Marcy's Santa Fé expedition the previous year. "You will be astonished when I tell you that he [Dent] is engaged to marry Louise Lynch. Louise is very tall; she curls her hair in ringlets, which gives her a girlish appearance, although in manner she is quite the woman. She attends all the parties and dances with her Captain most beautifully." The Lynch family, like many other families at Fort Gibson in 1850, had been stationed in Wisconsin at the time the Marcys were there.

The nine days that the Marcys spent at Fort Gibson were celebrated in the same exhausting fashion as their two days at Fort Washita—only much more prolonged. Dances, horseback rides, and dinners were the order of the day and night, with an occasional "concert" being presented by the post band, whose repertoire was limited but loud. The climax of the visit came with the presentation of a play produced by the soldiers at the post theater, and the next day (May 20) the visitors took leave of their friends and rode on to Fort Smith. "We were very tired nearly to death from passing over the worst road you ever saw," Mary wrote of the two-day journey. "We had been expected for several days and, as we are now people of some consequent [sic] in this part of the world, our arrival was quite an event. There is a very pleasant little circle within the Fort, and several most agreeable families who live in the town which surrounds the garrison."

While at Fort Smith, Randolph and Mary stayed with Captain Caleb Sibley and his family, whom they had also known in Wisconsin in earlier years. The visit was a short one, for by now the travelers had less enthusiasm for the strenuous social life which they recently had experienced so abundantly, and they were anxious to return home. The road from Fort Smith back to Fort Towson was the same one Mary had traveled the year before on her arrival in Indian Territory. "It was horrible and the houses we were obliged to stay in at night worse." But after an absence of five weeks, the Marcys soon reached home to find Fanny in good health and their quarters in proper order.

"We much fear that your father will be one of the officers

who will be sent with two companies from the Fifth to San Antonio," Mary wrote Mary Ellen a few days later. "Oh! this army life is dreadful. So much uncertainty about everything. I now have everything so delightful about me, just fixed to my mind—all must be left behind. My beautiful flowers, birds, and house, must be abandoned for the wilds of that detestable Texas."

When Marcy's orders finally arrived on June 12, 1850, contrary to expectations he and his entire company were transferred to Fort Gibson. Mary was considerably relieved: "I dread the journey," she remarked. "It will take us about twelve days to reach there, and of course shall have to live in tents during that time, though your father has arranged everything as comfortable as possible, still I do not expect to like it all together. Most fortunate for me, however, I can submit to circumstances as well as most persons. Colonel Abercrombie goes to Texas. Poor Mrs. Abercrombie with her large family have a month's march before them; it will be terrible [*sic*] tedious as the weather is warm. I shall like Gibson very much, the band is delightful and the society very pleasant, but yet I do not like to leave this sweet spot. Our quarters there will not be so good, but such is the fate of war and I must submit however hard it may be."

Almost two weeks were required for packing household furnishings, camping equipment, and supplies before the company was ready to begin the long journey to Fort Gibson. The Marcys' three servants, Uncle Andrew, Aunt Mary, and John, were to be taken along, but at the last moment Mary decided against keeping Katy, the young orphan: "I shall send her back to the mission. I do not like the child and would not keep her longer for her weight in gold."

At last, on June 25, 1850, everything was arranged for the departure, and the Marcys left Fort Towson—never to return. Captain Marcy, Lieutenant Updegraff, and Lieutenant Myers traveled on horseback at the front of the procession, but most of the fifty enlisted men and officers of Company D had no alternative but to walk, carrying their muskets and knapsacks. Behind the troops were four heavy supply wagons, each pulled by four mules. Mary, together with Fanny, Aunt Mary, and John, followed the wagons in an ambulance, while "Uncle Andrew brought up the rear with our two fine cows, which we could not consent to leave behind."

In the wagon with their furniture and personal belongings rode the Marcys' small flock of chickens; in her lap Mary held a willow cage which contained her "beautiful mocking bird, who compensated me many fold by his sweet singing."

The company trudged a weary, uneventful twelve miles the first day. That evening soon after the tents had been erected, supper eaten, and the travelers ready to retire, a soldier from Fort Smith galloped into camp with an express from General Arbuckle. Marcy's long years in the army had conditioned him to the unexpected, but he was hardly ready for the sudden turn of affairs. Upon opening the dispatch from General Arbuckle, he read with surprise that his transfer to Fort Gibson had been canceled. The General explained that a recent order from the Adjutant General in Washington had been received which directed him to establish a new post on the Canadian River. The enclosed copy of the general order read in part as follows: "The site will be selected as near the western boundary of the Reserves as may best insure protection against the depredations of the Indians, having due regard also to obtaining the necessary supplies. The post will be garrisoned by a company of the Fifth Infantry, drawn from any station except Fort Gibson, within the Department."[4]

General Arbuckle's dispatch to Marcy also contained an order for Marcy to locate and build the post in accordance with the instructions from Washington. "I was very unhappy over this piece of intelligence," Mary lamented, "for it threw me out of a home entirely. I had started to Gibson and hoped to have been there in a few days, when alas! I was doomed to disappointment."

Before dawn on the following morning the entire party was on the march once again, with Fort Washita (instead of Fort Gibson) as its immediate destination. As Marcy rode at the head of the procession, he silently pondered the question of what to do with his family until the new post was completed. The problem quickly solved itself when they reached Fort Washita, for there the Marcys' old friends, Captain and Mrs. Whitall, insisted that Mary and Fanny remain with them. The realization that she hardly had an alternative, plus the knowledge that Mrs. Whitall was pregnant, caused Mary to accept the offer—at least she could help with the household work to compensate in part for her keep.

4 General Orders No. 19, May 31; *General Orders X*, 1850, A. G. O.

99

The Regimental Returns (Fifth Infantry) show that Captain Marcy and his entire company left Fort Washita on July 1, 1850. They proceeded north along the Gibson Road as far as Gaines Creek, where Marcy left his troops encamped near the future site of McAlester, Oklahoma, while he rode on alone to Fort Smith. Much had to be done before the new post could be started, and for the next several weeks the Captain was busily engaged at Fort Smith procuring grain, ammunition, and food supplies. Also, carpenters and blacksmiths had to be hired, building materials to be obtained, and, finally, arrangements made with civilian teamsters to haul the materials and supplies to the site of the new post.

When the work at Fort Smith was completed, Marcy returned to his men and moved them immediately to a point on the south bank of the Canadian River. There, on August 25, 1850, he conferred with his former Indian guide, Black Beaver, regarding the best possible location for a garrison. Black Beaver recommended a site near the present settlement of Byers, Oklahoma,[5] approximately 150 miles west of Fort Smith and fifty miles east of the ruins of Chouteau's Trading Post, where Marcy's California immigrants had rendezvoused the year before. The position was about a mile south of the Canadian River and possessed plenty of grass, a year-round supply of good water, and abundant timber. In addition, it was near the settlements of the Kickapoo, Washita, Choctaw, Chickasaw, Delaware, and Creek Indians. Believing that the site possessed all the necessary prerequisites for a frontier fort, including the fact that it was near the route being taken by emigrants bound for California, Captain Marcy accordingly dispatched a letter to the Adjutant General in Washington.[6]

Work on the fort began at once, with the military troops put to cutting logs for the new buildings and landscaping the grounds. When the carpenters, blacksmiths, and building materials and supplies arrived from Fort Smith by ox wagons, work was pushed ahead at a rapid pace.

In the midst of all this activity Captain Marcy received orders, on September 10, 1850, from General Arbuckle to discontinue construction at once. The General explained that the War Department had decided that the post should be located farther

[5] Grant Foreman, *Adventures on Red River, viii.*
[6] August 25, 1850, Letters Received, File No. 492M–50, A. G. O.

south, so that it would be "nearer the direct route from Fort Smith to the crossing of the Red River." The new location, therefore, would afford better protection to the emigrants journeying between Fort Smith and El Paso, and at the same time would be more favorably situated "to exercise a controlling influence over the small roving bands of Indians, and perhaps eventually attract them to settle in the more fertile region and cultivate the soil."[7]

In view of the War Department's decision, General Arbuckle ordered Marcy to make a thorough reconnaissance of the region designated for the new location. The Captain received the intelligence in utter disgust, realizing that among other things it meant further postponement of his reunion with Mary and Fanny. The obvious absurdity of abandoning his present position so late in the season prompted him to protest the orders. In a return letter to General Arbuckle he pointed out that rapid progress on the log structures had already been made and abandoning the work now would result in much loss of labor and material, in addition to the fact that it was impossible for him to complete new buildings elsewhere before winter. General Arbuckle agreed with Marcy, permitting him to remain where he was until the following spring and to continue the work on the garrison through September and October.[8]

"This place is upon the border of the great western prairie where the Comanche and other wild tribes live," Marcy wrote to Mary Ellen on October 8, 1850. "The Creeks visit us every day and bring us game and often articles of marketing so that we are enabled to live very well. These Indians are very much civilized, having farms and cultivating the soil like the whites. They are very friendly and make good neighbors. As yet we are living in tents, but I am having log houses erected and we shall occupy them this winter. This one I am building for the reception of your dear mother and little Fanny has two large rooms with a wide hall between and a porch in front. The kitchen is in the rear and will be occupied by the servants, Andrew, Mary, and John. It will be quite comfortable, notwithstanding it is made of logs. I am

[7] General Arbuckle to Adjutant General Jones, September 2, 1850; Letters Received, File No. 147A–50, A. G. O.
[8] General Arbuckle to Adjutant General Jones, September 24, 1850; Letters Received, File No. 175A–50, A. G. O.

quite anxious to have it completed so that I can be with them again. They are still in Washita and I expect to visit them in a few days; it will be about a month before they join me here."

In the meantime, Mary's stay at Fort Washita was not altogether happy. The post commanded an unobstructed view of the surrounding country, which was principally a succession of rolling prairies. A small near-by village called Ruckesville contained several families with whom Mary, as usual, had become acquainted, but for the first time her life was drab, and she missed her many pets, gardens, flowers, and fruit trees which heretofore had always occupied her time during the Captain's absence.

Almost two years had passed since Mary had seen her elder daughter; during most of this period she had also been separated from her husband, and her letters to Mary Ellen now reflected her despondency: "There is little else but disappointment and sorrow for me," she wrote, "and if there is a set of people more than another who can feel the uncertainties of life, it is he who is attached to the army. We cannot make a single calculation for the future. We are here today and gone tomorrow. . . . I wish I could be with you once more, but Mercy only knows when that time will come, for the Big Bugs in Washington seem disposed to push us entirely out of the world and there is no telling where we will stop. I shall try my best to keep up good courage, however, as every soldier's wife should do so."

The cantonment on the Canadian (Camp Arbuckle) was only a two days' ride from Fort Washita, so that the Captain was able to make regular visits during the five months his family remained there. His arrival always lifted Mary's spirits, as invariably it was an occasion that called for a social function at the post. After one of Marcy's periodic visits, Mary observed: "This active manner of living just suits him. He looks as young and fair as when I first saw him; scarce a grey hair has made its appearance on his blessed pate."

A young army doctor recently arrived from Pennsylvania on his way to a new assignment at Camp Arbuckle met Captain Marcy during one of his trips to Fort Washita. The two men eventually became warm friends, and the doctor, Assistant Surgeon Rodney Glisan, subsequently wrote an interesting and delightful book in which he recounted his frontier experiences. Marcy and Glisan returned to Camp Arbuckle soon after their initial meeting at Fort Washita, and the young surgeon described the country through which they passed as follows:

"Our route . . . lay mostly through lonely, undulated prairies, covered with nature's carpet of green grass and wild flowers in profusion. . . . The view of the great meadows seemed to be confined only by streaks of cottonwood along the streams, and occasional groves of oak on the high grounds. Interspersed at intervals of a few miles were also patches of thickets of wild plum trees. The soil of this magnificent country is deep and rich, affording a future home for thousands of agriculturists, but at present rarely traveled over even by the owners of the soil—the Choctaws. After one gets a few miles [from Fort Washita], there is not to be seen a single hut, or other evidence of settlement, by these Indians. The nomads of the prairies have it all to themselves."[9]

Glisan likewise found Marcy a very interesting traveling companion: "It was truly amusing to hear him tell some of his choice anecdotes; which he always did without a ripple on his smooth countenance until he found his story appreciated by his auditor—then his expressive eyes and smiling face indicated a keen relish for the ludicrous aspects of human life."[10]

The two men arrived at the partially completed post on the Canadian several hours after sundown on their second day from Fort Washita to find everyone except the guard asleep, but the two junior officers roused themselves quickly, extending a hearty welcome to their commander and the young doctor. The occasion apparently warranted a minor celebration, for the whiskey jug promptly was brought forth and a round of drinks poured for everyone. When Glisan apologetically explained that he did not indulge, a companion laughingly replied, "My dear sir, you will lay this abstinence all aside after being in this dull place for a few months."[11] But Glisan would not find Camp Arbuckle a dull place, and apparently the others did not actually think so either.

The arduous work of cutting and trimming logs, shaping puncheon boards, and mixing clay and straw into plaster went on

[9] Rodney Glisan, *Journal of Army Life*, 47–48.
[10] *Ibid.*   [11] *Ibid.*

at Camp Arbuckle until early November, when the structures were sufficiently complete for the soldiers to abandon their tents in favor of the warmer quarters. Captain Marcy could now bring his family to their "cabin palace," and he left on November 11 to fetch them. Mary, meanwhile, had everything arranged and anxiously awaited the journey—not the least discontented by the realization that she would be the only white woman in the entire region—"a queen among the Indians," as she put it.

"We shall camp out one night, but we will have a fine tent with plenty of bed clothes, and I expect to have an agreeable pleasant journey," Mary wrote. Two days after the Captain arrived at Fort Washita the Marcys were on their way at last. Mary again carried her pet mockingbird (securely imprisoned in his willow cage) upon her lap and rode in the ambulance with Aunt Mary and Fanny. Captain Marcy and a small escort led the procession, and Uncle Andrew rode in the wagon carrying the household furniture which brought up the rear. John, the Mexican boy, was not present, for he had previously followed Marcy to Camp Arbuckle to take care of the cows and chickens and to wait upon the officers' table. The trip north took three days and was uneventful except for the disturbing howls of the prairie wolves each night, upon which occasions Fanny had to be constantly assured by her mother that the wolves, being arrant cowards, would not harm her.

Upon their arrival at Camp Arbuckle, Mary discovered that her new home in the wilderness was in a region strangely reminiscent of Wisconsin, and she was not unpleased. The double log cabin which Marcy had had constructed was one story high, floored with rough puncheon and covered with a roof of clapboard. It was not an imposing structure, but at least it was warm, for the cracks between the logs and puncheon flooring were "chinked" with mud and straw. It also contained a large fireplace faced with stone and a chimney made of short pieces of puncheon and plastered inside and out with clay. Surrounding the commander's quarters were three single-room cabins in which Lieutenants Frederick Myers and Joseph Updegraff and Assistant Surgeon Rodney Glisan lived. The enlisted men occupied a long building, twenty-five by two hundred feet, which contained a kitchen and four large sleeping rooms. Each sleeping room had a row of bunks built around the four walls, which were made of split logs and clapboards and placed two-and-one-half feet from the floor.

Once they were settled in their new home, the Marcys were happier than they had been in several years. Despite the remoteness and isolation of the place there was some social life about, particularly at mealtime when all the officers took their mess with the commander's family. The surrounding country abounded with wild game and fowl, and the table was burdened with the choicest of meats. "Besides this we have chickens, and of course eggs in plenty, also two cows which furnish us with butter and milk. We also have an icehouse and make ice cream every Sunday." It was at least no starveling land.

Mary's happiness at Camp Arbuckle during the winter of 1850–51 is reflected in the following letter to a former friend in Harrisburg, Pennsylvania: "We are now most comfortably settled in a log house. I wish with all my heart you could peep in on us, as you would be surprised to see how nicely we are fixed; our rooms are neatly white-washed and carpeted. My doors would, I think, be somewhat improved by paint—but as that article is scarce in this country, we let them rest with the coloring nature gave them. We are situated about a mile from the Canadian River in the midst of a beautiful prairie region—surrounded by several different tribes of Indians; all profess great friendship for the white men. They often come in to look at me as a curiosity, but you would laugh to see them tread on the carpets. They think them something too fine to walk on. I have no lady's society whatever, but strange to say I do not feel lonely. I would not once have believed that I could have been happy or contented living in the way we now do, but I believe that we can accustom ourselves to almost anything."[12]

Once the work on the buildings was finished, Marcy and his fellow officers were free to hunt as much as they liked. Wild geese and ducks were so plentiful on the Canadian during the winter months that they could be slaughtered by the hundreds. There were also deer and turkey in the immediate vicinity which Marcy preferred to shoot with his favorite rifle at long distances, but Gli-

[12] Mrs. Marcy to Mrs. Peacock, Harrisburg, Pennsylvania, December 13, 1850, Miscellaneous Marcy Letters, in possession of Mrs. M. J. Kernan, Clinton, New York.

san, his frequent hunting companion, used a shotgun exclusively. The two men carried on a spirited contest for game, but few could hope to surpass the redoubtable Captain as a marksman, and, indeed, few ever did. Army officers at this period had to supply their own ammunition and arms for hunting purposes, and most of them were expert marksmen. It was a different story for the soldiers, because they could not afford to buy powder and lead, and according to Glisan, "few of them could hit a man at a distance of thirty yards, in a dozen trials."[13] What the troops at Camp Arbuckle did for recreation, Marcy never reported in any of his writing.

Besides hunting, the small company of officers and the commander's wife frequently rode horseback through the woods and along the Canadian. When Lieutenant Myers presented Fanny with a small pony and sidesaddle as a gift, she also accompanied the riding parties on short excursions.

The evenings were not bad either, for then Randolph and Mary would sit by the fire and read the latest newspapers and magazines from the East. Frequently they took turns reading aloud to each other, especially Macauley's *History of England,* and they always enjoyed discussing the famous singer Jenny Lind, then making her first triumphant American tour. "My only chance to hear the Nightingale is for her to give a concert here at Arbuckle," Mary once remarked wistfully to Mary Ellen.

The mails reached Camp Arbuckle every two weeks in good weather, usually bringing a letter five or six weeks old from Mary Ellen, who was now seventeen years of age and apparently making rapid advancement with her studies. Mary Ellen's letters were always answered promptly by both Randolph and Mary. Unfortunately, the letters written by Mary Ellen during this period were not preserved, but the ones written to her by her parents are all in the McClellan Papers. Rarely did the anxious mother and father fail to caution their daughter to "take plenty of exercise and keep your shoulders straight." Also, they were much concerned about her music; Randolph, especially, insisted that she learn to play the guitar while at school: "It is much more convenient to take from one post to another than a heavy piano."

13 Glisan, *Journal,* 55.

"People of some consequence"

One anecdote about their experiences at Camp Arbuckle was repeated many times in the Marcy correspondence. It also was included in one of Marcy's later books and has been retold again and again by western writers. Soon after Mary reached Camp Arbuckle in 1850, she was honored by the visit of a Kiowa chief and a number of his braves who were scantily clad in buffalo robes. They had come to see the "white squaw," and Captain Marcy graciously invited them into his quarters. The chief and his followers entered very cautiously. Every object in the white man's "lodge" fascinated the red brethren, particularly a bright-colored oilcloth rug, which the chief carefully examined. He first scraped it with his fingernails and then wet his fingers in a vain effort to cut off the design.

After a few moments of silence he looked up at the Captain and inquired if the object was a present from the president of the United States. Marcy assured him that it was not. He then became attracted to a piece of delicate embroidery, which Mary let him fondle with his fingers. Upon learning that this was the work of "the white squaw," the old Kiowa immediately proposed to Marcy that they exchange wives. Marcy replied with a straight face that such a matter would have to be discussed with his wife, that the decision would be up to her.

Another few moments of silence followed, then at last the chief indignantly replied that he did not make trades with "squaws," but if the "Big Captain" would only say the word, he would "swap" at once. No doubt to Mary's relief, the honor was "most respectfully declined."

Fellow officers infrequently rode up from Fort Washita with the paymaster on his monthly tour of the western outposts and remained for three or four days—naturally such occasions were never dull. Sometimes a horse race on the prairie was arranged and small wagers made, or again, everyone would enthusiastically join in a wolf hunt until men, horses, and wolf were all utterly exhausted.

Mary was never in gayer spirits than on such occasions, and in one letter to Mary Ellen she gave a detailed description of the bill of fare with which one event was celebrated: "For dinner we had a delicious gumbo soup, then a fine large roast turkey (wild), a famous saddle of venison, together with a very fine boiled ham,

107

concluded the second course. The dessert consisted of mince pies, blanc mange, sweetmeats, etc., [which] together with a fine wine completed the dinner. At nine we had supper—stewed oysters, venison, ice cream, cake, sweetmeats, and coffee. Our oysters, of course we received them in cans, but quite fresh and very good. Our wine we get from New Orleans."

Little wonder that when the time came to move once again, Mary would write: "I am heartsick and discouraged that we must soon give up this little house of ours; although humble, we have been on the whole quite pleasant here." It seems a neat understatement.

VIII

"A handsome compliment"

1851–1852

THE FIVE MONTHS that Randolph and Mary spent together at Camp Arbuckle passed much too quickly, for they knew that with the arrival of spring they would have to abandon their present home. This would inevitably mean another long separation for them until new quarters could be constructed. Meanwhile, on January 9, 1851, Captain Marcy and a small detachment of troops and a few Creek Indian guides began an exploratory investigation of the country between the Canadian and the Red River to select a site for the new post.[1]

Although her husband did not plan to be away from home for an extended period, Mary was not happy with the idea: "I was much opposed to his going," she remarked, "but could not say a word, after Uncle Sam's wishes were expressed, of course." Indeed, Marcy was gone for only three weeks, but he did a lot of traveling. According to a map which he later drew of his route, he proceeded southwest from the Canadian for approximately thirty miles and came to the present Arbuckle Mountains. After exploring this rolling range of hills for some distance, he skirted their western edge, continuing in a southwesterly direction to the Red River. Thence, he pushed up the stream as far as the mouth of Cache Creek, a few miles north of present Wichita Falls, Texas. From there the explorer steered a northeast course back to Camp

---

[1] The name of the old Canadian post was changed from Fort Arbuckle to Camp Arbuckle after receipt of orders to establish a permanent post farther south; this new establishment was called Fort Arbuckle to distinguish it from the temporary post.

Arbuckle to complete a cross-country trip of approximately 330 miles without difficulty.

When Marcy returned to Camp Arbuckle, he found new orders from General Arbuckle awaiting him: The new post was to be erected "at the crossing of the Washita near the mouth of Wild Horse Creek" instead of at a point on Red River.[2] The mouth of Wild Horse Creek was near the Arbuckle Mountains which the Captain had examined during his recent reconnaissance. Marcy was pleased with the decision to erect a fort here, for he knew that the region possessed cool spring water, fertile soil, good timber, and an unlimited quantity of building stone.

Much preliminary work would have to be done before the post on Wild Horse Creek could be started, however, including as a prime requisite the marking out of a wagon road for moving supplies and building materials from Camp Arbuckle. This road Marcy ordered Lieutenant Myers to begin at once. Except for cutting a slash through the Cross Timbers and leveling the banks of one or two creeks, the job was easy and required less than three weeks to complete. When Myers reached the place which Marcy had pointed out to him on a map as the site of the new fort, he set his men to work to clear a plot of land near by and plant a garden before returning to Camp Arbuckle.

Meanwhile, Marcy had business at Fort Washita, and as he did not contemplate a final move from Camp Arbuckle until the middle of April, he and Mary departed on February 12, 1851. Again they left Fanny behind with Aunt Mary, and with their "faithful corporal" to drive the ambulance, they made the trip in two days of hard riding. The arrival of the Marcys at Fort Washita marked the first time in three months that Mary had seen another white woman, and she undoubtedly had much to talk about with her two friends, Mrs. Ruggles and Mrs. Whitall. Both insisted that she remain with them while her husband was building the new post on Wild Horse Creek. After some hesitation she decided that she would live with Mrs. Ruggles when the time came for her to move to Fort Washita, because, she explained, "I have already imposed upon Mrs. Whitall enough."

Ten days later the Marcys started back home. A few hours out from Fort Washita, a severe storm arose "which compelled

2 General Orders No. 44, December 16; *General Orders* X, 1850, A. G. O.

us to stay one day at a dirty Indian's house." But by now Mary could endure such an experience with a commendable degree of fortitude. In describing the return trip to Mary Ellen, she wrote: "I wish to give you a sample of some of the jaw-breaking names in this country. The individual in whose home we were obliged to stay on account of the storm was named *Stich a se ha i ka tabbu.* He is a Chickasaw of some note, though not, I believe, a chief."

Fanny's joy in seeing her parents must have been brief, for the very next morning after their return to Fort Arbuckle, the Marcys set out on another excursion. This time they headed for the region of the Arbuckle Mountains, where their future home was to be. Marcy also was eager to find out what progress Lieutenant Myers had made on the road and to show his wife the site he had selected for the new post. Uncle Andrew was taken along to do the cooking while they camped out, and, insatiable now, they were traveling once again.

Mary was pleased with what she saw, especially with the site of the new post which would be named in honor of the General: "It is about forty-five [thirty] miles from here through the most beautiful country I have ever seen in the South, it being high rolling prairies, with a grand range of mountains in view the whole distance. The country is quite green and lovely, and the site on which the new post is to be put is really beautiful. It will be on an eminence surrounded by a beautiful grove which is to be trimmed out to enable us to have a view of the lovely prairies. All around us there is a Kickapoo village of wigwams. Near by are the oddest looking houses you ever saw, built of bark and rush mats, and in the distance resembling beehives more than anything else. They are very unlike the wigwams of northern Indians." Before the Marcys left Camp Arbuckle for good in the spring of 1851, an incident occurred that caused them to realize that their future neighbors, the Comanches, who lived west of Cross Timbers, were far less civilized than the tribes in the immediate vicinity of the old post.

Soon after their return from the Arbuckle Mountains, a Delaware trader came into Camp Arbuckle on the Canadian with a fifteen-year-old Negro girl—"shockingly scarred and mutilated." The girl possessed barely enough clothing to protect her from the chill March wind, and her shrunken cheeks wore a telltale sign of near starvation. Horrified, Mary immediately had her brought into the kitchen, where she was given food and a place to sleep on the floor.

After a brief rest the young Negress related her story. In attempting to cross the Indian country to join the famous Seminole chief, Wild Cat, and his band on the Río Grande, she, along with her three sisters and their husbands and children, had been attacked by the Comanches. All of the party except the girl and two of the younger children had been killed. The girl had been forced to suffer miserable atrocities during the month that she was a prisoner, for her captors, never having seen Negroes before, made her the object of much "scientific experimentation." Among other acts the Comanches had scraped through her skin to see if the flesh was black like the exterior. Then they had burned their victim with live coals to learn whether fire produced pain, as with themselves. When the trader discovered the girl, he purchased her for a few paltry beads and mirrors and brought her to the garrison on the Canadian. "She is a bright girl," Mary observed, "and if I only had the money would take her myself. We are constantly hearing of such instances."

Toward their own women the Comanches appear to have been placidly tolerant, at least at times, judging from Marcy's observations. He later related a story of having stopped at a Comanche village during his reconnaissance to Cache Creek in January, 1851. Upon entering the tent of the principal chief, he was startled by an unexpected scene of domestic happiness, for seated upon the ground was a man of approximately sixty—Chief Ketumsee—surrounded by his four wives. The women were busily engaged in combing Ketumsee's long black hair, talking and cooing over him as if he were a baby. The chief was beaming blissfully!

After a brief conversation with his host, Marcy turned to one of the wives and showed her a picture of Mary. But when he asked for the photograph back, the young woman did not want to give it up. Indeed, she seemed to imagine that it was living, and pointed to the eyes and smiled, as much as to say that it could see her, too. Never one to let a humorous situation die of its own inertia, the Captain asked the Indian woman how she would like to go home with him. She immediately pointed to the photograph with one hand while drawing the other across her throat, significantly indicating that in her judgment the white man's household would be anything but a safe place for her. "I was rather inclined to the same opinion myself," Marcy reflected, "and I did not feel disposed to discuss the subject any further."[3]

The Post Returns for Camp Arbuckle show that the garrison there was abandoned on April 17, 1851, at which time Captain Marcy and forty-six members of his company set forth with all their stores and movable equipment for the new location. Lieutenant Myers, Lieutenant Updegraff, Dr. Glisan, and a few troops had already reached Wild Horse Creek and were awaiting the arrival of the remainder of the company. By April 19, 1851, the full command had arrived on Wild Horse Creek and were in their tents. The old camp was turned over to Black Beaver and his band of Delawares, numbering approximately five hundred, who eventually moved into the abandoned buildings on the Canadian and occupied them for several years.

At the new post the troops were put to cutting logs and gathering building stones as soon as they had rested, for most of the construction work was to be done by them and the few civilian carpenters and stone masons who could be hired at $2.50 a day. Meanwhile, Captain Marcy took his wife, small daughter, and Aunt Mary to Fort Washita (Uncle Andrew and John remained behind), and was back four days later to supervise the work.

Even today the Fort Arbuckle country is one of the most beautiful regions in Oklahoma. The site for the new post was well-chosen. Three or four miles above the mouth of Wild Horse Creek on the western edge of the Cross Timbers and near the northwestern slopes of the low, sprawling Arbuckles, it possessed many advantages over the former location on the Canadian River. Besides being more strategically located in regard to the Plains Indians, it likewise was more favorably situated in respect to the new California Road. Near by was a spring of fresh water that gushed from a hill with enough force to power a small mill.

The original plans for Fort Arbuckle were drawn by Captain Marcy, and when finally completed the buildings constituted "an oblong rectangular parallelogram."[4] Rows of barracks for the

[3] Marcy, *Army Life on the Border,* 50.
[4] Glisan, *Journal of Army Life,* 81.

enlisted men were located on opposite sides of the parallelogram, while the commissary and quartermaster building formed one side and the officers' quarters the other. Some distance away from this quadrangle was a long one-story structure which served as hospital, kitchen, steward's room, and ward. The sutler's store was also placed by itself and, like all of the other buildings, was built of hewn logs chinked with clay, with puncheon floors, a clapboard roof, and a stone chimney and fireplace.

Two weeks after Marcy returned from taking his family to Fort Washita, he received a dispatch from General Arbuckle stating that all remaining companies of the Fifth Regiment in Indian Territory would soon be withdrawn and transferred to the Texas frontier. The orders resulted from the War Department's recent decision to construct a line of forts from the Red River to El Paso, along the route which Marcy had explored in 1849. "It is a handsome compliment that they have paid his judgment in abiding by it, as they have done down in Washington by selecting all the sites he has recommended in his report," Mary wrote to Mary Ellen on April 26, 1851, "but yet I could wish with all my heart that they had postponed this compliment till some future time." Certainly it seemed that Randolph's and Mary's hopes for a permanent home were constantly blighted.

Marcy undoubtedly felt honored that the recommendations he had made in 1849 relative to the military sites had at last been accepted by the War Department. At the same time he must have had cause to reflect upon another and almost certain prolonged separation from his family. As yet, however, he had not grown tired of army life—he was but thirty-nine and still in his prime. With Mary it was different; she was daily growing more discontented with the long months of waiting and hoping, living with another family in crowded quarters, forever isolated from civilization. "The future seems so enveloped in darkness and closed to us who belong to the 5th. I am just now experiencing the inconveniences and discomforts of our army life. I would not complain if only I could be constantly with Randolph, but these separations are worse than death."

Mary was not the only army wife who was upset by the latest orders to move, as most of the women of the Fifth were in the same situation. Some began to make plans to return to the East,

Fort Arbuckle

Fort Washita
From Harper's Weekly, *March* 16, 1861.

but the majority were temporarily at a loss about what to do. The expense of keeping Mary Ellen in school for another two years left Mary with little choice but to remain at Fort Washita until the new forts in Texas were built. Yet she could not refrain from wishing for better things: "If I had the money, I would not remain in this dull stupid spot one day longer," she moaned.

Since the end of the Mexican War the majority of the troops and officers of the Fifth Infantry had led relatively easy lives at the various garrisons in Indian Territory. Captain Marcy was an obvious exception. Expeditions, reconnaissances, and the construction of new forts had kept him almost continuously engaged. Indeed, Mary had frequently and bitterly complained that "his duties have been more arduous than any other officer in the entire regiment." Now, with the rush of emigrants to California across the Texas plains and the rapid spread of settlers into western Texas, the federal government was pushing hard its ambitious plan to establish a new line of forts into the Southwest—and it would be a long time before any officer of the Fifth would again settle down to routine garrison life.

The Regimental Returns in the War Records Office, National Archives, show that on May 23, 1851, Marcy and a small portion of his Company D arrived at Fort Washita from the new post on Wild Horse Creek. There he conferred briefly with General Belknap regarding probable sites for the new military posts in Texas. Meanwhile, four companies of the Fifth Regiment were encamped near Fort Washita awaiting final orders to move farther out on the frontier. Before the end of the coming summer the entire Fifth Regiment, with the exception of part of Company D, would be in Texas. This latter detachment would remain under Lieutenant Myers' command at Fort Arbuckle until all of the principal buildings had been completed.

On May 25, 1851, Captain Marcy bade his family good-bye and, with Lieutenant Updegraff and eleven privates of Company D and detachments of Companies A and H, left for the Texas frontier. Accompanying them was General Belknap, who planned to make a brief personal inspection of the upper Brazos region. The long military train crossed the Red River near the mouth of the Little Wichita, then followed the same general route to the

Brazos that Marcy had blazed two years before while returning from New Mexico. The journey was tedious and slow, for it was necessary that the troops clear brush, level embankments, and mark their path well for the rest of the regiment and heavier supply wagons which would follow.

Back at Fort Washita, Mary had cause to worry about her husband's latest adventure, for word had recently come that forty or fifty troops at Fort Smith had died during the past spring of cholera, and a general uneasiness now prevailed among the entire regiment. "I feel some anxiety about him," she wrote. "It is so exceptionally hot, I fear he may get sick."

Mary's fears proved valid, for when Marcy ultimately reached the main fork of the Brazos (Red Fork) on June 22, he already was suffering from a "severe attack of intermittent fever—threatening congestion of the brain,"[5] and for eight days he would be confined to his tent. In the meantime, the troops remained encamped on the east bank of the Brazos, a few miles below the crossing which Marcy had first made on October 24, 1849, while General Belknap made a careful inspection of the surrounding region. Belknap had reason to be pleased with Marcy's judgment in having recommended the present site for a military establishment—a post which was to be named in the old General's honor.

When completed, Fort Belknap was approximately 150 miles southwest of Preston, Texas. Ultimately it would become one of the most important frontier posts in Texas; today its ruins are to be seen a short distance south of Newcastle. The swift, brackish waters of the Brazos near the site where the post was being built could be forded without difficulty, and there were many small streams near by to furnish an abundance of fresh water. Too, the site was strategically located in respect to the route to El Paso, and it was well enough in advance of Texas settlements to afford maximum protection against the Plains Indians.

For several weeks after the soldiers arrived at the Brazos, they were busily engaged in cutting logs and clearing new ground for the buildings. General Belknap completed his inspection of the country by July 1, 1851, and then departed for Fort Smith. By this time Marcy had recovered from his illness and was making preparations to reconnoiter and map the various tributaries of the

[5] Letters Received, July 25, 1851, File No. 334M–51, A. G. O.

Brazos and fix the sites for additional forts. The Brazos has several sources, the principal one being the Double Mountain Fork which flows into the main stream from a general southwestern direction. It will be recalled that Marcy had explored this tributary in 1849.

Now, two years later, he expected to chart all of the other principal branches of the Texas river. According to a map[6] of his various explorations, which he prepared in Washington some months later, he set out from Fort Belknap and traveled south for about ninety miles along Hubbard Creek until he reached Pecan Bayou, a tributary of the Colorado. But he was unable to continue farther, for sickness returned and he suffered from constant chills and fever. Reluctantly he turned back to the camp on the principal branch of the Brazos to rest and to consult the army surgeon regarding his health. He reached camp on July 17, when he was advised by the doctor to return to Indian Territory and apply for a leave of absence. Following the suggestion at once, Marcy began the lonely ride back to Fort Washita, which he reached on August 2—"thin and pale."

After a few days with Mary and Fanny, during which time he regained a little strength, he continued on horseback to Fort Gibson to report to General Belknap and to request the leave. According to Mary's correspondence with Mary Ellen, General Belknap promptly granted permission to Marcy to spend a few months in the cooler New England climate, and he left Fort Gibson by stage on August 15, 1851.

The long journey north was accomplished after much difficulty, for not only did Marcy continue to suffer from his recent illness, but he also fell victim to a severe and prolonged spell of dysentery. He later wrote to Mary that he had spent several days in Chicago recuperating and therefore was delayed in reaching his destination. But by September 20, 1851, he was at his old home in Greenwich, Massachusetts, and in a letter to Mary on that date he reported on his arrival and on his recent visit to Mary Ellen at Hartford, Connecticut:

"I found Nelly at school when I called. She soon made her appearance and was perfectly overjoyed at seeing me. I found her grown so much that I should not have known her, had I met her

[6] Map File, Map Q 74 (1852), "Records of the Office of Chief of Engineers," National Archives.

anywhere else. She is taller than you—good size and looks well. I could hardly realize that she was my daughter. She has grown from a girl to be a woman and a very sweet dear one too. I did not know how much I loved her until I saw her. I cannot be contented when she is out of sight and I desire her near me all the time. She is very dear indeed and loves me very much. She was disappointed when you did not come with me, but I consoled her by telling her you would come on next spring. . . . I purchased a guitar for her and hope she will learn to play it. She does not play the piano much better than when I left her in Harrisburg—indeed I think she has but little talent for music. She is a fine girl, however, and appears to be universally beloved, and she reminds me of you, my darling, when I first saw you."

Marcy added that Mary Ellen had accompanied him from Hartford to Greenwich, where she would stay a few days before returning to school. He further remarked that he had found his aged father and mother "looking much the same as when I left them." It was his first visit home in almost four years.

Before Mary Ellen departed for Hartford, she and her father took a brief sight-seeing trip to Montreal. Upon his return to Greenwich, Marcy reported to Adjutant General Jones by letter on November 8, 1851, that he was still unable to resume his regular duties. He also added the following remarks: "Having been engaged a great portion of the time for the past three years in examining the country west of the state of Arkansas, and having taken particular pains to learn the disposition, habits, and wants of the Comanches and other wild tribes frequenting that section of the country, at the same time believing that I am the only white man capable of giving much reliable information derived from personal observation relative thereto: It has occurred to me (as new military posts are being established in that country) that the facts which the Department might obtain from personal interviews with me, would carry a much better idea of the country than a written communication and would conduce the interest of the service."[7]

Two weeks later we find the Captain in Washington, evidently having been ordered there by the Adjutant General. "It has occurred to me," Marcy further explained in a letter to the Adjutant

[7] Letters Received, File No. 421M–51, A. G. O.

General written the day after his arrival in Washington, "that a map with such explanatory notes as I could furnish would be of service to the department. This map would embrace the country where it is proposed to establish a new line of posts between the Brazos and Colorado Rivers. As the notes which I have taken in my different explorations are in New York City, I should be pleased (if it meets your approbation) to receive an order to make the map and notes at that place."[8]

The proposal was promptly approved, and Marcy was told that he might remain on duty in the East until the report and map could be finished. His correspondence for the next three months reveals that he was doing his work in New York City while boarding with his brother's family. His brother, Dr. Erastus E. Marcy, was then a prominent homeopathic doctor and editor of the *American Homeopathic Journal*.

In a letter to Mary on March 6, 1852, Marcy wrote: "I should like to bring you out some dresses made according to the present styles but I do not know your measure, and from what Emeline [Marcy's sister-in-law] says I concluded you have grown so thin that I shall not know you when I see you. Poor Molly, I hope you have not grieved away your flesh on account of my absence, have you? The dresses they wear now are like the old-fashioned large mutton-sleeved ones with the sleeve cut off half way up and the large part turned upside down. This is the tone now with lace sleeves under these with ruffles. The bonnets are very short and small and I think very pretty. I have got one for you which Emeline says is pretty. I have it packed in a trunk and think it will go safe."[9]

The change of environment was good for Marcy's health and spirits, but by now Mary was feeling the effects of her lonely life at faraway Fort Washita. Not only had she not seen her older daughter during the past three years, but during this time she had been with her husband less than six months—small wonder that in her letters to Mary Ellen she began to unburden her soul: "I am sick and tired of this country. The truth is I am disgusted with this army life and feel deeply the disagreeable things connected with it. I long to be settled in life and have my chosen friends about me.

[8] November 21, 1851, Letters Received, File No. 432M–51, A. G. O.
[9] This letter is now in the possession of Mrs. M. J. Kernan, Clinton, New York.

There are some in this army whom I like and others whom I would fain trust with contempt, but policy dictates a different course and I must act a deceitful part when I despise it."[10]

A few weeks later she was even more distressed: "I was very glad to hear from you by yesterday's mail [January 24, 1852]. The letter had, however, been six weeks on the way. I received one also from your father, the first in two months, so you may readily imagine that I had come to the conclusion that poor little Fanny and myself were entirely neglected and forgotten. My spirits have been dreadful, and still are.

"I cannot arouse myself to look forward to any one bright thing on earth. My health has not been good for months. I cannot tell what ails me, but I feel miserable and my nerves are in a terrible state. I suppose I require change of scene more than anything. I am much more thin than you ever saw me and shall always feel that there never was so unfortunate a thing as that I could not have been permitted to take Fanny and gone North with your father. He gave me my choice to go with him and leave Fanny here, or stay behind with her. I chose the latter. I could not think of leaving her when she is subject to illness. She is and always has been a very delicate child, particularly in warm weather. And had I been gone without her I could not have enjoyed one hour of my visit.

"And why I blame your father is that he, without any reason on earth, took it into his head that she should not go, and of course she could not. And we have been left behind to suffer more than I can tell you in various ways. In the first place we have no one to provide anything for us. I have had to attend to all the outdoor as well as indoor affairs, which is something new for me. The officers are not worth a cent for politeness at this post. I am perfectly disgusted with them. Major Holmes, who is in command, promised to be very attentive and kind to us, but he is so lazy and indifferent to anyone but himself and family. Provisions of all kinds are so scarce, and exceedingly expensive. We have had no butter, milk, eggs, or a single luxury this winter, not a loaf of

[10] The McClellan Papers contain more than twenty-five letters from Mary Marcy to her seventeen-year-old daughter which were written between June, 1851, and April, 1852 (2nd Series, I).

white bread has been seen, for flour is very sour and you can imagine a little how we have been obliged to get along. I merely write you only a little, of what we suffer, that you may judge something how we get along. The weather has been subject to sudden changes, and of course, we suffer much when it becomes cold. Within the past week everyone has more or less been afflicted with influenza. Fanny still has it and is very thin. Your Aunty has been quite sick—I am glad you seem to be enjoying life so much."

Mary had other reasons to be unhappy. By the end of the summer of 1851, all of the Fifth had been moved to Texas and none of her old friends had remained behind. Mrs. Whitall had returned unexpectedly to the East, later to be followed by Mrs. Ruggles; and both General Belknap and General Arbuckle had died recently—"It is truly melancholy . . . both were warm friends and have done a great deal for us." The following fall and winter months (1851–52) were the most boring and lonely months that Mary had ever experienced, for the Seventh Regiment that now occupied Fort Washita had little or no society. Gone were the gay dinner parties, dances, and pleasant horseback rides; Mary's only source of pleasure during the period was the reading of *David Copperfield*, sent to her by a friend in Harrisburg.

As if things were not already bad enough, Mary's sister-in-law and her family arrived at Fort Washita in late summer en route to the Texas frontier. Being military people, they had found themselves somewhat in the same situation relative to living quarters as the Marcys—temporarily displaced persons. As the woman and her two children had become seriously ill during the journey from the East, Mary prevailed upon her to remain behind at Fort Washita until permanent quarters could be completed at the Texas post where her family eventually would be stationed. She decided to stay, and Mary Marcy now found herself caring for three virtual invalids, a grievous added burden. It is not surprising that by the time her husband returned to the southwestern frontier, she had already concluded that she would have no more of garrison life.

Captain Marcy finished the official report of his recent reconnaissance into Texas on November 25, but he did not complete the map of the region until February 14, 1852.[11] Although inaccurate in many details, especially the courses of various small streams, the map represented the most complete compilation of geographical information relative to present Oklahoma, western Texas, and southwestern New Mexico, that had heretofore been assembled. The map was particularly important because it showed for the first time the correct courses of the Colorado, Brazos, Pecos, and Canadian rivers. Furthermore, it contained information relative to the disposition of both civilized and wild Indian tribes and their villages and hunting grounds. Also, the many military roads, forts, trading posts, and settlements in the area were shown.

Marcy ultimately was able to correct some of the mistakes in the original draft as a result of his expedition to the source of the Red River in the summer of 1852. Not only did this expedition supply more accurate information regarding the course of the Red, but Marcy collected additional geographical information regarding the region of southwestern Oklahoma and the Texas Panhandle. The revised map of the area was subsequently printed and given wide distribution—judging from the number of copies still in existence. It must have been consulted by thousands of travelers, hundreds of army officers, and dozens of cartographers, for this was a day when detailed maps of the Southwest were indeed rare.

The information which Marcy had gathered before the Red River expedition and during his three previous travels through the Southwest from 1849 to 1851 furnished the basis of the War Department decision to locate a line of forts from Fort Smith to New Mexico. Fort Arbuckle, the first of the new forts, was completed in 1851. The second new post was the previously mentioned Fort Belknap on the Brazos in Young County, Texas. From this post the line of forts would be extended in 1852 toward El Paso by the construction of Fort Phantom Hill, Jones County, Texas, and Fort Chadbourne, Coke County, Texas. Two years later Camp Cooper in Shacklesford County, about halfway between Fort Phantom Hill and Fort Belknap, would be built as a result of Marcy's reconnaissance into this region in 1854. Indeed, Marcy

[11] See note 6 above. Marcy's "Report" was published for the first time in printed form in the *West Texas Historical Association Year Book*, XIV (1938), 115–36.

selected the specific sites for all of the above-mentioned forts except Fort Phantom Hill.

The line of forts was eventually completed to El Paso; however, none of the sites of the later posts was specifically chosen by Marcy himself. (After he returned from the expedition to the source of the Red River in 1852, Marcy also recommended a site near this stream for still another post, but it was not constructed until 1869—present Fort Sill near Lawton, Oklahoma.) The cordon of southwestern military posts when completed followed an approximate diagonal line from Fort Smith to El Paso, and ultimately they marked the abandonment of the old inner line of Oklahoma and Texas forts: Fort Towson, Fort Washita, Fort Martin Scott, Fort Grogan, Fort Gates, and Fort Worth.[12]

While Marcy was in the East working on the map and report for the War Department, he realized that practically no reliable information on the region of the headwaters of the Red River was available. Although he himself had explored the stream in January, 1851, as far west as Cache Creek, no American explorer known to him had ever gone beyond this point. From information obtained from the Indians during the journey to Santa Fé in 1849, Marcy had become convinced then that the true source of the Red was much farther east than was generally believed. Humboldt's map of New Spain, compiled from data in the City of Mexico in 1804, was highly inaccurate concerning the course of the Red River; yet fifty years later it remained the principal source of geographical information regarding this important stream. In 1806, the explorers, Freeman and Sparks attempted to ascend the Red from its mouth to its source, but without success, and one year later during his "confused" wanderings throughout the Southwest, the intrepid Zebulon Montgomery Pike missed the stream completely.[13] Major Long in 1820 likewise had been unable to find the Red, mistaking the Canadian for it until he had nearly reached Fort Smith.

No serious effort had been made to find the true source of

[12] M. L. Crimmins (ed.), "W. G. Freeman's Report of the Eighth Military Department," *The Southwestern Historical Quarterly*, Vol. LIV, 216.

[13] For an account of Pike's efforts to find the headwaters of Red River, see W. Eugene Hollon's *The Lost Pathfinder* (Norman, 1949).

the Red from Major Long's expedition in 1820 until 1852. On February 25 of that year, Marcy wrote to the Adjutant General: "In a report I recently had the honor to submit to the War Department, I alluded to the fact that a great portion of the country upon upper Red River has never been explored and that all information we have upon the subject was derived from the Indians." He continued by proposing that he be commissioned to lead an expedition from Fort Washita or Fort Belknap to the source pointing out that such an expedition could be undertaken with little cost to the government: "My acquaintance with the chiefs of several bands of Comanches frequenting that country, and the knowledge I have of their character and language will facilitate my intercourse with them and enable me to pass without molestation through their territory, when . . . another officer who did not understand their disposition might have difficulty with them."[14]

He further pointed out in the letter that an expedition to the headwaters of the Red River could have far-reaching results: it could determine the geography of "one of the most important rivers in the United States," reveal the mineral resources of the area, determine the practicability of establishing future military posts, encourage friendly relations with the natives, and prevent future depredations by the Kiowas and Comanches upon the peoples of Texas.

The result of this important communication was a special order which Marcy received on March 6, 1852, authorizing him to take the necessary personnel from Company D, Fifth Infantry, and "proceed without unnecessary delay upon an examination of the country between the mouth of Cache Creek to the source of Red River."[15]

Marcy lost little time in putting the order into execution; and his long journey from Washington to Pittsburgh by train, thence by boat down the Ohio to the broad Mississippi, brought him into the great Southwest for the third time. It was a country, this Southwest, which he both hated and loved—hated because it had deprived him of the culture and domesticity for which he longed; loved because he doubtless felt that he was now a part of

[14] Letters Received, File No. 44M–52, A. G. O.
[15] Special Order No. 37, March 5; *Special Orders* V, 1852, A. G. O.

"A handsome compliment"

the prairie ocean, the winding streams, the cool, bubbling spring waters, the great herds of buffalo, and the shy, elusive antelope. No matter that he adored his wife and daughters more than life itself, he was not destined to sit long by the family hearth.

It had been eight months since Marcy had seen Mary and Fanny, and now as he traveled south in 1852, he must have felt uneasy about facing his wife after such a long absence. He was eager to see her, but at the same time he wondered how she would take the news that he was commencing another extensive expedition. Perhaps he had a guilty conscience at having requested the assignment, but perhaps, too, he rationalized that his newly acquired fame as an explorer could not rest upon past achievements alone. Whether he knew it or not, he had a restless spirit; its thirst for adventure was great, and it constantly reached out for the unknown. In the struggle between the strong spirit and the sickly body, the results were inevitable—the spirit could not be denied.

IX

"A tierra incognita"

1852

"YOUR FATHER has not yet arrived," Mary wrote to her older daughter on April 2, 1852, "though I heard of him at Little Rock two weeks since. He must be here in a day or two. I think this is indeed a horrible way of living, not knowing what to expect or anticipate from day to day. I regret that your father has been ordered to survey Red River. I fear his health will suffer. I shall be constantly anxious all summer about him. My life has for the past four years been one of anxiety and trouble. My spirits are almost broken down, and how long this state of things is to last, God surely knows. Your father has done more active duty than all the officers put together in this southwestern region and still it appears he can have no rest."

Captain Marcy reached Fort Washita "in fine health" during the first week of April. Arriving with him from the East was one J. R. Suydam of New York, whose official status is not clear, but who later became a member of the company that explored Red River. The two men had been delayed at Fort Smith for several days while Marcy busied himself with plans for the forthcoming expedition. At Fort Smith he obtained the services of Dr. George G. Shumard as surgeon and botanist, a choice that would prove excellent, and he contracted with a civilian teamster for oxen and wagons to transport a part of the expedition's supplies and equipment. However, Marcy was ordered to procure most of his quartermaster supplies and additional transportation facilities from the military supply depot at Preston, Texas.

Mary was in poor health and low spirits when her husband

reached Fort Washita—her nerves completely shattered by a chronic toothache from which she could get no relief. For the past month she and Fanny had been living with Major Holmes' family, the Marcy relatives having recently departed for Texas. Now her husband was home at last, but there was small comfort in that; already he was eagerly pressing his preparations for the new expedition in the hope of getting it under way before the scorching summer months arrived. Mary felt more frustrated than ever.

Two or three days after his return Marcy rode down to Preston, forty miles south of Fort Washita, to make requisition upon the quartermaster "for a sufficient number of teams to transport supplies of subsistence, and baggage . . . for five months." While supplies were being readied, the Captain returned to Fort Washita for *one day*. How Mary must have loved that! Then he left again, this time riding north to the site of Camp Arbuckle on the Canadian to hire scouts and hunters.

His old friend Black Beaver declined the honor of serving as the expedition's chief scout and interpreter because of illness, and Marcy then hired another equally famous guide, John Bushman— "a true specimen of the Indian type, dignified, reserved, and taciturn, self-reliant, independent, and fearless."[1] Four other Indians —Jim Ned, Billy Boy, John Bull, and Wagon—were also employed as guides at one dollar a day.

All of these Indians ultimately rendered invaluable service to the expedition, for none were superior to the Delawares as guides and hunters. Their intelligence, skill, and knowledge of nature were constant sources of amazement to the white men, and Marcy subsequently told many stories of their feats as hunters, trappers, and horsemen. Captain George B. McClellan also was impressed with the five scouts whom Marcy had employed. "Jim Ned is the next [to Black Beaver and John Bushman] best Indian in the country," he wrote to his brother John soon after reaching Fort Washita. "Jim is a fine-looking intelligent Delaware, with a slight touch of Negro. He is probably the bravest warrior and most successful horse thief in the West. He frequently starts out alone and goes hundreds of miles among the worst of the wild Indians and returns with a drove of horses. They are all afraid of him, and he is not afraid of the devil or anything else.

[1] Marcy, *Army Life on the Border*, 87.

"John Bull and the rest are considered the best hunters and most honest Indians about here. John Bull is a small, slight made man with characteristic Indian face, full of humor and intelligence. He is about thirty-five. Wagon is a handsome laughing fellow of about twenty-two. We are very lucky in getting them, I can tell you."[2]

Young McClellan had reached the Choctaw Nation during Captain Marcy's absence on the Canadian River. It will be remembered that the Adjutant General had appointed him second-in-command at the time the Red River project was first authorized. The Captain was then in the corps of engineers, and since the Mexican War he had served, a bit fretfully, as an instructor of bayonet exercises at West Point. When he received orders to accompany the expedition, he quickly departed for the Southwest. An interesting and detailed account of his journey from New York to Fort Washita is found among his letters to his brother John, which are now preserved with the McClellan Papers in the Library of Congress.

The handsome, dashing, young officer, who would later become the most controversial military figure of the Civil War, was exuberantly pleased with the prospect of his adventurous new assignment. Although he had not yet met the man who later became his father-in-law, he already knew of Marcy's reputation as an explorer, and when the two eventually met at Fort Washita, they became warm friends. This mutual admiration would last as long as both lived.

"Washita is a very beautiful place," McClellan wrote to John on April 21. "It is built in a clump of trees on a knoll in the prairies —good quarters and nobody near it. Mrs. Marcy is here. She goes [north] by the first opportunity. She is a most pleasant and kind lady—hope you see her. We are only waiting now for the wagons from Fort Smith which are due today. We will probably start tomorrow. . . . I am to be quartermaster and commissary of the expedition, unless Marcy can get another officer at the Brazos, in which case, I can, if I wish, be relieved from the duty. As it gives me extra pay I may keep it, if I feel that it does not interfere with my other duties too much. We have 16 ox teams (8 oxen each),

[2] George to John, Fort Washita, April 21, 1852, McClellan Papers, 2nd Series, II.

one six pounder, one ambulance and one mule wagon. The ox teams will go from here [Fort Washita] by way of Fort Arbuckle to the mouth of Cache Creek on Red River and then wait for us. We will go with the guns, ambulance, etc., to Brazos for the escort, and then across to the north to Cache Creek."[3]

The supply train which McClellan mentioned departed from Fort Washita for Fort Arbuckle a few days later. It was to proceed from the Arbuckle to Cache Creek by the road Marcy had made during his brief reconnaissance into western Indian Territory in January, 1851. On the same day that the wagons left Fort Washita, April 22, 1852, Captain Marcy, Captain McClellan, Dr. G. G. Shumard, J. R. Suydam, five Indian scouts, and Captain J. H. Strain, a civilian merchant at Fort Washita, departed in the opposite direction for Fort Belknap. Also accompanying Marcy on the expedition was the young Mexican boy, John, and the aged Negro slave, Uncle Andrew. (Whatever became of Aunt Mary is not known, for neither Marcy nor his wife ever mentioned her in their correspondence after 1852.) The party rode straight south to Preston, where it turned toward the southwest, following the now well-traveled trail which Marcy had blazed on his return from New Mexico in 1849.

Mary and Fanny meanwhile remained at Fort Washita, prepared to leave for the North as soon as a military escort could take them to Fort Smith. On May 7, 1852, Mary reported to Mary Ellen that their escort had not yet left. "Your father went off in fine health and spirits," she added, "and will be absent until October. All that time I shall be unable to hear a word from him, as he goes into such a wild region, it will be unsafe for an express to attempt to come through. He started from here with every luxury that could be obtained, even took a cow to supply them with milk on their journey." One week later the escort was ready, and Mary and Fanny left the Southwest permanently. Although Mary reached New York late in May, 1852, she did not journey on to Hartford to see Mary Ellen for several weeks. The delay was caused by her anxiety to have a complete new wardrobe made before traveling farther.

When Marcy reached Fort Belknap on April 30, his old Company D, which had been under the command of Lieutenant Up-

[3] *Ibid.*

degraff during his absence, now joined the expedition. The fifty-five privates and noncommissioned officers of Company D, together with various servants, scouts, and civilians brought the personnel of the exploring party to about seventy men. On May 2, they took up their line of march and proceeded northward from Fort Belknap toward Red River, seven days later reaching the stream's south bank, opposite present Ryan, Oklahoma.

The party was now near the confluence of the Little Wichita (which flows from the southwest) with the Red. Marcy decided to cross the Little Wichita and continue toward the west, but at the same time he wanted to remain within sight of the south bank of the Red until he could find a suitable fording place. A twenty-five-mile march[4] over "elevated swell of undulated prairie" brought him in sight of the high bluffs of the Big Wichita on May 9. This stream flows into the Red a short distance northeast of present Wichita Falls, Texas, and its course is approximately parallel to the Little Wichita.

The muddy waters of the Big Wichita were in high banks, which together with the steep, barren cliffs made an immediate crossing out of the question. The commander had expected to continue along the south side of the Red to a point opposite the mouth of Cache Creek, some eight miles farther west of the mouth of the Big Wichita. He now realized the difficulty of such a course, since he would have to cross the hazardous Big Wichita, which would be as much trouble as crossing the Red itself. He could not afford a very long delay for his supplies now were dangerously low. The only alternative was to leave his company encamped at its present position, cross to the north bank of the Red River and locate the supply train which should be somewhere in the vicinity. Therefore, he took two Indian scouts and several pack horses and started at once. The small party swam the Red without difficulty and crossed over into present southwestern Oklahoma, where the commander hoped he could soon pick up the trail of the wagons.

The three men took a straight north course from the river for about twenty-five miles before they intercepted some recently

[4] All references to distance during the Red River expedition are based upon Marcy's own calculations, which are not necessarily accurate since he did not use a surveying chain.

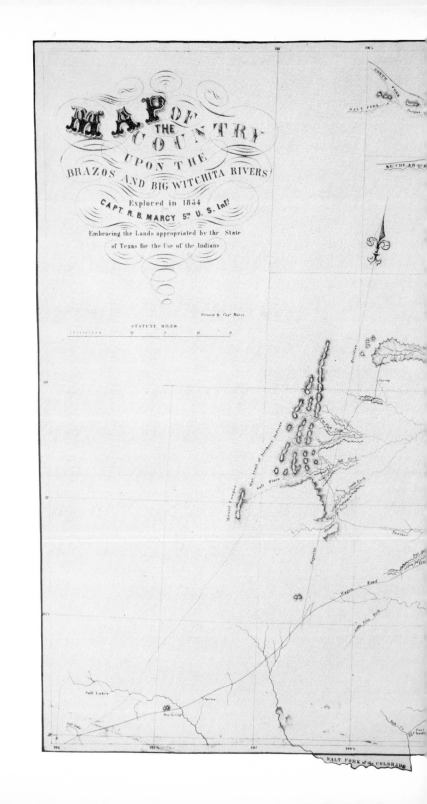

MAP OF THE COUNTRY UPON THE BRAZOS AND BIG WITCHITA RIVERS

Explored in 1854

CAPT. R. B. MARCY 5TH U. S. Inf.

Embracing the Lands appropriated by the State of Texas for the Use of the Indians

Drawn by Capt. Marcy

STATUTE MILES

made wagon ruts. Turning west, they came upon the supply train within a short while, slowly plodding through heavy mud toward the rendezvous point, Cache Creek. A substantial supply of bacon, coffee, sugar, flour, salt, beans, and molasses was taken from the wagons, packed in sacks, and tied on the backs of the half-dozen pack animals. The commander then gave orders to the civilian teamster in charge of the supply train to continue toward Cache Creek while he and the Indians returned to the expedition encamped on the south bank of the Red. By May 12, the river had fallen to a depth of from one to three feet and to less than two hundred yards wide. Its treacherous quicksand bottom still made crossing dangerous, but by the end of the first day after Marcy's return to camp, he and his entire command were on the north bank ready to move forward. Despite a torrential rain, nothing was lost or damaged in the day's arduous activity.

The expedition encamped for the first night in Indian Territory on an elevated prairie about a half-mile beyond the crossing, and on the following day, May 13, it pushed on to Cache Creek. This small stream begins in the Wichita Mountains in western Oklahoma and flows into Red River near present Taylor, Oklahoma. The mouth of the creek in 1852 was approximately one hundred miles west of the farthermost white settlement on the Red. At the point where Marcy's command came upon Cache Creek, it was swift, deep, and more than a hundred yards wide because of recent rains throughout the region. As they could not cross until the water had fallen, the commander availed himself of the opportunity to examine the surrounding country.

At this time one of the important events of the journey occurred: a member of the party found several pieces of metal ore containing a high percentage of copper, and much excitement prevailed over the prospect of the country's containing rich mineral resources. The excitement was further intensified when particles of gold dust were washed from the sands of Cache Creek; however, extensive additional search failed to turn up more of the precious metal. The ore containing evidence of copper was later examined by Edward Hitchcock, president of Amherst College and a prominent pioneer geologist, who pronounced it poor in quality. Hitchcock named the new ore "Marcylite" in honor of the explorer, but as far as is known it has never found a commercial use. Despite much prospecting in the Wichita Mountain area in subsequent decades, no substantial amount of gold or other precious metals has ever been uncovered there.

By May 16, the waters of Cache Creek had fallen several feet, and the expedition moved again, but the only progress made that day was the crossing of the stream. The country to the west now was a *"tierra incognita"*—to use Marcy's own terms. It was generally believed that no Anglo-American had ever been there before, and if Spanish or French traders had explored the country sometime during the distant past, Marcy did not know of it.[5] The importance of the journey beyond Cache Creek suddenly became evident to the whole company. Indeed, Marcy was now launched upon the most important exploratory venture of his career; perhaps he realized that his chief fame as an explorer would rest upon the successful completion of a task in which so many explorers before him had failed. The Red River expedition was not a particularly long one, either in time or distance, but to be the first to examine an unknown country and the first to define an important river was sufficient honor within itself.

A detailed day-by-day narrative of Marcy's journey to the ultimate sources of the Red does not need retelling. His own published journal, which, incidentally, contains one of the most accurate and lucid descriptions of a portion of the Great Plains ever printed as a government document, is available for those who have a curiosity for detail.[6] As late as 1937 this journal was considered to be still of sufficient interest to geologists, naturalists, biologists, and students of western history, that it was republished.[7] The editor found it unnecessary to add much to the original manuscript

[5] A map drawn in Santa Fé, October 18, 1787, by a French trader named Pedro Vial shows the two main sources of the Red River, the North Fork and the South Fork, fairly accurately. Marcy was undoubtedly the first Anglo-American to explore the two branches extensively, but whether he could claim credit for being the first white man to do so is questionable. Vial's map is now in the Museum of New Mexico (Santa Fé), Spanish Archives, and a photostatic copy of it is in the possession of the writer.

[6] Marcy's report appears as U. S. Senate *Exec. Doc.* (unnumbered), 33 Cong., 1 sess. (1854), 390 pp. It contains his narrative of the expedition, copious illustrations, and scientific reports relative to the various fields of science in which the expedition interested itself. Unless otherwise indicated, quotations in the present chapter are taken from this document.

[7] *Adventure on Red River*, edited by Grant Foreman (University of Oklahoma Press).

except to establish the route taken in 1852 in relation to present-day geographical place names.

Considering the brief time the commander had to prepare for the Red River expedition, it perhaps was one of the best organized, best conducted, and most successful expeditions that heretofore had ventured into any section of the Great Plains. Its scientific results would prove particularly notable, for Marcy had been instructed to give careful attention to things other than the course of the stream he was to explore and chart, and he obeyed orders in both letter and spirit.

The expedition to the upper reaches of the Red River in 1852 should be judged primarily in relation to its original purposes. In a letter dated March 6, 1852, which Marcy received prior to his departure from Washington, the specific objectives of the expedition were enumerated by Adjutant General Jones.[8] The communication is prefaced by an unusual compliment: "It is presumed that detailed instructions are unnecessary for an officer of your experience." Jones then went on to suggest that the explorer "collect and report everything that may be useful or interesting in relation to [the region's] resources, soil climate, natural history, and geography." Marcy was further charged with determining whether or not the region bordering the headwaters of the Red was capable of sustaining a considerable Indian population; to discover whether or not the various nomadic tribes could be induced to settle there and devote themselves to farming; to impress upon them the military powers of the United States; and to inform them that if they continued their depredations upon the inhabitants of Texas, they would surely be punished.

This was no small task, but it is doubtful if another officer in the Southwest, indeed in the whole army, was more qualified for the particular mission than Randolph B. Marcy.

Judging from the vast number of animal, plant, and geological specimens and written data which the company brought back, it must have been a busy experience for all. From May 17, when the travelers left Cache Creek, until they arrived back at Fort Arbuckle on July 28 (seventy-two days), Captain McClellan made four daily recordings of the weather: temperature, barometer reading, and wind. Dr. George G. Shumard kept a journal of the

[8] Letters Sent, XXVIII, A. G. O.

general geology of the region explored, at the same time collecting several hundred geological specimens, which were later examined and classified by President Edward Hitchcock of Amherst College.

The responsibility for collecting various plant specimens also belonged to Dr. Shumard, who later turned them over to John Torrey of New York, a well-known plant scientist who had previously classified the large collection made by Frémont in 1843–44. Mineral and soil samples were eventually analyzed by Professor C. U. Shepard and Dr. Benjamin F. Shumard. The samples of minerals obtained for the scientists included coal, copper (Marcylite), and two small pieces of gold. In addition, several large beds of gypsum were discovered, and the samples brought back caused Hitchcock to express the opinion that these deposits (one of the most extensive in the known world) would be of "utmost importance to the nation."[9] But nothing excited more interest among the party's scientific discoveries than the announcement that the millions of acres of mesquite trees found throughout much of the area contained a sap which would make an excellent substitute for gum arabic.[10] Indeed, the *Washington Star* called this "the most important western discovery since that of gold in California." Unfortunately the statement proved a little too optimistic.[11]

Marcy personally assumed responsibility for the assimilation of zoological information and was ultimately able to identify and describe in detail more than twenty-five different animals indigenous to the area. The last ranged from the larger quadrupeds such as the black bear, buffalo, deer, panther, and antelope, to the smaller animals such as the prairie dog, rabbit, and lizard. Also, more than ten species of snakes were collected. These, together with several species of lizards (heretofore unknown to science),

[9] The large deposits of gypsum in western Oklahoma and Texas furnish the raw materials for the manufacturing of tremendous quantities of sheetrock and gypboard which are used in home construction. Plaster of Paris and other products are also manufactured from this mineral.

[10] The world's supply of gum arabic is obtained chiefly from the Sudan and Senegal. Its principal by-product is mucilage. So far as it is possible to determine, no commercial use has ever been made of the gum from mesquite trees.

[11] This newspaper article is found in Marcy's Scrapbook.

fishes, shells, and various insects were eventually brought back to be examined and classified by two prominent zoologists, S. F. Baird and Charles Girard of the Smithsonian Institution.

Besides the above-mentioned fields of science in which the party interested itself, Marcy compiled a small dictionary of 168 common terms used by both the Comanche and the Wichita Indians. The collection of Wichita words proved especially important, for according to the well-known ethnologist, W. W. Turner, they constituted the first such vocabulary ever compiled and published.

After Marcy's command left Cache Creek on May 17, 1852, it moved westward for a short distance before ascending a smooth high ridge bordering the north bank of the Red. The land now changed into a series of broad, elevated swells and spacious intervening valleys, and except for the cottonwood, oak, and pecan trees that lined the river banks, the scenery all about was one vast, naked prairie. On the second day beyond the crossing of Cache Creek the travelers saw in the northwest a chain of mountains rising abruptly above the horizon to a height of eight or nine hundred feet. This range had already been made known to the explorer; it was within the hunting grounds of the Wichita Indians (after whom it had taken its name) and was composed of many granite boulders of various sizes and colors.

The course which the men and their slow, plodding oxen and pack mules continued to follow for the next few days was firm and level. Marcy still kept within sight of the north bank of the Red until he discovered that approximately fifty miles beyond Cache Creek the river divided into two forks: one branch flowed from the north and the other from the west, and both were enclosed by high red bluffs. After a brief consultation with his fellow officers and guides, the commander decided to follow the north tributary. This stream he estimated to be seven hundred yards wide, while winding crazily from bank to bank over its shifting bed of sand, and the small current of water proved to be as bitter in taste as it was red in color.

On May 23, somewhere between present Tipton and Snyder, Oklahoma, the company encamped near the foot of the Wichita Mountains. Here they remained for six days while an extensive examination of the area was made, and here numerous geological and scientific specimens were collected; also quantities of newly discovered coal and timber were obtained for future use as fuel.

Before leaving this encampment, Captain McClellan took a longitude reading with his pocket lever watch and computed the present position to be forty-five seconds east of the 100th meridian. This latter line had been established as the boundary between the United States and Spanish territory in the Treaty with Spain in 1819. When Texas was admitted to the Union in 1845, it became the boundary between that state and Indian Territory, and Marcy noted in his journal in 1852 that McClellan was the first surveyor to fix the line.

Furthermore, McClellan was determined to survey the line to its intersection with the Red; according to his calculation this point was approximately six miles downstream from the fork of the river described above. Near by was a tremendous cottonwood tree, and the officer blazed identical inscriptions on its four sides attesting the fact that it marked the beginning of the boundary line between the Texas Panhandle and Indian Territory. This action, instead of being an aid to geography, soon helped contribute to a prolonged dispute between the United States and Texas over the ownership of the region between the north and south forks of the Red.[12]

Soon after McClellan fixed the 100th meridian, Texas laid claim to the land immediately west of his 1852 line, but subsequent surveys showed that the meridian had been inaccurately located. Indeed, McClellan had placed the line fifty miles too far east. In 1886, Marcy testified before the Texas Boundary Commission in Washington that the error had been caused by an inaccurate pocket lever watch, which was the only surveying instrument available to him at the time on account of his inability to obtain a chronometer before the start of the journey in 1852. Although Texas was forced to concede the error and accept the loss of considerable land, she claimed that the north fork of the Red was the principal course of the stream, thus entitling her to the territory between the north and south forks (Greer County). Texas pointed out that in 1852 Captain Marcy had explored this branch

[12] B. B. Chapman, "The Claim of Texas to Greer County, *The Southwestern Historical Quarterly*, Vol. LIII, (1949–50), 19–34; 164–79; 404–21.

of the river first, thereby acknowledging it as the more important fork. On the other hand, Marcy asserted in 1886 that although he had found that the north fork contributed more water to the parent stream, it should not be considered the main course because it was much narrower than the south fork.[13] This testimony, perhaps more than anything else, eventually caused the United States Supreme Court in 1896 to award the area between the two forks (Greer County) to present Oklahoma by declaring the south fork as the western extremity of the Red River. The long dispute focused belated attention upon Marcy's extensive expedition of 1852.

Before the expedition abandoned its camp near the foot of the Wichita Mountains on May 29, it encountered its first party of Indians when one day a large group of Wichitas appeared unexpectedly on the opposite bank of near-by Otter Creek. The aborigines made signs that they wished to cross, and Captain Marcy obliged them by ordering two of his men to cut a large tree and let it fall across the small but deep creek. The visitors, about 150 warriors, then came across, and a formal talk with the chief of the tribe followed. Marcy explained to him that the inhabitants of Texas were now of the same nation as the whites in other parts of the United States and he and his braves would be held responsible for any depredations committed against Texas settlers. The chief professed his peaceful intentions as he eagerly awaited the receipt of the white man's presents. Marcy reported giving him and his braves quantities of flour and bacon, "for which we received their acknowledgments in their customary style—by begging for everything else they saw."

Marcy also took advantage of the occasion to inquire about the characteristics of the country into which he and his party were advancing. The Wichitas gave anything but an encouraging report. They assured the "White Captain" that no drinking water could be found beyond the present position because the waters of the Red were brackish and bitter, and therefore the entire command would perish before it could possibly reach the headwaters.

Although the news of such an inhospitable country was dis-

[13] "Report of the Texas Boundary Commission," *House Exec. Doc. No. 21*, 50 Cong., 1 sess., XVIII (2500), 9.

couraging, nevertheless Marcy was undaunted in his determination, and he pushed on again. Forty miles north of the Wichita Mountain camp he discovered that the stream which he had been following divided into two branches of about equal width. The tributaries were separated by a high bluff, with one stream flowing from the west and the other from the northwest. Deciding to examine the western fork first, the commander pursued it for a distance of about eight miles. Appropriately, he named it on his map the Salt Fork (now Elm Fork), but reasoned that it would be more convenient to explore its ultimate source later. He then returned to the junction of the two streams and continued along his former course as rapidly as possible. The stream seemed to flow from an almost level and uninterrupted plain as far as the eye could extend, and the farther the party traveled, the easier was the going.

By June 1, the course of the river had veered almost directly west, leaving the Wichita Mountains to fade from sight, and the change from the rustic scenery to the dead-level plains moved Marcy to write: "The beautiful and majestic scenery throughout the whole extent of that portion of the chain we have traversed, with the charming glades lying between them, clothed with a luxuriant sward up to the very base of the almost perpendicular and rugged sides, with the many springs of delicious water bursting forth from solid walls of granite and bounding along over the debris at the base, forcibly reminds me of my own native hills, and the idea of leaving these for the desert plains gives rise to an involuntary feeling of melancholy similar to that I have experienced on leaving home."

Sixteen days and 370 miles later the party neared its destination, the headwaters of the North Fork. Not far from the location of present Lefors, Texas, the river made a sudden turn toward the southwest, and the sandstone bluffs along the banks now began to come closer together until at last they formed a narrow canyon approximately three hundred feet deep. The travelers left their wagons on top, descended to the bed of the canyon, and continued upstream for another five miles until the canyon emerged upon the plains and branched off into several smaller gorges like fingers on a giant hand. At the end of the largest branch was an oasis-like grove of cottonwoods. Here the company pitched camp.

Almost the first thing that Marcy did after reaching the end of the trail was to bury under the roots of a tree a bottle which contained a memorandum of his visit. He then blazed the tree on both the north and south sides and penciled the words "Exploring Expedition, June 16, 1852."

Despite the Wichita chief's predictions that the travelers would surely perish for lack of adequate drinking water, the company so far had suffered very little. The water near the source of the North Fork and above the vast gypsum bed which underlay much of its route proved to be pure and sweet. Furthermore, the country was not as desolate as had been expected; the soil in many places was good, the grass was abundant, and the fringe of the river contained a variety of trees—pecan, elm, hackberry, cottonwood, and dwarf oak.

The country offered other surprises, too. In addition to a tremendous deposit of gypsum, there were also large quantities of sulphate of lime throughout the section, which ranged "in various degrees of purity from common plaster of Paris to a beautiful transparent selenite." But the most pleasant surprise of all was the fact that no hostile Indians so far had been encountered except occasional glimpses of small parties who made an obvious effort to avoid meeting the whites. Marcy was at a loss to explain their action unless they took his expedition for a warring party sent to punish them.

During the course of the journey along the North Fork, the travelers always selected a campsite at night, when possible, on high ground within the bend of a creek in order that the wagons and tents could be placed in a semicircle across the opening to form a makeshift stockade. The cannon was placed in the center of the barrier. After camp had been made, the mules, saddle horses, oxen, and beef cattle were taken out to graze, and a close watch was kept over them in case of marauding Indians. A few minutes before dark the animals were brought inside the enclosure; all the mules and horses were picketed for the night, and the oxen were tied to the wagons. Finally, sentinels were posted on all sides to keep guard throughout the night, while the remainder of the company went to sleep at an early hour. By three o'clock each morning the expedition had broken camp and the day's march was under way. A brief stop was made at six o'clock for breakfast and by eleven o'clock the expedition halted once again to make camp and to give the animals ample time to graze. Thus the intense afternoon heat of the plains country was avoided.

Except for fresh vegetables and fruits, the members of the expedition were well supplied with food by the Delaware hunters. Indeed, plentiful buffalo, deer, antelope, and turkey made fresh meat a simple matter. Marcy frequently joined with the Indian hunters in search of game, and according to his journal he rarely failed to kill two or three deer in a single afternoon. A number of greyhounds and an excellent bear dog had been brought along, the former capable of running down deer. The broad, level prairies afforded an excellent view of more than one such thrilling chase.

A total of more than one hundred deer were killed in one manner or another during the journey, as were several antelope, turkeys, and three or four bears. In addition, four panthers, all of which measured more than eight feet from nose to tail were bagged by the hunters. Marcy personally accounted for the largest of the four cats quite by accident. Having sighted a herd of antelope grazing among a grove of mesquite trees, he cautiously approached to within a few hundred yards before calling out to them with a "deer-call," an instrument commonly used by the Delaware hunters. It could be made to sound like a fawn, and sometimes it would decoy a doe within rifle range, which Marcy now succeeded in doing. The antelope naïvely approached the spot where the commander lay hidden, but just as Marcy raised his rifle and was ready to fire, he was distracted by a rustling in the grass to his left. Casting his eyes in that direction, he was startled by the sight of a tremendous panther bounding toward him at full speed. The animal doubtless anticipated making his breakfast on a tender fawn, but instead he received a fatal rifle shot in the chest. The Captain now forgot all about the tender antelope and let loose with several loud yells of exultation, but it was an experience he did not care to repeat.

It seems strange indeed that the travelers suffered in the presence of so much game, but the almost total absence of fresh fruits and vegetables caused several members of the party to have scurvy. Occasionally a patch of wild onion or a small grove of plums or grapes discovered upon the bank of a creek helped to combat the disease, and Dr. Shumard carried a limited amount of "anti-scorbutics" among his medical supplies, although the soldiers refused the medicine unless ordered to take it by the commander himself, for they were obliged to pay for it with a corresponding reduction in rations.

Before Marcy left the region of the headwaters of North Fork, he and a small party of "three gentlemen, five soldiers, and three Indians" struck out in a northern direction across the prairie to determine the proximity of the Canadian River. They had ridden several hours over the elevated plateau country, when their eyes were suddenly gladdened by the appearance of a valley bordered by several high bluffs. The commander recognized that he was again near the Canadian River, which he had followed on his trip to Santa Fé in 1849. The distance between the upper sources of the North Fork and the Canadian, according to Marcy's present calculation, was about twenty-five miles.[14] This discovery was a matter of much gratification to the commander, as it confirmed the accuracy of the theory he had formed in 1849 regarding the geographical positions of the Canadian and the Red—the two rivers which so often had been confused by earlier explorers as being one and the same.

John Bushman, Marcy's chief guide and interpreter, was visibly astonished by the proof of the commander's assertion that the Canadian could be found such a short distance north of the Red, and he was now prepared to believe in Marcy's unlimited supernatural powers. "I want you, Captain, to look at stars again, and tell me where Comanches gone," he earnestly requested. Repeated assertions by Marcy that it was impossible to deduce from the stars and the telescope the exact location of every Indian camp in the country could not convince the trusting Indian.

The small party returned to the camp by the grove of cottonwood on June 19, and made immediate preparation to continue across the plains in a due south direction. The entire command was in motion the following day, plodding over a great meadow of short buffalo grass, which gave the appearance of a boundless ocean. The principal fear that Marcy and his companions now

[14] According to Grant Foreman the actual mileage between the two streams at the present position was more nearly thirty-five than twenty-five miles. Foreman, *Adventure on Red River*, 66f.

faced was of not finding suitable drinking water; however, they had prepared themselves as best they could by filling all their casks with cool spring water before leaving the camp on North Fork. Thirty miles south of the fork the party came upon another stream whose course cut through the tablelands like the slash of a tremendous knife. This was the tributary of Red River which Marcy had previously explored on May 31, in the vicinity of its junction with the North Fork. It will be remembered that because of its taste he had named the stream the Salt Fork, but happily for the group, the water near the present upper region proved to be free from the usual unpalatable taste.

"The country in this region was much broken and cut up with deep gorges and abrupt ridges which are almost impassable for wagons," Marcy wrote. But by taking a circuitous route, he and his command got beyond the Salt Fork without difficulty and continued another fifty miles over a desert-like region until they arrived on the north bank of a third tributary of the Red, the South Fork, on June 26, 1852. This stream was partially distinguished from the previous branches of the Red by the near-by stretches of prairie-dog towns, and Marcy estimated that one such settlement of these curious little creatures must have exceeded four hundred thousand acres. Indeed, this fork was known to the Comanches as "Ke-che-a-qui-ho-no," or "Prairie-dog-town River."

The landscape in the vicinity of the "Prairie-dog-town River" (South Fork) assumed a rugged character, with jagged cliffs and deep gorges branching in all directions. At the point where Marcy's party first came upon the stream, which was in a general west-to-east direction, they could easily view the Staked Plain some distance to the west, "towering some eight hundred feet above the surrounding country and bordered by precipitous escarpments, capped with a stratum of white gypsum, which glistened in the sun like burnished silver." Somewhere within this vast expanse were the beginnings of the South Fork of the Red, and Marcy knew that he must search them out as he had done on the North Fork.

It was obvious to all members of the expedition that the upper sources of this branch of Red River would be difficult to reach with wagons unless the terrain on its south bank proved less rugged than on the north side. Accordingly, the party made a crossing in an effort to discover a smoother path, but they realized quickly that such a search would be in vain, and Marcy now had no alternative but to leave most of his men and supplies behind while he and a smaller command pushed on. For the next three days the party of thirteen men—officers, guides, and enlisted men—managed to endure a journey that took them over a constant succession of steep, rocky ridges and into deep ravines, but they reached their ultimate destination on July 1, 1852, the headwaters of the third and last principal branch of a previously unexplored river.

The rough country made their ride difficult enough, but this was not nearly as unpleasant as the bitter water they were forced to drink and the midday temperature, which frequently reached 110 degrees in the shade. However, the bed of the stream near the extreme source changed from sand to rock, and to the travelers' delight, they found the water there clear, cool, and free from the nauseating taste of gypsum. When they realized that the casks could be filled at last with good drinking water for the return journey, the morale of the small party took a sudden upward turn.

As Marcy's company approached the end of its journey, it traveled the last several miles along the bottom of a giant canyon through which the stream took its course. The sandstone bluffs along each side rose to a height of eight hundred feet or more and were sometimes separated by a distance of ten or twelve miles. This was the Palo Duro Canyon, where Colonel Charles Goodnight, a Texas cattle baron, later established his famous JA Ranch—a place where grass and water were to be had the year round. Marcy and his men rode the length of the great canyon and finally took a left fork into what is known today as Tule Canyon. They continued to pursue this gorge as its perpendicular walls drew closer together and its floor gradually rose to the surface of the surrounding plains.

At the very apex of the sandstone bluffs a spring of cool, sparkling water burst forth, and the travelers stood for several moments in hushed silence, believing that they were the first white men in recorded history to witness the scene before them now. This discovery was certainly a great emotional experience for Marcy and a high point in his career as an explorer, and he described it graphically:

"The magnificence of the views that presented themselves to our eyes as we approached the head of the river, exceeded anything I have ever beheld. It is impossible for me to describe the sensations that came over me, and the exquisite pleasure I experienced, as I gazed upon these grand and novel pictures. . . . All here was crude nature, as it sprang into existence at the fiat of the Almighty architect of the universe, still preserving its primeval type, its unreclaimed sublimity and wilderness; and forcibly inspired me with that veneration which is justly due to the high antiquity of nature's handiworks, and which seems to increase as we consider the solemn and important lesson that is taught us in reflecting upon their contrived permanence which contrasted with our own fleeting and momentary existence."

Before leaving the spot which they had labored so hard to attain, the travelers dismounted and climbed to the rim of the canyon to find themselves upon the level, shadowless prairie of the Staked Plain. At least they would not be required to cross that pitiless, hostile region with its oppressive dust and intolerable heat. Gratefully, they were now free to turn their backs upon it and to begin the long trek homeward.

X

"Melancholy and distressing news"

1852

THE JOURNEY from the edge of the Staked Plain back to the expedition's camp on the south bank of the river was approximately sixty-five miles, as the crow flies. Marcy's small party traveled the distance in two days, however, despite the roughness of the country. From his map and the description of the route found in his journal, Marcy evidently took a return course along the edge, and not the bottom, of Palo Duro Canyon. This giant chasm, which he had explored rather thoroughly while going upstream, excited the commander's curiosity and was the subject of much speculation in his journal. Was it formed by the continued action of the current, or was it produced by some great convulsion?

Some months later, after his return to the East from the Red River expedition, the explorer was invited to present a paper before the American Geological and Statistical Society in New York City. The *New York Evening Post* carried the full text of the speech (on March 22, 1853) which was more than eight columns in length.[1] In the speech Marcy devoted considerable time to the Palo Duro Canyon, which he had discovered and explored on his recent expedition. Like most travelers who came upon similar freaks of nature in the West during the nineteenth century, he now advanced the theory that the canyon could only have been formed in the remote past by a tremendous earthquake.

Dr. Hitchcock, the geologist, did not agree with Marcy. After listening to the latter's description of the canyon and reading his journal very carefully, the well-known geologist announced his

[1] Scrapbook.

unqualified conclusion that the giant gorge had been formed by erosion and not by fracture of the earth's surface. Hitchcock's theory, which, incidentally, coincides with that of most present-day geologists, was later discussed fully in his own report on the geological specimens collected by the expedition, which was printed as a government document along with Marcy's official journal.[2] It is interesting to note that Hitchcock believed the canyon on Red River the most gigantic one he had ever found described. Perhaps geologists had not then been informed of the Grand Canyon in Colorado and Arizona, for certainly it is much larger than the Palo Duro. Nevertheless, the Red River expedition in 1852 resulted in the discovery of one of the most unusual and grandiose geological phenomena in the great Southwest.

But let us return to Marcy and his companions on Red River. On July 4, 1852, the two parties of the command were reunited, and everyone had the same thought—to get home as quickly as possible. The road back was not to be an easy one, however, and Marcy soon realized that he would have to change his course if he wished to make more speed. The country along the south bank of the South Fork continued to be broken with deep gullies and abrupt ridges, so that to go around them with the heavy wagons would require more time than he was willing to take. Accordingly, the commander decided to move back to the north side of the stream once again, where he found a smoother prairie which provided an excellent road for the next eight days. The wagons rolled smoothly on, for their path was now paved with grama and mesquite grass that covered the dry, sandy soil like a thick carpet.[3] Except for a fleeting glimpse now and then of a small band of Comanches, which gave the company a few moments of uneasiness, the journey to the crossing of the North Fork was monotonous. But each mile meant a shorter distance home.

Wild game continued to be plentiful on the pristine prairie, but the water in the present region proved to be the bitterest and most nauseating that so far had been encountered. Scurvy again

[2] U. S. Senate *Exec. Doc. No. 54*, 32 Cong., 2 sess. The report appears also as U. S. House *Exec. Doc.* (unnumbered), 33 Cong., 1 sess.

[3] Marcy brought back a quantity of grass seeds (grama and mesquite). The seeds were later planted in various sections of the Atlantic coastal region, but the results of the experiments are not known to the writer.

John Bushman, in 1858, who was Marcy's chief scout on the 1852 Red River expedition. "A true specimen of the Indian type, dignified, reserved, and taciturn, self-reliant, independent, and fearless."

overtook several of the soldiers, and it became difficult for them to stay on their feet, but occasionally they would find a patch of wild onions or a thicket of plums and obtain temporary relief. On July 12, 1852, the command intercepted the same North Fork which it had previously explored. The men crossed over rapidly, for by now the stream was in low banks, and camped for the night near the base of the principal peak of the Wichita Mountains. This peak is the most conspicuous elevation in the western region of the state, and Marcy estimated that it rose to a height of approximately eleven hundred feet above the surface of the surrounding plains. In 1852, it was fringed with gigantic pecan, hackberry, oak, and elm trees. Before leaving the region Marcy gave the mountain its present name, "Mount Scott," in honor of his commanding general.

The travelers took up a southeast course from Mount Scott and passed through the valley of a small creek. Near the end of the valley they suddenly came upon an abandoned Wichita village where they camped for the night. "In my humble judgment," the commander wrote in his journal, "a military post established in the vicinity of these mountains, and garrisoned by a force of sufficient strength to command the respect of the Indians would add more to the efficiency of the army in checking the depredation than any other position that is now occupied by the troops in western Texas. This post would be about a hundred and forty miles from Fort Arbuckle; two hundred miles from Fort Washita; and one hundred and twenty miles from Fort Belknap; and being near Red River (which it is believed will prove navigable, at a good stage of water, nearly as high as this point), the troops could probably be furnished with supplies at a lower rate than at any of the military posts in this part of the country equidistant from the seacoast."[4]

Many additional examinations and reports of the region were subsequently made by army officials, but not until 1869 did the War Department finally accept Marcy's recommendation regarding the location of a post near the Wichita Mountains. Today, one of the most important military establishments in the United States, Fort Sill, near Lawton, Oklahoma, occupies this spot, and its per-

[4] Unless otherwise indicated, all direct quotations in this chapter are taken from Marcy report. See note 2 above.

manency stands as a tribute to the intrepid commander of the Red River expedition in 1852.

From the abandoned Wichita village the journey was resumed the following day, this time in a due east course. Each turn of the wagon wheels brought the travelers closer to Fort Arbuckle, and despite the grubby life that the soldiers generally led at the frontier garrisons, they now eagerly looked forward to returning. At least they would again have fresh vegetables, for wild game had long since become an old story. A rest from the trail and three month's back pay would soon make them forget the oppressive, hot winds which blew stinging sand in their faces, the early rising each morning, and the dumb oxen and stubborn mules which had so sorely tried their patience.

Every day now was much like the one before. Around two o'clock each morning the tents were taken down and placed, along with the baggage and supplies, on the wagons; the stock was fed and watered before being hitched for the day's drive. Soon the men and animals took their places in line and the scouts rode out to their positions on each wing. A last-minute inspection by the commander, and the signal was given to go forward. Marcy, McClellan, the other officers, and the civilian members of the party led the parade on horseback, followed by the main body of soldiers on foot. Immediately behind the soldiers was the six-pound cannon, dragged forward by a mule team, while the pack animals, supply wagons, beef cattle, surplus work stock, and drivers brought up the dusty rear.

An incident occurred one morning as the men prepared to break camp that made a profound impression on the commanding officer. Someone noticed that a mule had broken loose during the night and was still not to be found after a prolonged search by most of the expedition. The commander finally questioned John Bushman about his chances of recovering the lost mule and rejoining the party, for the animal was a good one. "I think maybe so find um—maybe not," was the laconic reply. Accordingly, Marcy ordered him to try to pick up the trail and to abandon it only when all prospect of success had vanished. The expedition then made its daily march as Bushman rode back toward the Wichita Mountains.

Near the end of that same day when the men had completed

their chores and were making ready to retire for the night, the Captain's attention was called to the distant approach of a lone horseman. It soon proved to be Bushman, driving the missing animal before him, and upon his arrival in camp he reported that he had overtaken the mule some twenty-five miles due north of the last camp.

Recalling the Delaware's noncommittal attitude earlier in the day, Marcy asked him if he had become discouraged before he caught up with the fleeing animal. Bushman seemed puzzled by the question and for several moments remained silent. Finally, he replied, in such a manner as to leave no doubt of his sincerity, that, if need be, he would have remained on the trail for several weeks. Such an example of obedience to orders caused the commander to note that evening in his journal that he had never met a man with "a more resolute character, regardless of his background," and he attributed the success of the expedition in large measure to this faithful guide: "He never sees a place once without instantly recognizing it on seeing it the second time, notwithstanding he may approach it from a different angle . . . he will almost invariably point out the particular localities where water can be found, when to others there seems to be nothing to indicate it."

Later, Captain Marcy also paid tribute to John Bushman in two of his books, and on one occasion spiced his tribute to the Indian's character with this anecdote: Soon after the Red River expedition had gotten under way in 1852 and the men and animals had adjusted themselves to the routine of the trail, Bushman approached the Captain one evening and bluntly inquired how much he was going to be paid for his services. Marcy answered in an equally blunt fashion that he had made it clear before leaving Fort Washita that each guide would receive one dollar a day.

"I no understand um that-a-way, Captain, Black Beaver he say maybe so give um two dollars half one day."

"Black Beaver is not authorized to make contracts for the army," Marcy snapped.

Bushman's refusal to talk during the rest of the day caused the commander to fear that his chief guide might quit, so he adopted a more conciliatory attitude and agreed to pay the Indian an additional fifty cents a day for his services as interpreter. Bushman received the news without comment, but his surly attitude left no doubt that he was still disappointed. Marcy by now was more than slightly chagrined, and he admonished his guide that "the government has no money to throw away by paying three prices for anything."

Bushman carried his bitterness on his face for several days, but eventually he softened up, and Marcy was happy to push the affair out of his mind; finally, he forgot about it entirely. When the work of the expedition was complete and the company had returned to Fort Arbuckle, the commander paid off all the civilian employees for their services. He then called Bushman aside and told him that he might go on another journey the following year and would be happy to employ him again. Bushman responded to the compliment with a resounding "No!"

"Why not?" inquired the astounded Captain.

"Because that government he ain't got no money to throw away."[5]

July 22, 1852, was a day which Marcy long remembered. The expedition was but a short distance from home, and every member of the party was anticipating the end of their arduous labors. That evening they encamped a short distance beyond two small villages of Wichita and Waco Indians, near present Rush Springs, Oklahoma. As usual, a delegation of warriors called upon the "White Captain," doubtless in hopes of receiving gifts. When they learned the identity of the commander and his company, they were visibly surprised and soon revealed that a report had been made to the commander at Fort Arbuckle several weeks before that Marcy and his entire command had been massacred by the Comanches. Marcy at first was only slightly amused by the story, deducing that it must have originated with the Comanches or the Kiowas, since these were the only two tribes that frequented the area into which he had gone. "This accounts for the fact of their avoiding us upon all occasions," he wrote.

Not until his return to Fort Arbuckle a few days later did the explorer realize how extensively the rumor of his massacre had circulated and how completely it had been believed. Indeed, the hoax had been the cause of a prolonged series of sensational

[5] Marcy, *Army Life on the Border*, 86–87.

stories, and when at last it was countered by the news of the command's safe arrival at Fort Arbuckle, Marcy's name and the details of the Red River expedition became even more widely known. The resulting publicity would have done credit to a modern Hollywood press agent's dream, and it is doubtful if any previous exploring party on the western plains ever received more immediate attention from the general public.

Before leaving the Waco and Wichita villages, Marcy observed the inhabitants very closely, and he concluded that they had less regard for the truth than any Indians he had ever known. The Wichitas and Wacos were similar in many respects and frequently intermarried and lived together, as the present groups demonstrated. During the early settlement of Texas the Wichitas gave more trouble to the pioneers along the northern border of the state than the more daring Comanches.

Marcy was now able to complete his dictionary of Wichita words. He also set down one of the best descriptions of a Wichita town that we have. The villages contained most of the approximately five hundred Wichitas then in existence. Their lodges were made by frameworks of poles placed in circles in the ground with the tops tied together to form conical-shaped structures. These, in turn, were thatched with grass and from a distance gave the impression of large haystacks. Each dwelling was built to accommodate ten or twelve people. "When seated around their fires in the center of the lodges [Marcy noted], they have an air of domestic happiness about them which I did not expect to find."

While encamped near the Wichita and Waco villages, Marcy also learned that the Indians held two Mexican prisoners, one a man approximately forty years of age and the other a young boy of fifteen. The Captain explained to the chiefs of the joint settlements that the United States was obligated to Mexico by treaty to return any captives found in the Indian country, and that if necessary he was prepared to take the two prisoners by force. The older Mexican, upon hearing Marcy's demands, immediately intervened in his own behalf and explained that he had been with the Wichitas since childhood, that meanwhile he had become "as great a rascal as any of the Indians" and therefore did not wish to leave them. But the younger prisoner had only recently been captured and was extremely anxious to return to his parents.

The Indian family that claimed the boy refused to give him up until Marcy offered to compensate them with a number of presents. They then grudgingly agreed, but only after they had stripped the young Mexican of all his ragged clothing—"to make his exit from them in the same manner in which he had entered the world." The boy was clothed in some castoff trousers belonging to one of the soldiers and, overjoyed with the happy turn of events, immediately joined the Americans to return to civilization. Eventually he was escorted to San Antonio from Fort Washita and from there traveled back to his home in northern Mexico. As for the old prisoner, Marcy was not to see the last of him until two years later when he and a group of Wichitas visited the officer's camp on the Clear Fork of the Brazos, August 22, 1854. The Mexican again boasted to Marcy that he was a "big rascal," and before he and his "brothers" rode away, he proved it by stealing everything he could lay his hands on.

It was also at the time of Marcy's visit to the Waco and Wichita villages in 1852 that he first heard the story of the capture of Cynthia Ann Parker by the Comanches. Cynthia Ann later became the mother of the famous Comanche chief, Quanah Parker. Although her tragic story has been told many times in the past century, Marcy was one of the first to write about it from first-hand knowledge. In his report to the Secretary of War regarding the Red River expedition, the Captain added the following comment: "There is at this time a white woman among the Middle Comanches, by the name of Parker, who, with her brother, was captured while they were young children from their father's house in the western part of Texas. This woman has adopted all the habits and peculiarities of the Comanches; has an Indian husband and children, and cannot be persuaded to leave them. The brother of the woman, who had been ransomed by a trader and brought home to his relatives, was sent back by his mother for the purpose of endeavoring to prevail upon his sister to leave the Indians, and return to her family; but he stated to me that on his arrival she refused to listen to the proposition, saying that her husband, children, and all that she held most dear, were with the Indians, and there she should remain."

The expedition turned due south from the Indian villages and continued in that direction for several hours until it reached

Wild Horse Creek, a few miles east of present Duncan, Oklahoma. The travelers followed the creek for a short distance eastward until they arrived at the edge of the Cross Timbers. Here they encountered a small band of Kickapoo hunters, who so impressed Marcy in contrast to the Wichitas that he later paid them this unusual compliment in his report: "They are fine-looking, well-dressed young men, with open, frank and intelligent countenances, and seemed to scorn the idea of begging; while the others [Wichitas] . . . are incessantly begging for every article they see, and do not possess the slightest gratitude for favors received."

From the western edge of the Cross Timbers to Fort Arbuckle was but a three days' journey, and as the soldiers caught sight of familiar landmarks along the way, their spirits lifted and they suddenly became imbued with renewed energy. At 1:00 A.M. on July 28, the command broke camp for the last time and arrived at Fort Arbuckle by daylight a few hours later. As the caravan rolled into the post grounds, the company was greeted by the soldiers and officers with open arms. Only now did Marcy realize how completely the rumor of his "massacre" had been accepted for the literal truth, and he also learned the reason.

An examination of contemporary newspapers from various sections of the United States reveals that no small amount of excitement resulted from the sensational news of Marcy's "death." These printed accounts were based almost entirely upon the official correspondence between the commander of Fort Arbuckle, Captain J. C. Henshaw, and Assistant Adjutant General F. N. Page, Fort Smith, Arkansas.

In brief, the story they tell is as follows: On July 7, 1852, a Kiowa Indian came to Fort Arbuckle and stated that a party of wagons from there had recently been destroyed by the Comanches. The wagon train, he continued, had been joined near the Red River by another party which had come from the Brazos, and both groups had continued on west of the Wichita Mountains. There the train divided, one part, which consisted of five wagons, going up the bank of a stream where it was met by a large band of warriors who attacked and destroyed it. Then the Indians were joined by another body and subsequently overtook the second company of Americans and completely destroyed them, also. All of this was supposed to have taken place sometime during the latter part of May, 1852. The accuracy of the informant's description of the company and the number of wagons, plus the fact that a very large band of hostile Comanches were known to be in the vicinity of the expedition, prevented Captain Henshaw from regarding the story lightly.[6]

Additional credence was given to the hoax two days later, on July 9, when a Waco chief came to Fort Arbuckle to inform the post commander that nine days before a large band of Comanches had arrived at his hunting camp on Red River and told him that they recently had killed the whole of Captain Marcy's company on the left bank of the Washita. They claimed to have visited first with the Americans and to have received various presents from the commanding officer. They had departed peacefully, but returned early the following morning, surprising and killing the entire command of approximately eighty men. The Waco chief told Henshaw that when the Indian party visited him, some of the warriors wore parts of army uniforms and possessed several leather belts and at least one cartridge box. Furthermore, they boasted to him that they intended to cross the Red River and attack the troops at Fort Belknap and then return and annihilate the garrison at Fort Arbuckle as well.[7]

Captain Henshaw concluded that the "massacre" must have occurred some twenty days' journey west of Fort Arbuckle and that Marcy's entire command had been slaughtered. A few days later Henshaw offered a reward of five hundred dollars to a party of Kickapoo Indians who lived near Fort Arbuckle if they would go to the scene of the battle and recover the bodies, but the offer was refused because the Kickapoos feared it would be impossible to escape detection by the Comanches while crossing the treeless prairies to the west.[8] Henshaw then wrote to the Adjutant General in Washington and requested sufficient funds to hire a large Indian force (from two to three hundred warriors) to accompany him and a small company of regulars into the region and wage a war of revenge upon the Comanches.[9]

[6] Henshaw to Page, July 7, 1852, File No. W62–52, A. G. O.
[7] Henshaw to Page, July 9, 1852, File No. W62–52, A. G. O.
[8] Henshaw to Page, July 16, 1852, File No. H22–52, A. G. O.
[9] *Ibid.*

Meanwhile, the first account of the massacre appeared in the *Fort Worth Herald.* The story carried these sensational headlines: MASSACRE! MELANCHOLY AND DISTRESSING NEWS! MURDER OF CAPTAIN MARCY'S COMMAND BY THE COMANCHES! "If this report proves to be true," the editor concluded after a gruesome and somewhat original account of the episode, "an Indian war is inevitable. . . . The lives of hundreds of soldiers and citizens are sacrificed upon our frontier annually, in consequence of the penuriousness of our government. Instead of sending Captain Marcy out with sixty or eighty men, he should have had about 300, as the importance of the expedition demanded it, the country being unexplored and unknown, and filled with bands of marauding Indians who make murder and robbery a business."[10]

From Fort Smith the story soon reached Little Rock, Memphis, and New Orleans, and from those places it was relayed by mail and telegraph to every corner of the United States. Some editors seized upon it as an opportunity to discredit President Fillmore and General Scott. The *New Orleans True Delta,* like most western newspapers of the time, predicted that "the long expected prairie war is now upon the country," and went on to declare that the Comanches were five thousand strong and determined not to stop until every soldier on the southwestern frontier had been killed. "Let the prairies be swept until no Comanche warrior lives to boast of the scalps he has taken from the innocent whom he has treacherously slain in the merciless forays," it concluded.[11]

Still another newspaper, whose editor claimed to have talked with a traveler who knew the details of the battle, bluntly placed the blame on the War Department's failure to provide adequate weapons for Marcy's command. The editor charged that the Indians had ascertained the fact that the Red River expedition had been supplied with only three percussion caps a man, and that this lack of ammunition was the principal reason for "the loss of 100 men and 18 teams."[12]

The eastern newspapers took up the controversy also, but removed as they were from the frontier, their approach to the whole episode was a bit more sane. Recalling that Captain Marcy had previously been on recruiting duty at Harrisburg, Pennsyl-

[10] Scrapbook.   [11] *Ibid.*   [12] *Ibid.*

vania, the local editor spoke philosophically of his unfortunate death at the hands of the Plains Indians. He described the commander as "a martyr to that spirit of enterprise which is pushing the tide of civilization from the Atlantic to the Pacific."[13]

"It should be recollected," he continued, "that the Indians . . . have not made an invasion of our soil or our rights. They fight only for the soil which the Almighty gave them—for their houses, their altars, and their gods. If we had not invaded them—if we had left them to pursue the even tenor of their ways . . . they would not have committed an act of aggression or consummated a deed of blood. But, for almost three hundred years, the Indian has been the object of the white man's capacity [*sic*]—he has been hunted as if he were a wild beast of the field; and, from Plymouth Rock to the shores of the Pacific, the soil is stained with the blood of that aboriginal and rightful owner of the earth, who has fallen at the hands of the canting and cruel Puritan, who with firebrand and missile—stiletto and musket—has carried a war of extermination to the door of the innocent, and all for the glory of God, in success of the religion of the cross, and that humane doctrine which finds satiety in rapine and murder only.

"In the midst of the bloody war, which is anticipated will soon be upon us, it will not do, however, to stop by the wayside and moralize. It must be supposed; and therefore, let a force equal to the demands made by the emergency of the case be sent to the scene of action—let the bloody hand of vengeance be stayed; and peace again restored, let us extend justice to the Indians. This done, the savage will easily be made a friend and neighbor."

As the subject gained momentum in the press, the country became alarmed and horrified over the "sickening fate" of the Red River command, and Captain Marcy's life and deeds became well known to almost every American reader. He was characterized by such adjectives as "gallant," "talented," "brave," "cultured," "accomplished," and "distinguished." All agreed that his untimely death would be universally mourned, and one journalist eulogized him as follows: "Outliving the period of the Mexican War, inexorable fate decreed that he should thus die, in a less glorious, but not the less patriotic strife."

A funeral service was actually held in Marcy's honor at Green-

13 *Ibid.*

wich, Massachusetts, which was attended by most of his relatives, including Marcy's more prominent cousin, Governor William L. Marcy of New York. Several years later Randolph Marcy wrote, appreciatively: "I had the novel satisfaction of reading in the press several quite complimentary obituary articles upon the death of Captain Marcy."[14]

If the situation had its humorous side, the War Department had more than one reason to be relieved over Marcy's safe return. It had become the scapegoat of the affair, and had taken pains to defend its course by issuing a categorical denial of the charges levied against it for failing to send a larger and better-equipped force to the source of Red River. "Captain Marcy had unlimited discretion as to the number of men to be employed in, and the equipment of, the expedition," the Secretary of War explained. "He had been detached on this service for several years, and it was left to him to take as many men as he wanted and such an outfit as was necessary."[15]

The furor raised by Marcy's "massacre," however, prompted the War Department to release to the press a short time later an announcement that Congress had authorized an immediate increase in the size of the army on the frontier. Commented the *Missouri Republican* on August 12, 1852: "Painful as the report [of the massacre] has been, it will not have been without its good uses. Nothing else than a calamity of some kind could induce legislative action in that body, where demogogueism [sic] and President-making have complete control, and all public business is necessarily neglected."[16]

Within a few hours after the return of the Red River expedition to Fort Arbuckle, Captain Henshaw despatched a special courier to the Seventh Military District Headquarters at Fort Smith. He reported that Marcy's command had just returned— "without having seen any Comanches during the entire journey." The news quickly circulated throughout the country, bringing relief to the friends and relatives of the members of the party. The *Little Rock Whig* in a special edition proclaimed in bold type across its front page, CAPTAIN MARCY AND HIS COMMAND SAFE!

[14] Marcy, *Army Life on the Border,* 164.   [15] Scrapbook.
[16] Newspaper Collection, Library of Congress.

Meanwhile, the returned travelers enjoyed the hospitality of their fellow officers and soldiers at Fort Arbuckle. After the many weeks on a steady diet of little else but wild meat and stale bread, they "wolfed" down the fresh vegetables with zestful appreciation, and the bountiful post garden was hard put to satisfy their cravings.

During the two days that Marcy remained at Fort Arbuckle he saw that his soldiers, guides, and civilian employees were paid and that the surplus supplies and stores were properly disposed of. The scientific specimens were carefully prepared for shipment to New York. Lieutenant Updegraff now took full command of Company D and made preparations to return to Fort Belknap after a few more days of rest. "I feel a sincere regret at parting with the company," Marcy wrote in his journal on July 28, "as the uniform good conduct of the men during the entire march of about a thousand miles merits my most sincere and heartfelt approbation. I seldom had occasion to reprimand one of them. All have performed the arduous duties assigned them with the utmost alacrity and good will; and when . . . we were obliged to make long marches, and drink the most disgusting water for several days together, instead of murmuring and making complaints, they were cheerful and in good spirits."

On the following day, July 29, Captain Marcy and a small party rode to Fort Washita, where one of the civilian members of the command, Captain Strain, rejoined his family. Another few days of rest and the company continued toward Fort Smith, where their arrival on August 12 created much excitement. The *Herald* editor observed that he had seldom seen healthier men than Captain Marcy, Captain McClellan, Mr. Suydam, and Dr. Shumard. "Were it not for their long beards and sunburnt countenances, we should not suspect them to have been for the last three months living upon the plains, eating and sleeping in the open air."[17]

Dr. Shumard, whose home was in Fort Smith, now bade farewell to his companions as they rode toward Rock Roe, the steamship landing on White River some two hundred miles eastward.

Years later, in *Army Life on the Border*, Marcy wrote of his journey across Arkansas in 1852 with his two remaining companions, McClellan and Suydam. The first day after leaving Fort Smith the trio traveled approximately twenty-five miles before

[17] Scrapbook.

stopping in midafternoon at a plantation house to inquire about the prospect of obtaining food. Upon entering the front parlor of the owner's colonial house, the Captain was met by a Negro servant. When he told the Negro that he wished to speak with his master, he was ushered into a bedchamber occupied by the mistress of the plantation. The poor woman was in bed, obviously suffering severe pain from what she later explained was rheumatism. Marcy spoke to her in his usual gallant manner, apologized profusely for the intrusion, and then explained that he and his companion were in need of nourishment.

The sick woman replied that her servants were in the field and that she was by no means willing to call them from their work, and Marcy did not press the subject further. Instead, he inquired if the woman had had a good physician to attend her in her illness. She replied that her doctor, who had lived at Fort Smith, had recently been killed by the Indians and that no other competent physician was available. Curious for more details of the man's death, Marcy soon learned that the physician was none other than Dr. Shumard. "There is no doubt about his death because he was with Captain Marcy's party," the woman assured him. This was the sort of situation that Marcy relished, and after a momentary pause he confronted his hostess with a proposition: Would she give him and his companion a warm meal in exchange for positive proof that Dr. Shumard was still alive and in good health?

"I have the honor, Madam," he retorted after the proposition had been accepted, "of presenting myself to you as the identical Captain Marcy whom you suppose to have been killed by the Indians, and I have the pleasure to inform you that your physician returned with me yesterday to Fort Smith, and in the best possible state of health." The surprised woman leaped out of bed, rheumatism and all, and screamed at the top of her voice: "You, Jim, go out into the field and tell Sally to come here quick, and get these gentlemen some dinner; do you hear!"

The next stop did not turn out as well. The three travelers came upon a less imposing farmhouse the following evening, and Marcy again politely inquired if he and his friends might obtain food and lodging for the night. They were taken in without further questioning and soon found themselves seated at the family table.

But alas! "The dishes before us consisted of fried bacon floating in grease, some corn bread in the shape of hand grenades, and a quantity of glutinous, half-baked hot biscuits, none of which seemed calculated to tempt the appetite of the gentleman from New York [Suydam] who called for toast. The farmer's wife replied that 'she had it on a frying, and she 'lowed it would soon be done.' . . . When it came on the table it appeared that she had taken the loaf, cut in in two parts, placed them in a pan, and fried them in grease for about half an hour. My friend did not seem to relish this method of cooking, and explained to the hostess in detail the proper method of making toast; whereupon she said, 'Oh, you want burnt bread; I thought you wanted toast.'

"The woman evidently did not know much more about making tea than she did the proper method of making toast," Marcy concluded. Indeed, she had taken the box of tea which Suydam gave her for "a mess of dried greens" and had boiled the whole lot accordingly.

The travelers somehow survived the meal and then asked to be shown to their sleeping quarters, hoping no doubt that a good night's rest would compensate for the miserable cooking. Their beds looked comfortable enough, but experience soon proved them otherwise. Try as they would, they could not get to sleep, and Marcy kept imagining that something was crawling up his legs and over his body, but all of his efforts to trap the intruders failed. After several fruitless minutes of playing "tag" with the baffling enemy, the Captain finally arose and lighted a candle. As he pulled back the covers, he discovered "a whole army of bed bugs marching and counter-marching in all directions."

Since prospects for any sleep there appeared dim indeed, Marcy took a blanket from his baggage and made ready to slip outside to spend the remainder of the night on the grass. About that time his companion Suydam called out: "What in thunder is it that tickles my leg so?" Marcy quietly assured him that it was only his imagination working—that if he remained perfectly still, he would soon drop off to sleep. But it did not take long for the gentleman from New York to realize that his imagination was "fighting a losing battle," and both he and McClellan fled their beds in terror to join their chuckling friend on the grass.

Apparently the remainder of the trip to Rock Roe was without incident, for Marcy makes no further mention of his Arkansas adventures. At Napoleon, Arkansas, not far from where the White River flows into the Mississippi, the three men parted company. Captain McClellan now took passage on a down-river steamer for New Orleans, thence he was to continue through the Gulf to Indianola, Texas, and from there to San Antonio via stage. A day or two later Marcy and Suydam took an up-river boat to St. Louis.

The explorer and his companion stopped for two days in St. Louis, and their visit there did not go unnoticed: "It gives us very great gratification to be able to announce the arrival of Captain Marcy, and another gentleman of his party in this city," the *Missouri Republican* stated in a front page story on August 27, 1852. "His presence here dissipates all apprehensions of his death and we are pleased to be able to say that he is in the enjoyment of excellent health. . . . It was intimated that there was cruel indifference on the part of the President and General Scott, not only to the success of the expedition, but to the fate of the men engaged in it; and if it had happened that the command had been cut off, there would have been a vast deal of indignation expended for political effort. As the expedition has returned in safety, some other grounds of accusation must be found . . . against the administration, and particularly General Scott, who, as head of the army, it was designed to hold responsible for it."[18]

From St. Louis, Marcy and Suydam continued by steamer to Cincinnati and Pittsburgh. They took the "cars" at the latter place and arrived at Philadelphia sometime in the early part of September, 1852. The exact circumstances of Marcy's reunion with his family cannot be described, for correspondence during this period is lacking. Since Mary and Fanny had remained in various places in New York or at Hartford, Connecticut, during most of Marcy's absence on the Red River expedition, it seems likely that they all met at Hartford where Mary Ellen was still in school.

In a letter postmarked Greenwich, Massachusetts, October 6, 1852, Marcy informed the Adjutant General that he had arrived there with his family on September 13, where he "was soon afterwards taken suddenly ill and remained so until now."[19] He further

[18] Newspaper Collection, Library of Congress.
[19] Marcy to Cooper, File No. 332M–52, A. G. O.

stated that he would shortly proceed to Washington and report in person the result of his recent expedition.

On November 4, he again wrote Adjutant General Samuel Cooper to report that he had left Greenwich on October 15 for Washington, but upon reaching New York was "stricken with a fever which has confined me to my room ever since."[20] Cooper promptly and sympathetically suggested to Marcy that he remain in New York until fully recovered and that while there he could complete his report and map of the recent expedition before coming to Washington for a personal conference.[21]

Several weeks passed before Marcy made a complete recovery, but meanwhile he was able to be about and to do some work each day on his report. To his now close friend, George McClellan, he wrote on December 9, 1852, that he had visited the latter's brother (John) while passing through Philadelphia some weeks previously. He remarked that he had settled McClellan's various accounts in New York, had had one of the panther claws mounted for him, and was looking about for the special type of hunting rifle which McClellan had asked him to purchase.

"I have had an interview with Professor Baird," Marcy continued. "He says the collection of reptiles is by far the most important that had been made except that of the Mexican boundary commission, and he is anxious to have many of them figured. . . . I have placed the herbarium in the hands of Doctor Torrey, and the minerals with Doctor Hitchcock, both of whom have promised to give me a full description of them. Doctor Hitchcock says that the gypsum formation is the most extensive in the North American continent."[22]

The forty-year-old Marcy by now had the West in his heart and was acclaimed as one of the most important military explorers in the United States. His fame as a western traveler and observer in 1852 perhaps was surpassed only by that of the more glamorous John C. Frémont, whose many exploring ventures had already ended. But Marcy's travels were far from being over. Indeed, he now stood midway in a career that ultimately embraced more adventure and excitement than ordinarily befalls a dozen men.

[20] Marcy to Cooper, File No. 377M–52, A. G. O.
[21] Cooper to Marcy, Letters Sent, XXVIII (1852), A. G. O.
[22] Marcy to McClellan, December 9, 1852, McClellan Papers, 1st Series, IV.

XI

"An uninteresting and forbidding land"

1853–1854

CAPTAIN MARCY remained in New York for more than a year before he returned to regular duty on the southwestern frontier. Meanwhile, the long exposure to uneven weather, bad water, and an unbalanced diet had taken its toll, and several months dragged by before he regained his health and was freed from intermittent chills and fever. Still, he was not altogether displeased with his present situation, for it afforded him the first opportunity since 1848 to be with Mary and the two children.

Throughout 1853, the Marcys stayed at the Madison House, one of the most fashionable boarding establishments of its day. By now Mary Ellen had completed her schooling at the private academy at Hartford and was a pretty, vivacious young woman of eighteen. Her time was taken up largely by dancing lessons and the cultivation of the social graces that society demanded of its fashionable young ladies. At the same time, seven-year-old Fanny attended a private school in the city, while Mary was fast becoming recognized as a prominent figure in local society. Marcy must have enjoyed this domesticity, for his correspondence reflects the feeling that fame and adventure were too high a price to pay for continual separations from his wife and daughters and his inability to have a permanent home like other people. Quite naturally he began to look about.

A recent vacancy in the Commissary of Subsistence Department offered possibilities, so Marcy set to work to obtain the position by asking his friend Congressman W. Cass Johnson to lend his support. Johnson wrote to the Secretary of War on November

13, 1852: "Captain R. B. Marcy's friends are anxious that you should appoint him in the Commissary of Subsistence Department where his duties will be less difficult to discharge."[1] Secretary C. M. Conrad tersely replied by return mail that the position had already been filled. That was the end of that!

On February 4, 1853, the United States Senate passed a resolution requesting "a copy of the report of the recent Red River expedition." Accordingly, the Secretary of War promptly wrote to Marcy in New York, urging him to complete the work as rapidly as possible.[2] Apparently Marcy's health continued poor, for he answered that he was yet unable to devote much time to writing and that he would be further delayed on account of the necessity of receiving the reports of the scientists who were examining the various specimens collected by the expedition. Indeed, the whole project was not completed until the following November, when it was forwarded to Washington.

The Captain's narrative of the Red River journey, together with maps, reports, and illustrations, was ultimately printed as Senate and House documents. The publicity given to the expedition at the time of Marcy's alleged "massacre" in 1852 by the Comanches had been widespread, and the general public apparently awaited his account with great interest. To meet this unusual demand, the War Department ultimately had a special edition printed, in 1854, which appeared in book form, under the title *Exploration of the Red River of Louisiana*, and sold for one dollar a copy. Judging from the number of copies still in existence, it must have had wide circulation.

Sometime during 1853, the American Statistical and Geographical Society held its annual meeting in New York City, at which time Marcy was invited to address "a large and brilliant audience" on the subject of his recent travels into the unexplored Southwest. The meeting, held in the chapel of Columbia University, was presided over by George Bancroft, the distinguished American historian. The *New York Tribune* carried the full text of Marcy's speech and observed that "it was received with close attention and much applause."[3]

[1] Johnson to C. M. Conrad, Letters Received, File No. 402M–52; A. G. O.
[2] Conrad to Marcy, Copies of Letters Sent, Vol. XXXIV, 1953; A. G. O.
[3] A newspaper clipping of the speech is found in Marcy's Scrapbook.

"An uninteresting and forbidding land"

"It has generally been supposed that the sources of the [Red] river would be found in lofty mountain ranges," the *Tribune* quoted Marcy, "where the melting of snows would account for the great amount of water passing through the channel during the month of June, but such is not the fact, as all the principal tributaries have their origin in the eastern borders of the tablelands of New Mexico, where there are no mountains." The explorer also observed that the Red did not flow through extensive salt plains, as commonly believed; instead, the bitter and disagreeable taste of its water was caused by the vast gypsum formations throughout the region.

Perhaps the most interesting part of Marcy's well-publicized lecture was that dealing with the inhabitants of the Great Plains, always a popular subject with eastern audiences. Few men could speak with as much authority about the "uncivilized tribes" of the West, whom Marcy now called "the Monarchs of the Plains," as he compared their nomadic customs to those of the Arabs in the Arabian desert and the Tartars on the steppes of central Asia.

"What will become of the prairie Indian who relies for subsistence, shelter, and clothing on the flesh and hides of the (rapidly disappearing) buffalo?" he asked. "He must either perish with the buffalo, or increase his marauding depredations on the Mexicans, or learn to cultivate the soil. As the first law of our nature is self-preservation, it is not probable that he will sit down and quietly submit to starvation; he must therefore resort to one of the latter alternatives; but as he has no knowledge of agriculture, considers it the business of a slave, and very much beneath the dignity of a warrior, it appears reasonable that he will turn his attention to the Mexican, over whom he has held the mastery for many years. Heretofore, his plunder of them has been for pastime and for glory; but when he is obliged to resort to this as a means of subsistence, woe to the poor Mexican. . . . It will be necessary to devise some measure to do away with the inveterate prejudices which the Comanches entertain against the habits and customs of the whites, before they will be induced to remain in any fixed abodes, or cultivate the soil.

"It is not, at this late day in our power to atone for all the injustices inflicted upon the red man; but it seems to be that a wise policy would dictate almost the only recompense it is now possible to make, that of introducing among them the lights of Christianity and the blessings of civilization, with their attendant benefits of agriculture and the arts."

Marcy was to have a part in devising a solution to the problem of the Plains Indians; within one year after making these remarks, he was arduously engaged in locating the first Indian reservation ever established in the West. This work, plus his long and friendly association with the Comanches and other western Indians and his frequent public remarks regarding their hopeless predicament, marks his importance in regard to the reservation concept. Although it is difficult to determine his exact influence on the federal government's decision in 1867 to put all the Plains Indians on reservations, his pioneering undoubtedly had its effect.

On March 1, 1853, the *Washington Intelligencer* carried a brief news story of the arrival in that city of "the gallant officer and gentleman, Randolph B. Marcy," and at the same time pointed out that "the grade of Captain is too low for such a brave and valuable officer." Indeed, the subject of his rank was precisely what had brought Marcy to the capital city. Despite assurances from the Adjutant General that Marcy was to be made a brevet major, the recent list of promotions had failed to carry his name. Almost eight years had passed since the explorer had been made a captain, and meanwhile he had carried out three major expeditions and had experienced more active service than any other officer in his regiment. Not only did he feel that he had been neglected by the War Department, but he also needed more money to support his increasingly expensive family. (A captain of infantry in 1853 received fifty dollars a month, plus four rations a day and one servant.)

Marcy was not without influential friends in Washington, and he lost no time in appealing to them for help. At his request, Congressman Charles Chapman wrote immediately to General Scott on March 1, 1853: "You know his services and worth as a gentleman and soldier, and my purpose is to ask that he may be placed upon the list for brevet if you think it consistent with your interest and the public interest."[4] And on the same day Congressman James C. James also wrote to General Scott in the explorer's

[4] Letters Received, File No. M98–53; A. G. O.

behalf: "It would be gratifying to his friends to see him receive the compliment he so richly deserves."[5]

These two letters carry the following endorsement in General Scott's handwriting: "I earnestly recommend Captain Marcy for the Brevet of Major for his highly meritorious service." For some reason the new secretary of war, Jefferson Davis, refused to approve Scott's recommendation, and six years and two more major exploratory ventures passed before Marcy advanced in rank. No wonder he became discouraged and sometimes talked of quitting the service for some other type of employment.

In 1852 a subject that was receiving much attention from Congress and the general public was the proposal to construct a railroad across the continent to the Pacific Coast. Indeed, Congress had debated the matter ever since the beginning of the Mexican War, but unfortunately the proposed project always became ensnarled in sectional politics. The North and South could not agree upon the route that the railroad should follow, for the obvious reason that the road's eastern terminus would secure a tremendous economic advantage. Southerners generally were in favor of a route roughly parallel to the one along the Canadian River that Marcy had blazed from Fort Smith to Santa Fé in 1849. Or they would be willing to accept his return route from Doña Ana by way of the Brazos and Red rivers. (It will be recalled that the explorer had previously pointed out the advantages of both courses as possible railroad routes.) On the other hand, politicians and businessmen from the North strongly argued in favor of a road to California by way of South Pass in present Wyoming.

Congress did not take any definite steps regarding the building of the proposed transcontinental road until March, 1853, when it amended the Army Appropriation Bill to provide $150,000 for surveys. Five separate surveying parties were to examine the various possible routes to the Pacific, and supposedly the road would ultimately be constructed along the route that offered the greatest advantages. Several congressmen from Arkansas and other southern states lost no time in drawing up a petition requesting that Marcy be put in charge of one of the surveying parties. The peti-

[5] *Ibid.*

tion cited the officer's long experience as a western explorer, arguing that he was better qualified for the particular job than any other man in the United States Army. The sensitive Jefferson Davis did not take kindly to the suggestion; not only did he bitterly resent such political pressure, but he charged Marcy with unethical conduct as a party to the affair.

Marcy subsequently learned of the Secretary's charges through his old friend General Duff Green, and he hastened to repair the damage: "I beg leave to state," he wrote Davis, "that I had no agency in originating or getting up this petition or any other of a similar character. Neither did I know that it was the intention of these gentlemen or any other to present such a petition."[6]

Davis replied one month later that he was gratified to know that the officer had no part "in proceeding in such an unprofessional and inexcusable manner."[7] Nevertheless, he did not see fit to make the appointment and, instead, selected Captain John Pope.[8] From this and other actions toward Marcy, it is evident that Davis held a personal grudge, for he appears to have thwarted Marcy's career on other occasions, too. It could have been that Davis disliked Marcy because of his kinship to William L. Marcy, then the secretary of state. Although both men were members of the same cabinet, Secretary Marcy frequently disagreed with Davis, who could not tolerate opposition.

Even though Marcy denied any part in the scheme to assign him the command of the surveying expedition, nevertheless he soon became eager to return to his first love—exploring. On June 30, 1853, he wrote to Adjutant General Samuel Cooper in Washington proposing an extensive exploration of the Colorado River from its mouth to its source in the Rocky Mountains. He pointed out that the Colorado was the longest unexplored river in the United States and that it should be examined and accurately mapped. Indeed, Marcy had been interested in exploring the Colorado ever since his visit to Santa Fé in 1849, at which time he discussed the matter with the famous mountain man, Kit Carson. Carson had trapped beaver along the Colorado several years

[6] April 25, 1853, Letters Received, File No. M52–53; A. G. O.

[7] May 16, 1853, Copies of Letters Sent, War Department, Vol. XXXIV, 276.

[8] Except for a few short stretches, Pope traversed the same route described by Marcy in his journal of the Santa Fé expedition in 1849.

before, and his description of the Grand Canyon country had made a profound impression on Marcy.

Cooper favored the proposed expedition up the Colorado and recommended the project to Secretary of War Jefferson Davis, but there the matter abruptly ended when Davis turned the proposal down flatly on July 27, 1853. In the meantime, the Captain continued with his report of the Red River expedition and by November, 1853, he was done with it. From then until the following April, 1854, he had no further official duties to perform. Meanwhile, a year and a half had elapsed since Marcy had returned from the Southwest, and he was impatient for something to do. By the early part of 1854, he had recovered his health, yet he did not relish returning to the humdrum life at a frontier garrison. Opportunity for further travel and exploration would come soon, however, and his restless spirit would again find satisfaction.

By 1854, Texas had been in the Union for nine years, and already her western frontier had been pushed beyond the ninety-eighth meridian. Permanent lines of settlements were feeling their way through the Cross Timbers and gradually reaching out into the broken country of present northwestern Texas. Along the upper reaches of the Trinity, Brazos, Concho, and Colorado rivers military posts stood guard: Fort Worth, Fort Belknap, Phantom Hill, and Fort Chadbourne. These far-flung frontier posts had been built slightly in advance of white settlement to preserve order on the frontier, but the southwestern Indians in 1854 were not yet ready to submit in mute silence to the inexorable flood of restless pioneers. Settlers frequently felt the sting of the Indians' wrath. The red men often swept down upon their homes and farms to kill, pillage, and capture, but before troops could reach the scene of action, the marauding bands were many miles away.

On February 6, 1854, the Texas Legislature took steps to put an end to the frontier disturbances when it approved a measure which provided "eighteen leagues of unlocated lands to form a reserve for the settlement of all Indians within the State's borders."[9] At the same time the federal government agreed to cooperate in the project by locating and surveying the reservation lands and by attempting to induce the Texas Indians to discon-

[9] W. B. Parker, *Through Unexplored Texas* (Philadelphia, 1856), 9–10.

tinue their predatory habits and settle down as peaceful farmers. The federal government also agreed to supply the Indians with agricultural implements and seeds without charge and to hire instructors who would attempt to teach them modern methods of farming and stock raising until they could become self-sufficient.

The first step in getting the projected experimental program under way was taken on April 20, 1854, when Adjutant General Samuel Cooper wrote to Marcy in New York that he had been selected to explore the Texas frontier for the purpose of locating suitable sites for the Indian reservations. Marcy left immediately for Washington, where he was informed by Cooper that he would obtain the necessary supplies and equipment to conduct the Texas reconnaissance from the quartermaster at Fort Smith. From Fort Arbuckle where he would be furnished with an escort "not to exceed 40 men," he would continue to the Brazos post, Fort Belknap, and pick up Major Robert S. Neighbors, special Indian agent for Texas, who would assist in the location of the reserve lands in the near-by region where Texas settlers had not already established claims. By the terms of the agreement between Texas and the federal government, no Indians were to be located "more than twenty miles south or east of the most northern line of military posts . . . and extending from Red River to the Pecos River."[10]

Soon after receiving the details of his new assignment, Marcy hastened back to New York to collect his belongings and bid his family farewell. Together with W. B. Parker, a civilian friend with ambitions to see the West, the experienced traveler entrained for Pittsburgh. The long journey by steamer down the Ohio and the Mississippi marked the third such trip to the Southwest in four years for Marcy. The landmarks must have been familiar.

The explorer left the Mississippi steamer at Napoleon, Arkansas, where he and his companion took passage on a smaller boat and went up the Arkansas River to Little Rock. The water in the Arkansas must have been too low for the steamer to continue, for the travelers purchased saddle horses at Little Rock for the remainder of the journey, reaching Fort Smith fourteen days after leaving New York.

[10] George W. Manypenny, commissioner of Indian affairs, to Robert S. Neighbors, April 26, 1854, Bureau of Indian Affairs, Copies of Letters Sent, Vol. XLIX, 1854.

At Fort Smith, Captain Marcy immediately sought out his old friend, Dr. G. G. Shumard, who had accompanied the Red River expedition in 1852 as physician and naturalist. Dr. Shumard readily agreed to go adventuring once more. Marcy then turned to the task of requisitioning the necessary supplies and hiring civilian teamsters. This time he had to take not only the usual camping and scientific equipment but also, since he would hold several conferences with the Texas Indians, a bountiful supply of presents for them. Indeed, the items necessary for such an expedition were many and varied: tents, water barrels, calico, knives, mirrors, beads, blankets, powder, lead, tobacco, coffee, flour, biscuits, salt, sugar, molasses, medicine, soap, salt pork, rope, corn, tea, rice, dried beans, and whiskey, among others.

By May 31, 1854, plans were complete. Marcy, Parker,[11] and Shumard left Fort Smith before sunrise the following morning at the head of a caravan of wagons and civilian teamsters and arrived the next day at the Choctaw Agency, a few miles west of Fort Smith. From there Marcy followed the Fort Gibson road southwest to Fort Washita, but bad luck dogged him the entire distance. The civilian teamsters not only proved inexperienced but quite unreliable, while torrential rains turned the rutted road into a river of mud. The wagons seemed in constant need of repair, the oxen and mules required frequent rest from their burdensome loads, and to delay progress further, all of the streams overflowed their banks, so that crossing them was slow and hazardous. Normally the journey could be made in a little more than a week, but eighteen days passed before the company reached Fort Washita—yet the expedition had hardly begun.

While waiting a few days for the stock to rest before pushing on from Fort Washita to Fort Belknap, Marcy rode northwest to Fort Arbuckle for the military escort. While the troops there were being readied for the expedition into Texas, Marcy had other duties to perform: namely, to hire Indian guides and hunters. Of course there was the usual round of social engagements at Fort Arbuckle and Fort Washita to honor the officers and gentlemen accompanying the expedition. And there were letters to write.

In the last letter which Marcy wrote to Mary at Hartford

[11] Parker later wrote a very interesting book on the journey (see note 9 above), a copy of which is now in the Rare Book Room of the Library of Congress.

before departing for Texas, he informed her of a recent communication he had received from his friend McClellan, now in the East. "I am glad to learn that he was pleased with my dear Nelly," he remarked. "I hope she will like him for he is talented, good-looking, agreeable, and in every respect preferable to another officer that I know of, and I cannot conceive that she can think otherwise. He is generally regarded as one of the most brilliant men of his rank in the Army and one that any young lady might justly be proud of. His family connections are unexceptionable and his staff position is such that his wife would always have a good and comfortable home."[12] Marcy could not know that by these remarks he was planting seeds that would indeed be slow in maturing.

The military escort arrived at Fort Washita from Fort Arbuckle on June 28, and on the following morning the entire command departed for Fort Belknap. Exploring an unknown country was an old story to Marcy by now as he led out his fourth major expedition in five years. This one was different, however, in that the commander for the first time did not have the services of his old Company D; instead, his escort was an independent one commanded by Lieutenants N. B. Pierce and N. Chapin. These two young officers were capable enough, but they were woefully inexperienced in the art of maintaining discipline among a wretched crew of forty privates and noncommissioned officers. Most of the troops consisted of veteran Irish and German soldiers, all of whom had volunteered for the special service—apparently in the hope of finding some relief from routine garrison duties.

"We flatter ourselves that, should we get into a fight, we should have good material to depend upon," wrote the civilian W. B. Parker."[13] The veterans soon demonstrated their fighting qualities all right, but not against a band of savage Indians. During the first day's march from Fort Washita the soldiers somehow managed to obtain a supply of whiskey that proved sufficient to enable them all to get drunk, and efforts by their officers to find and destroy it were in vain. Fighting soon broke out among the drunken rabble and became so general before the day was over that discipline collapsed completely. The next day's march was

12 June 18, 1854, McClellan Papers, 2nd Series, I.
13 Parker, *Through Unexplored Texas*, 67.

like the first, but the third day was even worse when two Irish privates engaged in a bloody brawl that lasted for more than two hours. The men mutilated each other so severely that for a time they were thought to be dead, but unfortunately they lived "to fight again another day." Either Marcy had not experienced such a complete breakdown of discipline on his previous excursions, or else he deliberately failed to mention such incidents in his journal. But whiskey makes a considerable difference in men's behavior.

By 1854, it was fairly easy to obtain liquor in Indian Territory since large quantities of corn whiskey were being smuggled from Texas and sold illegally in the Choctaw Nation. When the expedition crossed Red River to Preston on its way to Fort Belknap, Marcy's friend Parker engaged the man who operated the ferryboat in a conversation, asking him among other things what he charged to transport a man across the river. "Why them as buys whiskey we don't charge nothing," was the laconic reply. "Them as doesn't, it's a bit." The traveler from New York later discovered that whiskey sold for fifteen cents a gallon at Preston, but easily "fetched" two dollars a gallon on the north bank of the stream in Indian Territory.

Eventually the company got the wagons safely across the Red, but the three previous days of drinking and brawling had left it in a sad state. Several soldiers were unable to walk and had to be placed in the ambulance and on top of the cargo in the freight wagons. Others could walk only with great difficulty, but at least the whiskey was all gone by now. Consequently, Marcy left Preston as quickly as he could, and as his expedition advanced along the Fort Belknap road, the sick and wounded gradually recovered. On July 4, the party was overtaken by two Delaware guides whom Marcy had hired before his departure from Fort Washita (one of the Indians had accompanied the Red River expedition two years before), and everything at last was in order to advance more rapidly.

The country through which Marcy now passed was no longer a land unspoiled by time. Indeed, this part of Texas was already filling up rapidly with settlers, so that for several miles west of Preston one regularly encountered isolated farmhouses and small settlements. Near the spot where the explorer had camped on

October 30, 1849, while returning from Santa Fé, he now discovered a town of five or six cabins which dignified itself with the name of Gainesville. This village in 1854 was literally a "one-legged" town, for it had the unusual distinction of having four men who had only one leg.[14]

From Gainesville, Marcy once more pushed beyond the Cross Timbers, and by July 7, 1854, he and his men were on the rolling plains country where nothing disturbed the broad landscape except scattered groves of mesquite. The journey from here on was much like the others—the caravan of men, animals, and wagons coming to a halt each day around 11:00 A.M. in order to avoid the blistering Texas sun, which brought temperatures above 100 degrees. On July 11, 1854, the command reached a place called Cottonwood Springs in present Young County, and there Marcy left the party encamped while he rode on to Fort Belknap, some fifteen miles to the southwest.

At Fort Belknap, Marcy talked with several representatives of various tribes in regard to the plan to locate reservations for them. He also obtained from the commander of the post a map previously prepared by the Texas Land Office which indicated the lands in Northwest Texas already claimed by white settlers, as well as the unclaimed lands upon which reservations could be established.

Four days later the explorer was back at Cottonwood Springs, having brought Major Neighbors, the Texas Indian agent, and four additional Delaware and Shawnee scouts with him. Neighbors proved to be a "fine-looking man, in the full vigor of manhood, about six feet two inches in height, with a countenance indicative of great firmness and decision of character." During the past several years he had lived and worked among the Texas Indians and perhaps knew their traits and character as no other man did. Indeed, his long experience on the Texas frontier, and, equally important, his ability to tell fascinating anecdotes made him a welcome addition to the expedition.

On July 16, the command moved from Cottonwood Springs in a northwest course across the trackless Texas plains. Advancing through the southwestern corner of present Archer County, it soon crossed over into Baylor County and continued until reach-

14 *Ibid.,* 71.

ing the Little Wichita River. Parker observed that this portion of Texas was ideally suited for stock raising, and he accurately predicted that in the distant future "Texas would be the stock yard of our country." The roughness of the Little Wichita valley combined with the stifling heat placed an impossible burden on the work animals. Fortunately a cool spring of water was discovered near the river, and Marcy wisely decided to leave the main company encamped there while he and Neighbors and Shumard took a small party of soldiers and scouts and continued on horseback. Accordingly, they turned almost due east and followed the Little Wichita toward its mouth for approximately twenty miles, but finding that the region had little to offer in the way of suitable timber and uncontaminated water, they soon changed their course to the north.

The next day the company arrived at the Big Wichita, approximately fifteen miles west of present Wichita Falls, Texas. It will be remembered that Marcy had explored the region near the mouth of the Big Wichita in 1852, and since he already knew that it was unsuited for his purposes, he decided to examine the country near the source of the stream. The party therefore crossed to the north bank and rode westward for several miles before coming to present Beaver Creek, a tributary of the Big Wichita. The travelers then pursued this stream to a point near the present Wilbarger County line. There they turned southward, gradually working their way through the cedar breaks and gullies until they were back at the main camp on July 20. The reconnaissance of the Big and Little Wichita took five days, during which time Marcy and his companions had traversed the four sides of a quadrangle. Except for the fact that the work stock had had a chance to rest for a few days, nothing else had been accomplished by the eighty-mile jaunt, for the country explored showed itself void of satisfactory building timber and drinkable water.

On July 26, all the wagons were in motion, this time rolling west along the ridge which separates the Big Wichita from the Brazos through the middle of present Baylor County. As the land gradually changed from semiarid to arid, Marcy resolved to leave the train once again at the first watering place and continue as before with a few mounted men. Accordingly, an Indian scout was sent forward to select a campsite, and he returned a few

hours later to report the location of water (Red Springs) in sufficient quantity and quality for an encampment.

When the camp had been established, Captain Marcy, Major
Neighbors, Dr. Shumard, Parker, four soldiers, and five Indians
left at sunrise on July 29. Taking good mounts and pack mules and
a twelve-day supply of provisions, including four five-gallon,
India-rubber water sacks, they "set out with the firm resolve to
see the heads of the Big Wichita and Brazos Rivers before returning." Marcy wrote that he was now advancing along a tortuous
course almost due west of and parallel to the South Fork of the
Wichita River—"into the heart of a rough country infested with
lawless Indians."

The travelers eventually reached the summit of a high bluff,
which towered some 250 feet above the deep stream. The present
elevation afforded a broad panoramic view of the surrounding
country, which moved Marcy to write later: "The different con-
fluents of the Wichita . . . united in forming a landscape pleasing
to the eye. But this is the only feature of the country which has
left an agreeable impression upon my memory and I bade adieu
to its desolute and inhospitable borders without the least feeling
of regret, for it is in almost every respect the most uninteresting
and forbidding land I have ever visited. With a barren soil affording little but weeds and coarse unwholesome grass with an inter-
mixture of cacti and most uncommonly grotesque shapes studded
with a formidable armour of thorns which defies the approach of
man or beast, added to . . . the scarcity of wood or grass, would
seem to render it probable that this section was not designed
by the Creator for occupation; and I question if the next century
will see it populated by civilized man. Even the Indians shun this
country . . . so that the bear (which are numerous here) are left
to undisputed possession."[15]

By now the small party had ridden almost forty miles across
present Knox County since leaving the encampment at the springs.
Already several members of the command had "diarrhea and
cramps in the bowels," and their condition had steadily grown

[15] Marcy to Colonel Samuel Cooper, adjutant general, January 15, 1855,
Letters Received (no file number). This document, in Marcy's handwriting
and containing more than 100 pages, constituted his official report of the
expedition through unexplored Texas in 1854. All quotations herein relating
to the Texas expedition, unless otherwise indicated, are taken from the above.

worse because of bad water. A large quantity of spring water had been brought along in the rubber bags, but it had become unusable because the hot sun had caused a partial disintegration of the inferior rubber. As a result, the water turned into a rank and disagreeable brew" and had to be poured out.

As Marcy stood on the bluff overlooking the great expanse of eroded lands, he concluded that it was useless to continue in the present direction and decided to turn southward through a mesquite grove toward the headwaters of the Brazos. Some six miles later the travelers came upon a miniature spring of fresh water dripping slowly out from under a rock: "I am not prepared to say that it was equal to Croton water cooled with Rockland ice . . . yet I doubt if the people of Gotham ever enjoyed their boasted and justly renowned beverage more than we did," Marcy remarked. With this thought in mind and to commemorate the occasion of their first drink in two days, Marcy appropriately named the small tributary into which the spring flowed "Croton Creek," the name which it bears today.[16] Being familiar with the writings of Lord Byron, Marcy must have recalled his famous words—"Men really know not what good water's worth."

Greatly refreshed after this soothing drink, the command now changed its course toward the southwest in the direction of a conical peak (Kiowa Peak) which was barely visible above the distant horizon. About twenty-five miles below the spring, they struck a branch of the Brazos which was spread out over a broad bed of loose sand. After following along the north bank of the shallow creek (North Croton) for a few miles, they again came face to face with the problem of drinking water, for this new stream possessed the most nauseating water heretofore encountered. And worse yet, the horses by now were almost exhausted, and two of the pack mules were practically unfit for further use. "In addition," Dr. Shumard later wrote, "the small stock of bread had become beautifully variegated in color, assuming all shades, from the brightest green of the prairies, to the darkest blue of heaven . . . more beautiful to contemplate than to tempt the appetite."[17]

[16] There are three creeks that flow into the Main Fork of the Brazos in this area that today are called Croton Creek: Little Croton, North Croton, and Croton. Marcy discovered the spring on Little Croton.

[17] Dr. Shumard, the geologist and physician, wrote an interesting ac-

The scenery in this inhospitable country at least was compensating, and the travelers ascended a near-by knoll to obtain a more extensive view of it. Consequently, they were able to follow the course of the stream with their eyes for several miles to the northwest. It appeared through the clear air like a cord of silver, meandering through the prairies in serpentine fashion until it seemed to disappear at the foot of two cone-shaped mounds. On beyond the mounds could be seen a broken line of high bluffs—the familiar *Llano Estacado*—resembling a tremendous cloud floating on the horizon.

The untrampled expanse of arid wilderness was in its own fashion impressive enough, so the small party turned away from the spacious scene to renew its exploring to the south. From the eastern edge of present Stonewall County the command passed the Salt Fork (Main Fork) of the Brazos and continued over a smooth valley toward a distant elevation (Flat Top Mountain near present Sagerton, Texas). Marcy later recognized the miniature mountain as one he had first seen in 1849 upon his return from New Mexico, for it was near the Double Mountain Fork of the Brazos which he had previously explored.

Major Neighbors now expressed a strong unwillingness to continue the exploration. He pointed out the obvious improbability of finding good water, upon which the fate of several men depended. Also, he argued, the weakened condition of the horses and pack animals and the scarcity of supplies made an immediate return to camp imperative.

Marcy was not blind to the situation, and the health of his men overruled his desire to go farther. He reluctantly turned back toward the northeast, and for the next few days he and his men pushed across a rolling plain dotted with mesquite trees and carpeted with several varieties of grama grass. (They were now crossing present Haskell County.) On August 6, nine days after leaving the escort, the reconnaissance party returned to the main camp near present Red Springs (Baylor County). During the journey up the Wichita and Brazos the small command had followed a circuitous route that extended over two hundred miles.

count of the Texas reconnaissance in 1854 in a letter to his "Friend Wheeler," dated August 10, 1854. The lengthy letter was published in several newspapers and a clipping of it is found in Marcy's Scrapbook.

Throughout the whole trip the travelers had been forced to drink bad water, to suffer torrid temperatures and multitudes of flies and mosquitoes, and to subsist almost entirely upon meat and fish. They had had no choice but to drink the bitter water found in the region explored, but had to forego its use in cooking rice and making coffee. Indeed, the lack of coffee proved the greatest hardship they encountered.

"Yet the trip had not been without its attractions, and we trust the information we have obtained concerning this hitherto unknown region will be of sufficient importance to compensate us for our trouble," Marcy wrote cheerfully.

Once the men were back in camp, their spirits lifted as rapidly as their suffering was forgotten, and they were thankful for the few luxuries that their remaining stores afforded.

On August 7, the entire command was in motion again, drifting in a southeasterly direction for three days over a broken, mesquite-covered plain. While encamped on a tributary of the Brazos (Elm Creek), not far from present Throckmorton, Texas, on August 10, the Americans had their first meeting with a party of Indians: "Quite a sensation was created . . . by several strangers whom we saw in the distance, crossing the valley and coming toward us. On their arrival they proved to be a Comanche Chief (Ketumsee) with two of his (six) wives who came to pay us a visit."

The chief was later described by the civilian Parker as a "fine-looking man, about fifty years old, six full feet high, with a dark brown complexion. His wives . . . were mere children, the one about eighteen and the other not sixteen years old."[18] Ketumsee was a picturesque character. He was dressed in corduroy leggings and moccasins, an old, torn, greasy, checkered-cotton coat, and "a sixpenny straw hat," while his horse's bridle was ornamented with at least "fifty dollars worth of silver." Both his wives were attired in dark calico skirts, with one-piece leggings and moccasins. Their clothes were thin, dirty, and common, and their bare heads revealed mats of short, uncombed dark hair. The younger, who appeared to be the chief's favorite, wore a girdle studded with heavy silver brooches that were not only striking, but very costly.

The Chief informed Marcy that a war party of 250 Northern

[18] Parker, *Through Unexplored Texas,* 180.

Comanches, Apaches, and Navajos had followed his small command for several days during its wandering toward the source of the Brazos. When the Indians discovered only thirteen in the party, they reasoned that a larger command was somewhere in the neighborhood; otherwise, according to Ketumsee, they would have destroyed the "white intruders." Thus, Marcy reflected, had his entire command been together during the reconnaissance, it undoubtedly would have been attacked and possibly annihilated. In weakness the explorers inadvertently had found safety.

Captain Marcy entertained the visitors with a simple dinner of deer meat, rice, bread, and coffee, after which the Chief and his wives retired to a near-by shade to sleep. At sundown, Ketumsee returned to the commander's tent, announcing his desire to make "big talk," and in customary fashion swore eternal friendship for the whites and assured Marcy that he was extremely anxious to follow any suggestion which the "White Captain" wished to propose. Marcy explained the purpose of his visit to the region and remarked that the "Great White Father" in Washington wished to see his red children living peacefully with each other and with their white brothers. He added that he personally desired to smoke the peace pipe with all Comanche chiefs in the region and to explain to them why they should abandon their nomadic ways.

Ketumsee remained silent for several moments, then arose and dramatically presented his host with a bundle of seven stalks of grass. Each stalk represented a Comanche war captain, he said, four of whom possessed high standing and three very low standing. Then, with a sudden gesture of anger, he twisted the latter three stalks together and dashed them upon the ground—contemptuously grunting "no 'count." The meaning was made clearer a short time later when Marcy discovered that the various bands of Southern Comanches were extremely jealous of one another and were constantly bickering among themselves.

On the morning of August 11, the expedition was again on the move—the wagons this time taking a southwest course toward a high ridge which divided the Salt Fork (Main Fork) from the Clear Fork of the Brazos. The country about seemed clothed with "innumerable flowers of a yellow hue." By 10:00 A.M. the train had come to the old road which Marcy had blazed from Doña Ana to Red River five years previously, and the travelers turned west on it for ten miles before arriving at the Clear Fork of the Brazos. Here Marcy decided to establish a permanent camp until the immediate surroundings were explored, for the country appeared to have all the qualities necessary for a reservation—fertile land, building timber, and good water. The Americans established their encampment near a "cold delicious spring of water gushing forth from a bank."

The place of the encampment was on the future site of Camp Cooper. The valley of the Clear Fork exhibited a rich and verdant herbage, which indicated an amazing fertility of the soil, and the near-by stream itself was lined with pecan, hackberry, black walnut, and elm trees. Marcy examined the Texas Land Commission map and spotted a tract of unclaimed land a short distance north. He prepared to make a preliminary survey of it, for the present encampment was too close to lands already claimed by Texas settlers. When it subsequently proved to be an ideal site for a reservation, his search at last had come to an end. The next thing to do was to order an accurate survey of the land, mark its boundaries, and then call the Comanches together for a general powwow.

Accordingly, one of the officers attached to the expedition and a party of soldiers were sent forward to establish the boundaries of the reserve, while the Comanche chief, Ketumsee, who had remained with the whites for the past several days, was sent to summon the various Southern Comanches and their leaders.

Although Marcy's recently completed expedition had not been ordered for the same exploratory purposes as some of his previous ones, yet it had taken the trail blazer through a region that was little known to the white man. It therefore had added to Marcy's extensive geographical knowledge of a large portion of the Southwest and enabled him to chart and name many streams heretofore unknown. Indeed, he knew this broad area of the Southwest and contributed to the nomenclature of it more than any other man of his time. Today his own name is almost forgotten, for no mountain, plain, river, or military post immortalizes it. The many trails he left behind have long since been obliterated by the march of civilization.

XII

"The pride of my heart"

1854–1856

BEFORE THE INDIANS ASSEMBLED at Marcy's encampment on the Clear Fork, the explorer and his companion Neighbors spent two full days (August 16–17) in a careful examination of the six square leagues selected as a reservation for the Comanches. Marcy was now more pleased with the region than ever, for it "comprised every essential of upland meadow, with fine water and timber."[1] Upon his return to the encampment on August 18, Marcy saw that many Indians had already arrived. By the next day several hundred had established their camps near the spring close to the Americans. Among the various Comanche chiefs present was Senaco, whom Marcy had met five years before in the same region. He was about fifty years of age, prepossessing in appearance, and, unlike his fellows, wore no ornaments. For many years, he and Ketumsee had been in a constant wrangle for power, a situation which boded ill for the future harmony of the proposed reservation settlement.

Perhaps no man present was more excited by the colorful gathering than Marcy's friend from the East, Parker, who fortunately has furnished us with a graphic account of the occasion. He described the Comanche women as being "ugly, crooked-legged, stooped-shouldered, squalid and dirty, with haggard and prematurely old countenances; their hair was cropped close to their heads and they possessed scarce a rag to cover their nakedness." As for the men—except for some of the young warriors who were "decked out" in war paint and feathers, they were scarcely more imposing than their wives.

[1] Parker, *Through Unexplored Texas*, 192.

182

The campsite where the powwow was to be held was situated in a valley shaded by great elm and pecan trees. The Americans had arranged their tents and wagons in a large semicircle; and as the Indians arrived, they erected their brush arbors in such a way as to surround the whites completely. As usual, the first thing the Comanches expected when coming into social contact with whites was something to eat, and Captain Marcy quickly put them in good spirits by ordering an ox killed.

A bustling scene of activity ensued as the women lost no time in preparing the carcass for present and future use. "Every edible part was consumed, even the entrails which are considered a choice delicacy, were drawn through the coals and devoured, reeking with excrement. The women boned the flesh and then split it, haggling and carving it into long chains of lumps and then throwing it over poles, dried it in the sun, when it looked like links of stale sausage. The caul, suet, and other inside fat was dried whole, and the cannon bones and hoofs were first scorched before the fire and then hung up in the sun.

"The portions of meat intended for present use, were prepared by placing them upon a wide scaffold over a slow fire. . . . It dries the meat without depriving it of its juices, and prevents decomposition. A supply of corn . . . together with some coffee and sugar, capped the climax of their happiness, and their bivouac wore a very cheerful appearance during the day."[2]

On August 20, Captain Marcy opened the grand council for the purpose of ascertaining the Indians' views about the new settlement. He told the assembled warriors that their "Great White Father" had sent him to select a permanent home for his red children where they would be more comfortable and not suffer for want of food. He reminded them that the buffalo and deer were rapidly disappearing from the plains, and that soon they and their children would be compelled to resort to some life other than the chase. At the same time he told them that they would not be permitted to prey on their neighbors, and that their only alternative now was to till the soil.

The speech was followed by several minutes of complete silence. Then the warriors passed the pipe and conferred with each other in low tones until Senaco finally arose to speak. He declared

[2] *Ibid.*, 196.

in his usual dramatic manner that he would be straightforward and true, that what his friend Captain Marcy had told the Comanches has sunk deep into their hearts and they would not soon forget it. "We feel happy that our Great Father remembers his poor red children in the prairies. We accept the talk, and shall endeavor to accede to that that is required of us," he concluded.[3]

Senaco then seated himself, and many questions were put to him and his followers by Marcy and Neighbors. Until now both had been fearful that the Comanches would not really be disposed to make a trial at farming, but as they questioned the red men at length, their doubts began to be dispelled. Many warriors rose, one by one, to express their desire to remain permanently on the lands that had been selected by the "White Captains." All this time Ketumsee sat statue-like, evidently displeased that Senaco and not himself had been chosen to be the spokesman. Ironically enough, he was the only chief present who in the end made a sincere effort to carry out the reservation experiment.

The principal business of the council was finally concluded, and Major Neighbors distributed presents among the braves and their women—printed cottons, handkerchiefs, blankets, knives, strouding for leggings, armlets of silver, long wampum beads, tobacco, and paints. Captain Marcy then issued rations of corn, sugar, and coffee—all of which put the visitors in a happy frame of mind, and during the remainder of their stay their camp was a scene of feasting and dancing.

On the morning of August 22, Marcy and Neighbors rode to Fort Belknap to discuss with the post commander the matter of a separate reservation for the minor Texas tribes. These were the Caddos, Anadarkos, Wacos, Towakonies, and Tonkawas, and were generally referred to as the Brazos Indians. Within a brief time the officials agreed upon a tract situated a few miles south of the post. The unclaimed land there, which consisted of approximately twelve leagues, lay just below the junction of the Clear Fork in present southeastern Young County. A hurried examination revealed that for the most part it was bottom land, covered with luxuriant grama grass and bordered by oak trees. In addition, the abundance of good water in all seasons of the year seemed to make it ideal for the purpose.

[3] Marcy, *Army Life on the Border*, 212.

The various tribes concerned with the reservation were shortly summoned to Fort Belknap, where a second powwow was held, with the usual "big talks," feasts, and presentation of gifts. Captain Marcy's task was now complete, and he had only to attend to a few details before commencing his long journey home.

It seems pertinent here to include a brief summary of the results of the first restricted reservation experiment for the Plains Indians. The major task of supervising the two Texas projects devolved upon the able shoulders of Neighbors, but it eventually proved too difficult for one man. Texas settlers soon charged the Comanches with stealing their horses and demanded that Major E. Steen, post commandant at Fort Belknap, send troops to recover the stolen animals. When Senaco received warning of the proposed campaign, he and his followers scattered over the plains, and in the end only Ketumsee and 180 followers remained to make a try of reservation life.

Meanwhile, only a scattering of Brazos Indians ever settled upon the second tract of land. Dust, drouth, and grasshoppers ruined their first crops, and the Indians were convinced that the Great Spirit was displeased with them. To add to their troubles, bands of nonreservation Indians frequently used the reserves as bases for their sporadic forays against the whites. The settlers accused the reserve tribes of participating in these ventures also, and on December 7, 1858, a large force of settlers attacked and killed a number of Indians from the Brazos reservation. Warriors from both reserves now joined forces in preparation for all-out war, and during the next few months the frontier was in constant panic.

Major Neighbors urged peace between the two races and not infrequently criticized the white settlers for their refusal to act with moderation and patience. For this he paid with his life. On August 22, 1859, the following story appeared in the *Austin* (Texas) *State Gazette*: "On Wednesday, the 14th ultimo, while Major R. S. Neighbors was crossing from his hotel, at Belknap, to the old garrison, he was intercepted by Messrs. Murphy and Cornet. The former asked Major N. if he had reported that he (Murphy) and certain others, had themselves, stolen certain others' horses, charged to have been stolen by the Indians. Major N. said, 'No, I never did,' and was in the act of explaining when young Cornet shot him. He exclaimed 'Oh Lord!' and fell dead. Cornet, at last date, was at Murphy's, and not arrested."

Even before Neighbors' death both reservations had been officially abandoned on June 6, 1859. The Texas Indians would eventually be rounded up and escorted to a new home in present Oklahoma.

By the end of August, 1854, Marcy's work was done, and he and all his company (without Major Neighbors) now made ready to return home as rapidly as possible. Since the military escort was commanded by officers from Fort Arbuckle and the danger of attack by Indians between Fort Belknap and there was slight, Marcy decided to take the ambulance and with Shumard and Parker push on alone.

The trip back across the prairies was not without incident, although of a different sort from any Marcy had encountered in recent weeks. One day, as he and his two companions approached the western edge of the Cross Timbers country, they chanced upon three girls and a young man picking wild grapes beside the road. They stopped and engaged the group in conversation, inquiring among other things about a suitable campsite. The young people told the dusty travelers that they lived a few miles down the road and that a spring could be found near by. As there was one vacant seat on the ambulance, Marcy politely inquired if any member of the party wished to ride, and one of the girls accepted the offer. Parker graciously leaned forward to assist her to the seat, but she ignored his chivalrous gesture and literally leaped from the ground over the side of the vehicle and landed beside him.

The New Yorker, who had never witnessed such a display of acrobatic skill outside of a circus, quickly recovered from his surprise and engaged the prairie belle in a lively conversation. The girl appeared to be about eighteen years of age, was very graceful and feminine, and her fascinating laughter and overflowing exuberance of spirits proved irresistible. She wore a closely fitting bloomer costume and a jaunty little straw hat which was held upon one side of her head by a pretty pink ribbon, while a luxurious crop of brown ringlets reached down to her shoulders. Marcy later observed that she was "just as wild, untamed, and free from the absurd, tyrannical conventionalities of society as the mustangs that roamed over the adjacent prairies."[4]

Parker lost no time in trying to impress his pretty young companion with accounts of his recent experiences among the Comanches, but she repeatedly interrupted him with such pithy remarks as, "Oh, git out!"—"You go-along now!"—and "Look at him." Finally, she burst forth with a wild yell, gave him a violent slap upon the knee, and shouted, "The hell you say, stranger!"—giving particular emphasis to the second word. The New Yorker was so astounded that he was at a loss for words. But not the Texas belle—she chattered on incessantly.

The girl asked the travelers a great number of questions and became particularly curious about their camping arrangement, observing that she had never seen a tent. Up to this point Marcy had maintained an amused silence, but now he remarked graciously that as soon as they had put up their tent for the evening they would be pleased to have her pay their camp a visit. The invitation proved to be a mistake, and the girl changed her gay mood at once. She glared at the startled officer furiously, stuck out her tongue at him, thumbed her nose, and shouted in a savage voice, "I'm afraid of wolves, old hoss!"

Marcy's efforts to explain were useless.

The trip across the prairies took fifteen days. At Fort Smith, Dr. Shumard bade his friends farewell, and Marcy and Parker prepared to continue alone. A private conveyance was rented, and the two proceeded overland across Arkansas and Missouri, reaching Jefferson City on October 24, 1854. Here they obtained passage on a small boat to St. Louis, thence by a large steamer to Pittsburgh. In exactly one week after leaving the lively city of St. Louis, they were back in New York City, having been absent almost six months to the day.

Once more Marcy was able to settle down with his wife and daughters. Although it is likely that he visited his parents and friends in Greenwich during the next few months, there is no record of his activities from November, 1854, to April, 1855, except concerning his work on his report and map of the recent expedition. These papers were eventually sent to the War Department and

4 *Ibid.*, 372.

ultimately published as a Senate document.[5] Marcy also had occasion to vent his spleen—a rare practice indeed for him.

On April 22, 1855, a long article entitled "The Necessity of the Increase in the Army," signed "Captain Marcy," appeared in the *New York Herald*. Departing from his usual caution in keeping out of public controversies, Marcy castigated the critics of a proposed bill to increase the size of the army. This article, in contrast to his well-publicized speech in 1852 before the American Geographic and Statistical Society—at which time he had attempted to rationalize the conduct of the Plains Indians—criticized the Indians and defended the actions of the army. Marcy first refuted the charges that present difficulties with the Apaches and Navajos in particular were the result of bad management by the government authorities and the "dreadful misconduct" of army officers. And, most surprisingly, he rallied to the defense of Secretary of War Jefferson Davis: "Those members of Congress who proclaim that the Secretary of War does not want new regiments for the suppression of Indian hostilities, but for the operation in Cuba, are mere political demagogues.

"It has become popular with some men," he continued, "to speak of the 'poor Indians' as an injured and persecuted race, who have never met any other treatment from the whites, but that of the most unjust character, and that in every instance they have been provoked to hostilities. Undoubtedly there are now, and there always has been some cases where the whites are the aggressors; but the man who makes the broad assertion that this is always the fact, must be regarded under the most charitable aspect, as speaking upon a subject that he knows nothing about.

"The natives of the prairies are altogether different in their dispositions and habits from the tribes that formerly occupied the the Eastern States. They perform no agricultural labor, but live by pillaging their neighbors, and murder without hesitation or provocation, and are unquestionably as faithless and treacherous a race as exists upon the face of the earth, and it is only necessary to know them a short time to lose all sympathy that we may have

[5] *Senate Doc. No. 64*, 33 Cong., 2 sess. Although the report of the tour through Texas was not as carefully prepared as the Captain's previous narratives, yet it affords interesting reading. The map is of special importance because it represents the first "accurate" details of an important section of the Southwest.

before imbibed from the speeches and letters of the hero of San Jacinto [Senator Sam Houston], or the great statesman of Missouri [Congressman Thomas Hart Benton] . . . the sympathy which has heretofore been evinced in behalf of the 'poor red man' of the prairies, might with very great propriety be transferred to the 'poor pale face' who are obliged to come in contact with them."[6]

A month elapsed after the appearance of this letter before Marcy was heard from again. Apparently his recent expedition through Texas marked the first time he had escaped serious ill effects from such a journey. Nevertheless, he still toyed with the idea of transferring to another department of the army where his duties would be less arduous than those he had been called upon to perform during the past twenty-two years on the frontier. On May 25, 1855, he and Captain A. W. Reynolds, Quartermaster Department, jointly requested the Adjutant General for a mutual exchange of positions.[7] General Samuel Cooper forwarded their request to Secretary of War Davis with the recommendation that it be approved, but Davis did not reply until August 29, 1855, when his answer was that if the two men exchanged military positions, then Marcy would have to be transferred to the Quartermaster Department with the same seniority held by Captain Reynolds. The latter stood twenty-sixth in that department, whereas Marcy ranked sixth in the list of captains in the Fifth Infantry.[8]

Meantime, Marcy must have already given up hope of transferring from the infantry. On July 13, 1855, he wrote to the Adjutant General from Corpus Christi: "I have the honor to report that I arrived at this place today with a detachment of four hundred and eleven recruits from New York Harbour. No deaths or desertions have occurred and the detachment is in excellent health."[9]

Soon after reaching Corpus Christi, Marcy escorted the new troops to Laredo, approximately 150 miles to the west, but he was back at the Texas Gulf Coast town on August 2. For the next four months he remained on detached service—inspecting various Texas harbors for the possible location of a new military depot. Theoretically, he was still attached to Company D, Fifth Infantry,

[6] Scrapbook (clipping).
[7] Letters Received, File No. 342M–55, A. G. O.
[8] *Ibid.,* (endorsement on back).
[9] Letters Received, File No. 590M–55, A. G. O.

now engaged in patrolling the Texas-Mexican border, but actually he had been separated from the company for almost three years. As Marcy's duties at Corpus Christi were light and allowed him much leisure, his letters to his family were fairly regular.

Mary and Fanny were now boarding in Hartford, but Mary Ellen had gone to the resort town of Milford, Connecticut, on the coast to recover from a touch of tuberculosis. Naturally, the anxious father was quite concerned over his beloved Nelly's health, and in his letters to her he invariably warned, "Take a plenty of exercise and restore yourself to respectable dimensions." And at least on one occasion he observed, "You are like me, naturally lean and long and require all the health and flesh you can muster to make you look to advantage."[10]

Corpus Christi by 1855 had grown from the rustic settlement of three or four dozen families when Marcy had first seen it in 1846 to a small city of fifteen hundred inhabitants, "who were from all parts of the world and are about as lawless a set of scamps as can be found." Marcy complained that there were not more than half a dozen families "fit to associate with," but at the same time he rejoiced that the climate was not as hot as he had expected, "as the gulf breezes render it quite comfortable."

In most of his letters to Mary Ellen he rarely failed to mention the subject of her future marriage. Mary Ellen in 1855 was twenty and already considered a "celebrated beauty." One gleans from Marcy's correspondence with her that she had many suitors, and also that they did not always measure up to the standards of the proud parents, particularly if they happened to be college students: "From what I have seen of their habits," Marcy wrote, "I do not believe any good can result from your association with them. You know, my dear Nelly, that I have your best interest at heart and nothing in this world would afford me so much sincere happiness as to see you married to a man who occupies an honorable position in the world . . .young people are prone to look only to the present, and if they are happy today, they care not for the future."

[10] Marcy wrote more than a dozen letters to Mary Ellen during his stay at Corpus Christi in 1855, and several times that number the following year while stationed at Laredo, Ringgold Barracks, and Brownsville. This correspondence, together with some of Mary's letters written during the same period, are now in the McClellan Papers, 2nd Series, III.

The Captain remained in Texas until December, 1855, during which time he traveled up and down the coast by steamer and ambulance with General P. F. Smith, military commander of the Department of Texas. These periodic sojourns took the two officers as far south as Brownsville and as far north as Indianola, Texas. On one such trip they stopped at the small village of Lamar (some fifty miles north of Corpus Christi), which consisted of approximately ten houses situated on a high bluff. "The people treated us very hospitably. . . . We were shown a very pretty cottage occupied by Mr. Hale and his wife. He is the son of Mrs. Hale the authoress [Lucretia Peabody Hale, sister of Edward Everett Hale and daughter of Nathan Hale] and is a very intelligent gentleman. His wife is very accomplished and refined and we were highly delighted with our visit. They gave us an excellent dinner with champagne and other delicacies which one would not expect to find at such a very remote and new place."

Despite the more than usual number of letters which Marcy wrote to his family during this stay in Texas, several months passed before he received any in return. "If you are not dead," he remarked on September 2, 1855, "you must have forgotten that I am in existence, or else you are enjoying yourself so much that you have not time to write. I wish I could step in and make you a call this morning. I am not sure, however, I should be well received. You might not be at home to me, or I should suppose if you desired to continue the acquaintance you should leave a card at my door once in a while." A few weeks later he received a bundle of letters from both Mary and Mary Ellen which had been misrouted, and his spirits lifted accordingly.

On November 28, 1855, General Smith ordered Marcy to return to Washington and report in person to the War Department the results of their recent tour of inspection.[11] The Captain secured passage on the first steamer, and thus was able to reach New York by the middle of December. Meanwhile, Secretary of War Jefferson Davis somehow had been informed of Smith's order sending Marcy to Washington, and he instructed the Adjutant General to write to the commander of the Department of Texas: "The Secretary of War now directs that Captain Marcy be ordered to join his

[11] Special Order No. 121, *Orders and Special Orders Book, Department of Texas,* 1855–56.

company without further delay. The report of his survey can be forwarded from that station."[12] Fortunately for Marcy, the order to return to Texas did not catch up with him for several weeks, and until it did, he could enjoy being with his family again.

On May 1, 1856, he wrote Mary Ellen that he had just arrived by steamer at Corpus Christi and expected to leave for Fort McIntosh, at Laredo, on the following day. The Post Returns reveal that he reached the border post two weeks later and assumed command of it on May 24. Recently enlarged significantly because of political disturbances in Mexico and occasional forays by Mexican banditti across the border into Texas, Fort McIntosh at this time had a complement of 483 officers and men, including Marcy's own Company D.

Marcy was not happily situated at Laredo. The quarters at the post were few and of "the most wretched character." Most of the grass-roofed adobe buildings were without floors, glass windows, or screen doors. Every building was filled beyond capacity, with three or four officers to each small room, while the troops for the most part were quartered in tents.

The commander frequently complained in his letters of the lack of ice, fresh vegetables, and fruits, of the oppressive Texas heat, the intolerable sand "which covered everything twenty times a day," and the swarms of flies. "After what I have seen," he remarked to Mary Ellen, "I should never give my consent for you to marry in the army." This conviction was not a sudden whim, to be sure. Indeed, Marcy had been especially worried ever since his recent discovery on his visit in the East that Mary Ellen seemed more than slightly attached to a young officer stationed in Washington. Although she had assured him that she would not let the affair become serious, still he was not certain that she could always control her emotions.

Sure enough, on May 28, 1856, Marcy was staggered by the receipt of a letter from Mary Ellen announcing her intention to wed the young officer—Lieutenant A. P. Hill, later a famous Confederate general.[13] The news hit like a bombshell. Since 1854, the

---

[12] December 15, 1855, Copies of Letters Sent, Vol. XXX, A. G. O.

[13] Lieutenant Ambrose P. Hill, who was graduated from West Point in 1847, eventually entered Confederate service and rose to the rank of lieutenant general. On July 1, 1863, he initiated the attack that began the Battle of

"The pride of my heart"

Marcys had repeatedly urged Mary Ellen to accept Captain Mc-
Clellan's persistent proposals of marriage, despite the fact that
he, too, was in the army. This handsome young officer had been a
great favorite of Marcy's ever since the Red River expedition, and
both Marcy and his wife were pleased when McClellan fell "head
over heels" in love with Mary Ellen a short time later, for even
though McClellan was a professional soldier, he belonged to a
wealthy and socially prominent family and was destined to go far.
George McClellan was indeed a "catch."

Like Robert E. Lee, against whom he later fought, McClellan
had finished second in his class at West Point in 1846, where, ironically enough, his roommate was none other than A. P. Hill. Despite his handsome face, charming manner, brilliant mind, and
promising future, Mary Ellen just did not love him. In addition
she was several inches the taller of the two, and she resented her
parents' efforts to force the match.

After McClellan first met his former commander's daughter
in 1854, the two carried on a correspondence until the officer was
sent to Europe in 1855 as military observer in the Crimean War.
About this time Mary Ellen met young A. P. Hill, and although
McClellan continued to write to her for a while, she flatly refused
to answer his letters. He sought mightily to effect a reconciliation
by courting her parents, but his efforts to win Mary Ellen's affections seemed futile.

A note found among the McClellan Papers from Mary Marcy
to her older daughter about the time she announced her engagement to Hill reveals the mother's disappointment: "Oh, Nell, such
a treasure as you have lost forever," she wrote in reference to Captain McClellan. "You can't realize it now, but the time is coming
sooner or later just as sure as you live when you will regret it—if
ever a woman did. Mark my word, I see it, I know it! Yet your
perverseness will in the end make you miserable. I have done all
that is in the power of a mother to do, and now whatever your
fate may be hereafter, I cannot reproach myself. The more I dwell
upon that affair in Washington, the more I am convinced that I am
right and you will be convinced of it by and bye. You are laboring

Gettysburg. Douglas Southall Freeman called Hill's division the best in either
army during the Civil War. On April 2, 1865, one week before the end of
hostilities between the North and South, Hill fell in action before Petersburg.

193

under a delusion that perfectly astonishes me. I cannot account for it. You certainly have shown less good sense in this matter than I ever knew you to before."

When Marcy's suspicions of "the affair in Washington" had been confirmed by the receipt of Mary Ellen's letter at Laredo, he hastened to reply: "I could never have supposed after the repeated conversations I have had with you upon the subject of marriage, and your knowledge of my opposition to your uniting yourself to a profession which has caused so much privation and separation in families, that you would desire to do the very act of all others that is the most objectionable to me. . . . I know what the situation of ladies in the army is, and I know that many of them regret that their husbands are in the army, and I believe also regret that they ever placed themselves in a situation where they suffer so much. Several ladies here have had to live in one room without doors or windows, with the sun pouring in upon them continually. . . . Yet this is but a fair specimen of many frontier posts.

"Suppose you were to marry a Lieutenant. You would have to go to a company where his pay could hardly give you a miserable living, with a house that a man in civilized society would actually be ashamed to keep a horse in. . . . It is a perfect vagabond life, and one that is hard enough for a man to bear without incumbering himself with a family, and if I were to live this life over again, I never, never would think of marrying as long as I remain in the life of the army.

"In regard to Mr. Hill: I know but little of him. He seemed to be a gentlemanly man, and if he was not in the army but engaged in some business that would insure you a comfortable home, I should not have so much objection. . . . There are plenty of men who have wealth and position in society, who are equally as agreeable as Mr. Hill and would make you full as good a husband. . . . I do not desire you to marry a man that you cannot love, but there are a plenty of men whom you can love who are perfectly unobjectionable to me and your mother, and I am confident you will be able to find such.

"You have only to wait until you meet such a one and you will be happy. You have been gratified in every wish except this, and I think it is no more than right that you should pay some little regard to the opinion and wishes of your parents. I feel too

Mrs. Randolph B. Marcy

Fanny Marcy

Mary Ellen Marcy

Courtesy Mrs. Michael J. Kernan

proud of you to have you throw yourself away or to marry a man
who cannot place you in a prominent position in society, and I
was greatly grieved when I learned that you had allowed yourself
to go directly in opposition to my wishes. . . . If I am not mistaken,
I asked you if Mr. Hill was not with you too often and expressed
my entire disapprobation of such attention from him, and that
you led me to believe that you would not encourage him or any
other officer. I thought I could confide in you and that I had
nothing to fear, but I find instead of that you must have been
holding out encouragement to him from the time I left. . . .

"This matter has made me exceedingly miserable, and I resolved when I first read your letter to leave you to your fate, but
subsequent reflection has changed my feelings and I am sorry
that you should suffer for a moment, but I think that when you
reflect upon it you will say that I am right. . . . I have written a
letter to your mother and given instructions to go with you into
the country and remain there. I forgive you, but I shall expect
that you at once abandon all communications with Mr. Hill. If
you do not comply with my wishes in this respect, I cannot tell
what my feelings toward you will become. I fear that my ardent
affections will turn to hate. Do nothing therefore, my dear, dear
child, without choosing between me and him. If I cannot trust
you, whom can I trust?"

One week after Marcy wrote the above letter, he regretted
his stern remarks and attempted to make amends. "I have passed
many unhappy moments in thinking that I caused you pain," he
stated on June 3, 1856. "If Mr. Hill has sufficient means to support
you without his pay, I should look upon the matter more favorably.
. . . I think you had better wait for several months and then see
what your feelings are toward Mr. Hill, and what his are for you.
In the meantime, I will make inquiries about his circumstances
and shall make no promises except that if I find he has not enough
money to make you independent in the event of his death, I shall
refuse my consent. I have myself but little besides my pay and
that is very small. If I had only expended my pay since you commenced going to school, I should not have been able to meet half
my expenses, and while I was with you last winter our expenses
were three times the amount of my pay, so that you see the importance of wealth. You do not know the suffering attended upon

want or poverty because you have never experienced it, but they are great."

As the next few weeks moved slowly on, Marcy anxiously awaited further news from Mary Ellen, particularly concerned about her reaction to his strongly worded letter of May 28, 1856. Although he tried hard to avoid the subject of Lieutenant Hill, he never let an opportunity pass in subsequent letters to Mary Ellen to mention some sordid aspect of army life: "There is another consideration . . . which will, I am confident, have some influence with you. It is the almost total absence of anything like religious services or observances of the Sabbath."

Marcy apparently made no effort to be subtle in his attempts to impress upon his daughter the advantages of wealth and position in society. "After a girl is married to a man, she identifies herself with him, and if he is poor or occupies a low position in society, she goes down irretrievably to the same level. But on the contrary, if she makes choice of a man of high standing or wealth, she is courted by all and all are her friends. . . . For instance, look at the ladies connected with people of elevated positions in Washington and see how much more they are courted than others more deserving. What do you suppose would be known of Miss Cass if she were not General Cass's [Lewis Cass, then senator from Michigan] daughter, nothing. . . . This you will say is a very cold and heartless world, and this is true, but nevertheless, it is very pleasant to be looked up to and flattered, and if I am not mistaken you are of a temperament like others in this respect and would not wish to be treated coldly."

Meanwhile, Lieutenant Hill presented his own case to his prospective father-in-law. "I have received a letter from Mr. Hill," Marcy informed Mary Ellen a few days later. "He says he is worth about $10,000. This is something, but not much. I have not yet answered his letter."

How much Marcy objected to Hill because of McClellan is difficult to determine, but his attitude toward Hill obviously was partly the result of his disappointment in respect to McClellan. "Although I should not have objected to your marrying Captain McClellan," he observed in a letter to Mary Ellen on June 12, 1856, "yet I had no great desire for it after he went back into the life of the army, as the same hard fare would have awaited you as with other officers. His talents and well-known high character, with the warm friendship which exists between us would have caused me to discard all other considerations and given you to him."

At last the father's persistent efforts to break up the "affair in Washington" began to bear fruit. Mary Ellen succumbed to family pressure, writing her father that she would be governed by her parents' wishes in regard to Lieutenant Hill. Marcy was overjoyed and replied by return mail on July 31, 1856: "My dear daughter, I always had the most unbounded confidence in your integrity and purity of purpose and this act of sacrifice on your part only tends the more fully to confirm my opinion. You are a noble, generous girl and I long to take you in my arms again. You are the pride of my heart and a dear good girl."

XIII

"Tired of being kicked about"

1856–1857

T̲HE̲ ̲MATTER̲ of Lieutenant Hill apparently settled, Captain Marcy was happy to let the subject rest. Throughout the remainder of his stay at Laredo he wrote to Mary Ellen about other things, particularly the day-by-day trivia of garrison life. Indeed, several months passed before the subject of marriage for Mary Ellen was mentioned again.

At Fort McIntosh during the summer of 1856, the Texas weather continued hot, and the thermometer hovered around 110 degrees day after day. From June to September there was no rain, and the earth turned into a bed of ashes. Marcy complained that "every wind causes a perfect cloud of dust to blow through every room in the house and even penetrate our trunks." He shared a single room with a fellow officer, Captain James A. J. Bradford, which was not even dignified by the presence of a carpet, while the sum total of the furnishings was a small bureau, dressing glass, three cane-bottomed chairs, one mess chest, a pine washstand with an earthen water jar on top and bottles of claret below, and two narrow cots covered with mosquito bars.

Most of the officers at the Texas post had Mexican servants and maintained their own mess. Food was costly, and ice was almost unknown. Practically every item of food was shipped from the North except the few vegetables that were bought locally at "enormous prices," but the brush country near Laredo abounded with wild quail and deer, and Marcy occasionally found time to supplement his larder of army rations.

198

Each day at the fort followed the same pattern. The commander arose regularly at 6:00 A.M., then bathed, dressed, and ate breakfast. At 7:00 he took dress parade, and by 8:00 was in the Adjutant's office transacting his daily routine duties. By 10:00 A.M., Marcy had retired to his room, "as it is too hot to do anything else." From 4:00 to 5:00 P.M., he studied Spanish with a Mexican tutor, whom he in turn taught English. As sundown approached, the broiling temperature quickly dissipated, and the officers gathered around after mess to exchange stories or to converse with the wives of two of their fellow officers.[1] By 9:00 P.M. another day had passed, and everybody retired to his quarters.

In August, 1856, Marcy received the distressing news from Mary that Mary Ellen's health had taken a turn for the worse and that she had been forced to send her to the seacoast once more for rest and recuperation. Meanwhile, Mary and Fanny remained at Amherst, where Fanny was enrolled in the same school that Mary Ellen had attended and Mary boarded with friends. Such an arrangement proved expensive, and Marcy became concerned about his inability to pay his bills as well as about the state of his daughter's health. His salary, rations, allowances, and extra pay at Fort McIntosh amounted to approximately one hundred dollars a month, all of which he was forced to send to his family. "My income is totally insufficient to sustain the manner of living which we have followed for the past three years," he wrote on August 20, 1856, "and it now becomes necessary to commence a course of life which will accord with my means."

But if Marcy had cause for worry at this period, he at least was to be relieved from the dullness of post life at Laredo by a change of environment. On July 3, 1856, Colonel Albert Sidney Johnston, commander of the Department of Texas, ordered him to attend a court-martial at Ringgold Barracks.[2] This post was located about one hundred miles southeast of Fort McIntosh on the north bank of the Río Grande River, near the small village of Río Grande City. Marcy and his garrison mate, Captain Bradford, arrived there on September 28 to find several old friends

---

[1] One of the ladies was Marcy's sister, the wife of an army officer. It will be recalled that she spent several months with Mary Marcy at Fort Washita in 1851.

[2] Special Order No. 49, *Orders and Special Orders Book, Department of Texas,* 1856, A. G. O.

of early days: Brevet Colonel Caleb Sibley, who had been stationed in Wisconsin and later in Indian Territory with the Marcys; Brevet Colonel Robert E. Lee, whose home in Arlington the Marcys had frequently visited during their trips to Washington; and Major George H. Thomas (later known as "The Rock of Chickamauga"), with whom Marcy had been acquainted since the Mexican War. Indeed, the company was both extensive and pleasant, for most of the officers at the post had their families with them, and as several who came for the court-martial brought their wives along, parties and other social events preceded the serious business at hand.

The matter to be considered by the court was the charge of repeated acts of drunkenness while in the performance of duty against Major Giles Porter, Fourth Artillery. The trial commenced on October 1. Twenty-four days later Colonel Lee doubtless expressed the views of his colleagues when he wrote his wife that "the case is protracted by the presence of two Texas lawyers accustomed to the tricks and stratagems of special pleadings, which of no avail, absorb time and stave off the question."[3]

Despite the tedious prolongation of the trial, Marcy was not exactly without entertainment. The court stayed in session only from nine in the morning until three in the afternoon each day, after which there was time for social calls and many friendly conversations. On October 20, 1856, Colonel C. A. Waite, commander of Fort Ringgold Barracks, gave a large dinner party for the visiting officers and their wives, and Marcy wrote that "the food was very good, consisting of mock turtle soup, roast chicken, ham, boiled chicken, turkey, etc., with potted vegetables from abroad."[4]

When not otherwise engaged, Marcy could always find diversion across the river in northern Mexico. "There are two armies, one of 2500 and the other about half as large, and it is expected they will have a battle today [October 20] at three o'clock," he informed Mary Ellen. "We have a fine position in the Fort to see them and as they are about five miles off we shall be entirely safe.

[3] Douglas Southall Freeman, *R. E. Lee* (New York, 1935), I, 369.
[4] Marcy to Mary Ellen, October 20, 1856, McClellan Papers, 2nd Series, III. Marcy's letters to Mary Ellen written in 1856 and 1857 from Ringgold Barracks and Fort Brown are found in the above volume.

We have seen one of the commanders, General Vidaurri, and as he treated us very politely, our sympathies are rather on his side."

A few days later Marcy referred to the battle again: "The two belligerents are contending for possession of the town of Camargo, which is a miserable place not worth fighting for. Several of us went over there a few days since and called upon the Commanding Officer, whose name is Guadalupe Garcia. He received us very politely and gave us a glass of wine, saying that he was sorry he had not known of our coming as he should have received us more in accordance with his wishes, giving us a dinner. All of which we took for a compliment, as it was intended. . . . I hope my friend Vidaurri will be victorious, as I believe his policy is best for the people."

On October 30, 1856, the trial was transferred to Fort Brown, near present Brownsville, Texas. The journey from Ringgold Barracks to the fort was made in one of the river steamboats then owned by Captain Richard King, subsequently founder of the King Ranch. The arrival at Fort Brown must have brought back memories to Marcy, for some ten years before he had helped construct the log post and a short time later had seen his first military action near by in the early engagements of the Mexican War. But the place had changed some during the past decade. "This is one of the most beautiful and comfortable posts that I have seen on the frontier," Marcy wrote on November 15 to Mary Ellen, who was now fully recovered and back in Amherst. "It is upon the bank of the Río Grande, is built in a square form with cottages all around for the officers and their families and is immediately adjoining a very respectable town."

Major Porter's trial was supposed to have been resumed on November 4, but again there were long delays while the court awaited the arrival of various witnesses from different parts of the country. Fortunately, Marcy was in no rush and took the opportunity to make periodic visits to near-by Matamoros, "a fine city for Mexico." On one occasion he made friends with the local *padre*, who conducted him on a tour of his church gardens and buildings: "We saw quite a few signorittas [*sic*] at their devotion, but they were not entirely devoid of that attitude of your sex [referring to Mary Ellen], as we saw several black eyes turned toward us as we passed. They were prettily dressed with rebosas over their heads and shoulders and were all kneeling gracefully upon the hard tile floor. They are certainly very devout in appearance. The Mexican men do not go to church often and are much more abashed in all respects than the women."

On Sundays, Marcy and his colleagues on the court usually attended in a group either the Catholic, Episcopalian, Methodist, or Presbyterian church at Brownsville. Each afternoon after the court the Captain took a stroll along the banks of the Río Grande, admired the millions of blossoms, the green patches of tomatoes, beans, lettuce, radishes, and potatoes, and sometimes picked a handful of fresh oranges. Occasionally there was a military wedding to attend, and he observed to Mary Ellen that it always made him feel sad to see "a young lady in the fresh bloom of life unite her fate with one who can neither give her a home or his society for any length of time." Obviously Marcy was still worried about Mary Ellen's affair with Lieutenant Hill.

In his frequent letters to his older daughter during this period, Marcy made occasional reference to people Mary Ellen had met. One was a Dr. McCormeek, who arrived at Brownsville in November, 1856, from New York to serve as a witness in the trial. "He said he met your mother and yourself in Washington last spring, and he complimented your mother very highly, but I do not know as you had better tell her of it or she might get very vain. But I will let you try her this time and see how she bears it. He did not compliment you very much, but Colonel Lee does every day, so that is just as well. He says his wife wrote him that you were just the girl he would like. So you see, my darling, that you make an impression sometimes. Colonel Lee is an elegant gentleman and his opinions are worth something."

Brownsville, Texas is located near the Gulf of Mexico, and in the middle of the nineteenth century kept in contact with the outside world through weekly steamers bringing travelers and the latest news. During Marcy's sojourn exciting political events were crowding all other news from the forefront, for 1856 was an election year and the young Republican party was making its first big noise. Marcy's political views appear to have conformed to those of most of the officers in the army in the pre-Civil War years. "We have just received some of the election returns," he remarked on November 15, "and thus far Buck [Buchanan] is ahead, which rejoiced us all and we hope he may triumph and defeat the miserable set of abolitionists, as they are most contemptible and their success could be a most serious calamity to this country. I have no doubt many of the southern states would immediately separate from the Union and form a Southern Confederacy. God grant that this may never happen, as there would be no end to war and bloodshed."

Eleven days later, on November 26, word reached Fort Brown that the Democratic candidate Buchanan had been elected. "What do those abolitionists say now about the President?" Marcy asked. "How do they like the idea of Frémont being defeated? They must be very disappointed. I believe his election would have ruined the army, if not the Union."

Meanwhile, the trial dragged on until Christmas, when Marcy's thoughts turned to memories of home and he longed to be with his wife and daughters. Even so, he and his colleagues were not without the holiday spirit in faraway Texas. "On Christmas and New Year's Day everybody set to work making excellent entertainment set out upon very prettily arranged tables." There were other types of entertainment, too, for a short time before Christmas a shipment of six hand organs reached Brownsville from Germany, and Marcy complained that he and his friends were serenaded "at all hours of the day and night."

By now the Captain had become inured to the life of court-martial duty. For one thing, rumors that he would be sent to Florida caused him much anxiety, and he frankly confessed to Mary Ellen that he would be happy if Porter's case "continued for a full year." On November 25, 1856, the Fifth Infantry had been transferred from Texas to Florida, and those officers of the Fifth who were also members of the court sitting at Brownsville realized that the more quickly they reached a decision in Porter's case, the more quickly they would join their respective companies. "As we shall not be stationed there, but probably be campaigning and marching after Indians through the Everglades, I do not much like the change," Marcy wrote on January 10, 1857. Indeed, he had reason for not wanting to go to Florida, for officers who had served there had complained bitterly about campaigning in the unhealthy swamps against an "invisible enemy."

The struggle in Florida was an old one, dating back to 1836, when the United States attempted to remove the Seminoles to a new home in Indian Territory. The removal was slow and costly—in both lives and money. Although many of the most highly trained United States officers and troops were used against the Indians from time to time, they were never able to bring hostilities to a definite conclusion, and Florida became known as "the graveyard of the army." By 1843, all except an estimated five thousand Seminoles had been removed, but the remainder stayed on to become a thorn in the flesh of Florida settlers. On August 7, 1856, the Seminoles in present Oklahoma agreed to do "all in their power to persuade their brethren in Florida to emigrate and join them in the West." Accordingly, a Seminole delegation went to the Everglade country, but when the members failed in their mission, federal troops proceeded to hunt down the stubborn Indians "like wild beasts."[5]

At long last the trial of Major Porter appeared near its end. On February 18, 1857, the court found him "guilty of the charge of conduct to the prejudice of good order and military discipline." Porter was sentenced to be dismissed from the army, but the court respectfully recommended that he be given favorable consideration for clemency by the president of the United States; and President Buchanan later mitigated the sentence to "suspension for one year from rank and pay."[6]

A few days before the court adjourned, Marcy received a package of letters from Mary and Mary Ellen—the first he had had from them in three months. The event proved most disconcerting, however, for Mary Ellen now reminded him that almost a year had passed since he had promised to reconsider his attitude toward her marriage to Lieutenant Hill. She also suggested that, if allowed to marry Hill, she would no longer be a financial burden to her father.

The letter opened an old wound, and Marcy curtly replied to his daughter on February 4, 1857: "I can take care of my family. . . . You are still young and cannot appreciate the vast importance of making a judicious selection of a husband, but if you live ten

[5] Charles H. Coe, *Red Patriots, the Story of the Seminole* (Cincinnati, 1898), 214.

[6] General Order No. 5, *General Orders, War Department*, 1857, A. G. O.

years longer you will say I am right. I really wish I had an opportunity to take you to one of our military posts for a few days to see what manner the married ladies have to live." Not too subtly, he ended his remarks with this statement: "I am very happy to learn that McClellan has left the army. He will do much better in the business he has taken up. He gets $3,000.00 the first year and $5,000.00 afterwards. This is much better pay than a Captain in the army receives." McClellan had become chief engineer of the Illinois Central Railroad, and in 1858 was elevated to the vice-presidency of the company.

Two weeks after Marcy answered Mary Ellen's latest request, he left Brownsville by steamer and arrived at New Orleans on February 25, 1857, where "many sweet and cheerful letters" from his family awaited him. Two weeks' stay at lusty New Orleans was most welcome to Marcy. He met many old friends, attended the theater, took in the sights of the French Quarter, and "looked in on" several masquerade balls at the St. Charles Hotel. Indeed, every minute was precious, for Marcy realized that soon he would be facing hardship and possible sickness.

During his trip to the North several months previously, the Captain had disposed of part of his landholdings in Wisconsin, and he now discovered that two thousand dollars had been deposited for him in one of the local New Orleans banks. He informed his wife of the sale and that he was "sending the money to a friend in Chicago to put at interest at ten per cent."

The stop-over at gay New Orleans passed much too quickly, and on March 20, 1857, Marcy and a small company of officers set sail on a schooner for Florida. The Captain shared a cabin, six by eight feet, with his old friend Caleb Sibley. The rough sea gave them "a most uncomfortable time indeed," but after ten days they reached Tampa Bay in safety. "I gave General Harney to understand that I wanted active service," Marcy wrote to his friend McClellan a few weeks later, "and was ordered at once on a scout. I started with eight days' rations, a rifle, blanket, pistol, knife, and sundry little fixings, all of which would have made a respectable load for a mule, and waded through the cypress swamp for nine days, but did not find any Indians. This is the most severe service we have ever seen. The 5th has been most actively employed ever since it arrived here and has had several fights, but always without seeing the enemy. They have every advantage and only come to battle when everything favors them. They have killed two men in my company and captured four musician boys. It is not known whether they have killed them or not."[7]

Throughout the months of April and May, 1857, Marcy carried out several scouting forays against the Seminoles, but the army was never able to engage the foe in an all-out battle. It did destroy many of their villages and crops and forced the Indians to be constantly on the move. During the six months of "fighting" probably no more than twenty-five Seminoles were killed.[8] Meanwhile, the Fifth lost twenty-one men in action, while 378 others deserted.[9] After being forced to subsist entirely on alligator meat and palmetto cabbage for several months, the Seminoles finally began to show signs of capitulating. By late spring, 1857, peace at last seemed assured, and Marcy and his fellow officers rejoiced at the prospect of leaving the swamps. Billy Bowlegs, chief of the Florida Seminoles, accepted the terms offered by the federal government a short time later, and the Second Seminole War came to a close.[10]

Marcy gained experience during his brief stay in Florida, for it was only his second time in actual combat in twenty-nine years of military life. Although he was unable to appreciate it at the time, the Seminole campaign supplied physical and spiritual training for the desperate years ahead. Indeed, at the moment Marcy wanted more than ever before to resign from the army. "Should you see any place for me on your road that you think would suit me, I shall take it as a great favor if you will write me," he told McClellan. "I am getting tired of being kicked about and separated from my family."[11]

The Captain remained in Florida for several weeks while negotiations were being conducted with the Seminoles. Meanwhile, the problem of Lieutenant Hill cropped up again. On June 14, 1857, Marcy received a letter from young Hill which read in

[7] Marcy to McClellan, April 24, 1857, McClellan Papers, 1st Series, XI.

[8] *Ibid.*

[9] "Annual Return of Alterations and Casualties Incident to the Fifth," Regimental Returns, 1857, Record Group 94, A. G. O.

[10] Cole, *Red Patriot*, 217–21.

[11] Marcy to McClellan, April 24, 1857, McClellan Papers, 1st Series, XI.

part: "I have heard from truthful lips and with delicacy that Mrs. Marcy's objections (to me) (one at least, and the only one to which I reply) . . . is, that from certain early imprudencies (youthful indiscretions, I suppose) my health and constitution has become so impaired, so weakened that no mother could yield her daughter to me, unless to certain unhappiness. This is the substance, the rest may be imagined. . . . I ask it of you as one gentleman from another, as one officer who has been grievously wronged, from a brother officer who can right him, that you put this matter right in the proper quarter, and that your wife correct this false impression with whomever she may have had any agency in learning it."[12]

Marcy quickly dispatched Hill's communication to Mary, along with a letter which was couched in the most severe language he had ever used with her. "I cannot believe that you would give circulation to such a scandalous rumor, even if it were true. . . . I cannot imagine you endeavoring to injure a man in such a manner. . . . The report is absurd and ridiculous and should meet with a prompt refutation as it would, if made public, injure Mr. Hill very much, and if I could suppose that you would give currency to such rumors, I should insist upon Ellen's marrying Mr. Hill at once, as a just reparation."[13] Mary must have succeeded in explaining the matter to her husband, for no further correspondence on the subject is found among the McClellan Papers.

On the same day (June 16, 1857) that he wrote this letter to Mary, the Captain and the whole Fifth Regiment embarked from Fort Myers, Florida, landing at New Orleans four days later. Marcy promptly informed his family of his arrival and added that he would be at Jefferson Barracks at St. Louis on June 27. He urged Mary and Mary Ellen to meet him there as he expected to be sent to Utah, where he would probably remain for several months.[14]

Marcy did not reach St. Louis until July 2, for his company

[12] A. P. Hill to Marcy, May 29, 1857, McClellan Papers, 2nd Series, IV.

[13] Marcy to Mrs. Marcy, June 16, 1857, McClellan Papers, 2nd Series, III.

[14] Marcy's various letters to Mary and Mary Ellen written during the Mormon campaign are found among the McClellan Papers, 2nd Series, III, IV, and V.

was the last in the regiment to leave New Orleans. Mary and Mary Ellen arrived about the same day, and for the first time in more than a year the Marcys were together, except for Fanny, who had remained in school at Amherst.

The army had been transferred to Missouri at the close of the Seminole War because of impending events on the far western frontier. When in 1848 the United States acquired from Mexico the vast area of land known as the Mexican Cession, there was automatically brought under its control a large Mormon colony in present Utah. The Mormons had left the United States the previous year and had pushed across the Great American Desert to establish an independent nation. Now, with the Mexican War over, they were again a part of the United States and viewed with alarm the altered situation.

Brigham Young, the Mormon leader, decided to act quickly; he called the Saints together to propose a petition to the federal government asking for immediate statehood. In this way, he reasoned, his people could continue to govern themselves, their religious practices would remain unmolested, and they could guard their institution of polygamy. The idea was good—too good, in fact.

From almost every pulpit, platform, and printing press in the United States a chorus of angry protest arose. The Saints saw quickly that Congress would not grant them statehood, and they hastened to change their request to territorial status. The petition was granted on September 9, 1850, when the Territory of Utah was created by Congress. President Fillmore named Brigham Young governor, with three "Gentiles" and three Saints appointed to the six additional territorial administrative posts. But no sooner had the new government been set up than discord arose. The "Gentiles" found themselves outvoted on every issue and treated with contempt by the populace. Accordingly, two of the three "Gentiles" resigned and returned to the East. They claimed that the Saints ignored the official government and looked to Brigham Young alone; they maintained, furthermore, that the Mormons were secretly plotting to establish an independent nation within the United States. The charge touched off another storm of protest against Brigham Young and his disciples, and within a few months the country was flooded with propaganda proclaiming the Mormons to be "lewd, lawless, sinful, and immoral people."

The federal government eventually succumbed to this nation-wide clamor, and in 1857 the President named non-Mormons as governor and other administrative officials for Utah Territory. Also, Congress ordered a strict and immediate enforcement of federal laws and prepared to send several hundred troops to escort the new officials to Salt Lake City. The Saints interpreted the action as a declaration of war.

Thus, the stage was set for what looked like a full-scale battle if the Mormons carried out their threats to resist. Accordingly, the War Department ordered some 2,500 infantry and cavalry troops to Salt Lake City to escort the new officials and to enforce United States laws. The first infantry companies left Jefferson Barracks on July 4, 1857, their immediate destination being Fort Leavenworth, Kansas, while the remaining forces followed in groups of two and three companies. Marcy's own Company D did not depart for the Far West until July 9, 1857. Mary and Mary Ellen accompanied the Captain as far as Fort Leavenworth, as did the wives of several other officers, but all the women save one turned back once this frontier post was reached. Mary and Mary Ellen eventually returned to Amherst to stay until the close of the Mormon war.

Each new separation from his family proved more difficult than the previous one for Marcy. On August 6, 1857, he wrote Mary Ellen from "Camp on Little Blue, 225 miles west of Fort Leavenworth" that he expected to reach Fort Kearney in five days. "We have had rather a pleasant march thus far, but it will soon become cold and I presume we shall suffer much therefrom. . . . I fear that this vile dogs life that I am obliged to lead will prevent me from ever knowing the happiness of having a home. We are nothing more than gypsies, wandering from place to place and living in the open air. How much I wish I had chosen some other profession."

Four days later, on August 10, he was able to send another letter, by a courier returning to St. Louis, in which he reported that his company had just arrived at Fort Kearney. He described this frontier post as "a rock in the midst of the ocean," situated in the center of a desolate prairie without timber or mountains to relieve the monotony. In 1857, Fort Kearney consisted of three stone and log buildings occupied by one company of the Sixth Infantry, two officers, and one assistant surgeon and his wife. The latter, incidentally, was the only resident white woman in a radius of several hundred miles. Marcy observed that Mrs. Burns, wife of one of the officers in his company and the only white woman who accompanied the army to Utah, was the first female, other than Indian women, whom the assistant surgeon's wife had seen in six months.

After a few days' rest at Fort Kearney the troops continued along the old Oregon Trail toward the next outpost, Fort Laramie. Each morning the men were called out from their sleep at 5:00 A.M., and the first duty for the day was the watering of the animals for the long march ahead. Meanwhile, fires were built, breakfast prepared, and the tents and baggage loaded in the heavy wagons—every man having a specific duty to perform. After a quick meal of bacon, coffee, flapjacks, and molasses, the mules were packed, horses saddled, and oxen hitched to the wagons. By six o'clock every man, animal, and wagon had taken his position in line, and the signal was given to move forward. Some fifteen or twenty miles farther on, the train halted for the day. Again the stock was watered and grazed, wagons unloaded, tents erected, and the noon meal prepared.

Marcy and two fellow-officers camped together, and it was their good fortune to have two Negro servants—Simon and his wife, Charlotte—to manage their meals. "Our lunch usually consists of cold ham, bread and butter. . . . We then lay [sic] down and take a nap for a couple of hours and have dinner and tea about sunset."

The next outpost along the monotonous trail was Fort Laramie, which they reached on September 2, 1857; here the train rested for four days. "This is a little better place than Fort Kearney, but still it must be horribly lonesome in winter," Marcy reported to Mary Ellen. "They tell us that they do not have a mail for six months sometimes. . . . Living at such a place as this is a perfect state of banishment. They spend every winter here without seeing a face except those about them and they might all die or the remainder of the world might all die and be buried for six months and they would know nothing of it."

This post, like the others on the road to California and Oregon, had been a stopping place for immigrants for more than a decade. Situated in the valley of the Laramie River, it contained one large

Salt Lake City, Utah, one year before the Mormon War.

From Frank Leslie's Illustrated Newspaper, *August* 23, 1856.

Fort Bridger, Wyoming, named for the famous scout, Jim Bridger. From this fort Marcy's relief expedition traveled 634 miles to Fort Massachusetts, New Mexico.

two-story house occupied by the commanding officer. Surrounding this building were several smaller structures which served as quarters for the officers and enlisted men, and the whole appearance was much like that of a plantation—except for the absence of fields of cotton and tobacco. Colonel Hoffman, the commander of the post, and two of the other officers there had their families with them, so that there was a very limited amount of social life at Fort Laramie in 1857.

The more Marcy saw of army life, the more determined he was to protect his beloved daughter from it; by now the matter was becoming an obsession with him. "I hope my sweet child," he wrote, "that you will reflect maturely before you ever think of uniting your fortune to anyone in the line in the army. For I should be much pained to see you placed in the situation that Mrs. Burns is at present. She is dragged along from day to day with her child. They suffer exceedingly and are very sick of the trip as I expected they would be. It serves her right as she had no business to come. She is in the way and a nuisance to the regiment at the present time as any other lady would be."

Five hundred miles west of Fort Laramie stood the famous old Fort Bridger, but this leg of the journey was the most difficult yet and took seventy-four days. Not until November 22, 1857, were all of the infantry companies safely through the South Pass and assembled near the site of the trading post that Jim Bridger had built in 1843 on the Green River. At near-by Camp Scott the troops went into winter camp. Although the present cantonment was only 112 miles east of the Mormon capital, several factors prevented the army from making further progress now, the principal difficulty being the lack of mules and horses. In crossing the mountains between Fort Laramie and Fort Bridger, more than half of the seven thousand animals had frozen to death or starved because of the deep snows and the impossibility of obtaining fodder.

Marcy poignantly described the events: "It was most pitiful to see the suffering of the poor brutes as we abandoned them to die on the road and left them to the tender mercies of the wolves, and many glances of commiseration and sympathy were cast toward them as we passed on and left them. I presume there was not a hundred yards of road that was not strewed with the poor

211

dead or dying creatures for several days of the march, but unfortunately we had not the power to do anything for them. All this might, however, have been avoided if Colonel Alexander, the former commanding officer, had followed my advice, as I predicted this several weeks before it occurred and showed him how to avoid the catastrophe which has come upon us, but he was then controlled by other councils and he now believes that I was right in the course I recommended."

Meanwhile, the Mormons had not been sitting idly by. Several months before, Brigham Young had issued a general proclamation to the people of Utah: "We are invaded by a hostile force, who are evidently assailing us to accomplish an overthrow and destruction. . . . Our opponents have availed themselves of prejudice existing against us, because of our religious faith, to send out a formidable host to accomplish our destruction. . . . We are condemned, unheard, and forced to an issue with an armed mercenary mob, which has been sent against us at the instigation of anonymous letter writers, ashamed to father the base, slanderous falsehoods which they have given to the public—corrupt officials, who have brought false accusations against us to screen themselves in their own infamy, and of hireling priests and howling editors, who prostitute the truth for filthy lucre's sake. . . .

"Therefore, I Brigham Young . . . forbid: First—All armed forces of every description from coming into this Territory, under any pretense whatever. Second—That the forces in said Territory hold themselves in readiness to march at a moment's notice to repel any and all such invasions. Third—Martial law is hereby declared to exist in this Territory from and after the publication of this proclamation and no person shall be allowed to pass or repass into or through or from this Territory without a permit from the proper officer."

There is little wonder that the tension-wrought Mormons were guilty of a number of atrocities, in view of the Governor's bombastic proclamation. The most brutal incident occurred at a place called Mountain Meadows in September, 1857, when the Mormons ambushed and massacred 140 immigrants en route to California. A few days after the event, news of the massacre reached Colonel E. B. Alexander, commander of the troops to which Marcy's company was attached. And as the army approached Fort Bridger, it was intercepted by a Mormon courier who presented Colonel Alexander with a copy of the proclamation and a letter from Brigham Young. Young declared that the officer was violating his orders forbidding entrance into the territory, and at the same time candidly remarked that he was still the chief executive of Utah. "I now direct that you retire forthwith from the Territory by the same route you entered," Young continued. "Should you deem this impracticable, and prefer to remain until spring . . . [near Fort Bridger] you can do so in peace and be unmolested on the condition that you deposit your arms and ammunition with [the] Quarter-Master General of the Territory, and leave in the spring as soon as the condition of the roads will permit you to march."[15]

Colonel Alexander ignored Young's dictatorial words, and despite the loss of his animals he pushed on to Fort Bridger. Not long thereafter news of the incident reached the rest of the country; reaction was swift and direct. "While we may regret the loss of life that is likely to follow this madness of these deluded people," wrote the editor of the *Santa Fé Weekly Gazette*, "yet we cannot but regard their action as a blessing to the cause of truth, for it must result in their extinction as a people in the United States. The honor of our country, and humanity itself, imperatively call for the assertion of the supremacy of our land, let the cost be what it may. The day of doom of Mormonism, we trust, is fast approaching."[16]

Even though Colonel Alexander was not particularly frightened by Brigham Young's threats, he nevertheless was forced to accept the "invitation" to spend the winter on the Green River. This action was dictated solely by expediency, for not only was the army woefully short of animals, but the weather was unusually severe and the troops faced a desperate shortage of supplies.

Soon after winter quarters had been established, Colonel Albert Sidney Johnston of the famous Second Cavalry arrived at Camp Scott to assume command of all the military forces. Marcy had known Johnston by reputation during his recent services in Texas when the latter was commander of the Department of Texas

---

[15] Brigham Young's proclamation and letter to Colonel Alexander were published in full in the *Santa Fé Weekly Gazette*, December 26, 1857.

[16] *Santa Fé Weekly Gazette*, December 19, 1857.

(from April 1, 1856, to May, 1857). "Colonel Johnston . . . has not been with us long enough for us to form an opinion as to how we like him," Marcy observed on November 20, 1857. "He is a very gentlemanly social man but has not yet had much experience as a military man."[17]

The day after Johnston's arrival, Colonel Philip St. George Cooke reached Fort Bridger with Alfred Cummings, the new governor of Utah, and six companies of the Second Dragoons. The total forces at Camp Scott now included ten companies of the Fifth Infantry, ten companies of the Tenth Infantry, eight companies of the Second Dragoons, and one light and one heavy battery of Forty-fifth Artillery. "We have a long winter before us and shall no doubt find it exceedingly dull. . . . When all the troops reach here we shall have quite an army, and if we were in Salt Lake City in good quarters we might have as pleasant a winter as could be expected away from our dear ones at home. I think the Mormons will all run away and leave the country next spring. If so, we shall not be kept in Utah long."

By the time all the companies had reached Camp Scott, Mormon guerrilla forces had already carried out several harassing attacks and had destroyed at least two supply trains carrying a large quantity of stores. The enemy had also succeeded in driving off some cattle and mules, and the position of the troops now was precarious.

Soon after his arrival Colonel Johnston saw that his situation could become desperate, and he began to consider the feasibility of sending a force southwest across the mountains to New Mexico for additional animals and supplies, which would enable him to renew the march to Salt Lake City in the spring. The most pressing need was for horses for the Second Cavalry (dragoons), pack-mules for the infantry, and salt for both men and animals. The last item was so scarce that on one occasion two quarts fetched fifteen dollars in camp. The Quartermaster Department had thoughtfully supplied the army with large copper kettles for evap-

---

[17] Colonel Albert Sidney Johnston was graduated from West Point in 1826. He resigned from the army in 1834, but re-entered for a brief period in 1846. Again in 1849, he was back in uniform and served on paymaster duty until 1855, when he transferred to the Second Cavalry. Marcy's evaluation of the officer's military experience at this time seems valid. Johnston was killed in the Battle of Shiloh, Tennessee, April 6, 1862.

orating salt from the saline waters of the Great Salt Lake, but it had neglected to include a single pound for immediate use. "If we are compelled to eat our bread without salt," one of Johnston's soldiers wrote, "we can do so at least with the consolatory reflection that we are not likely to die of scurvy—for old Jim Bridger says that the reason why the Indians and mountain men are not subject to the disease is, that they never use chloride of sodium as a condiment."[18]

Before long each man was rationed to three-quarters of a pound of bacon and thirteen ounces of flour each week, but even this ration could not be maintained for many weeks. Rumors began to circulate through the camp that Captain Marcy would be ordered to march at the head of a small force to New Mexico and bring back relief supplies. The prospect of an arduous journey across the Rocky Mountains during the middle of winter did not daunt the experienced and competent Marcy: "If I go I shall have three officers and (100) men and I think it will be much to my credit," he told Mary Ellen. "Moreover, I shall be much more comfortable there than here. . . . We have had some severely cold weather and the thermometer stood one morning at 16 degrees below zero. I had a great many clothes on my bed but was quite cold. I pity the poor soldiers who have but few clothes."

Colonel Johnston issued the anticipated order to Marcy on November 24, 1857, and three days later the Captain struck out across the snow-covered wilderness at the head of a company of forty soldiers (all volunteers), twenty-five mountain men, and sixty-five mules. The command carried rations for thirty days, and its immediate destination was Fort Massachusetts, New Mexico, 634 miles southeast of Camp Scott. Jim Bridger pronounced the venture impracticable, and Bridger was not a man whose opinions on such matters could be taken lightly. But Marcy knew that the welfare of his comrades, indeed the successful outcome of the whole Mormon campaign, depended upon his ability to reach New Mexico. "The gallant Captain will have a hard road to travel," remarked a correspondent for the *New Orleans Picayune*, "but no better officer for the service could have been found."[19]

[18] (Unsigned) December 1, 1857, *New Orleans Picayune*, Marcy's Scrapbook.
[19] *Ibid.*

215

XIV

"A very heavy responsibility"

1857–1858

CAPTAIN MARCY'S JOURNEY from Camp Scott in present Wyoming to Fort Massachusetts, approximately ninety miles north of Taos, New Mexico, has seldom been surpassed in human privation, hardship, and suffering. With good reason, newspaper editors throughout the country in 1858 proclaimed it one of the most remarkable and successful ventures on record.

The general course which the relief expedition took was southwest from Fort Bridger across the northeastern corner of present Utah, over the Uinta Mountains and through the southwestern part of present Colorado to the Cochetopa Pass, thence due south to Fort Massachusetts. In addition to the forty soldiers, twenty-five mountain men, four or five Mexican packers, and two guides, one woman was also a member of Marcy's party and shared in all the hardships. She was the Indian wife of the then well-known Tim Goodale, one of the guides. The other guide was Jim Baker, an even more famous mountain man and a former companion of Kit Carson and Jim Bridger.

When the command departed on November 27, 1857, six inches of snow had already taken uncontested possession of the entire valley surrounding Camp Scott, but Baker and Goodale were of the opinion that no more than two feet of it would be encountered in the mountains. As they also believed that the journey to Fort Massachusetts could be made in twenty-five days, Marcy felt confident that a thirty-day supply of rations would be ample.

"A very heavy responsibility"

The expedition reached the base of the first range of mountains, Uinta, in one or two days, to find the path obliterated by two feet of snow. Mere survival now became the foremost concern of all. Marcy followed the advice of his mountain men to divide his large company into small groups of two or three persons and directed them to construct separate bivouacs at night. Each party dug a hole through the snow and ice about seven or eight feet square and covered the bottom with soft pine twigs, over which a blanket was spread. A forked stick was set upright at each end of the pit to support a horizontal pole, and pine limbs and brush were placed on the windward side to make a "lean-to." A fire in one corner warmed the occupants, and indeed they were much more comfortable in these snug shelters each night than on the march during the day.

Upon reaching the far eastern bend of the Green River in the extreme northwestern tip of present Colorado, Marcy rediscovered the sheltered valley known today as Brown's Hole. Here, twenty-five years before, Fort David Crockett had been built as a fur-trading post, but all that remained in 1857 was the crumbled walls—"mute evidence of the passing of the hectic days of the fur trade."[1] From Brown's Hole the party ascended a winding canyon for several miles until it emerged upon a large plateau which separated the waters of the Green from the Grand (Colorado) River. "Here we found three lodges of Digger Utes," Marcy recorded, "and engaged one of them to act as guide over the mountains."[2]

The Ute rapaciously took the knife, powder, lead, and paint that was offered him in advance for his services, but despite the caution the commander had taken in placing a guard over him, he deserted during the first night in camp. The loss of him was sorely felt, for none of the mountain men had traversed this country during winter, and the deep snows now disguised all the fa-

[1] See LeRoy R. Hafen, "A Winter Rescue March Across the Rockies," *The Colorado Magazine*, Vol. IV (1927), 7–13, for an account of Marcy's journey through Colorado in 1857–58. By identifying many of the landmarks along the way, Professor Hafen has succeeded in establishing the approximate route of Marcy's party.

[2] Marcy's narrative of the journey was subsequently published as *House Doc. No. 88*, 35 Cong., 2 sess. The story of the adventure is also told in his *Army Life on the Border*, 224ff. Unless otherwise specified, all quotations in this Chapter are taken from the official document.

miliar landmarks beyond recognition. Nonetheless, Marcy had no alternative but to continue, knowing that the men at Camp Scott depended upon his reaching New Mexico. The expedition trudged through the thick blanket of snow in single file until it reached the southernmost edge of the plateau, where the tablelands ended abruptly. Some two thousand feet below the top of the present Book Cliffs (approximately twenty miles west of Glenwood Springs, Colorado), the travelers could see the Colorado River slowly meandering toward the southwest.

The evening shadows were already approaching rapidly, and Marcy knew that it would be foolish to attempt a descent to the valley until morning. Therefore, he ordered his men to make camp on the edge of the plateau; meanwhile, the mountain man Jim Baker was sent forth to search for a possible trail that could be taken the following day. Baker did find a trail and returned triumphantly to camp late in the evening to report his fortunate discovery and to receive the warm compliments of his commander and the hearty backslaps of his comrades. The following morning the most dangerous part of the journey thus far began. Cautiously the men and animals picked their way down the narrow, slippery trail; occasionally, one of the pack mules lost its footing and rolled thirty or forty feet before lodging on a tree or large boulder. But eventually the base of the precipice was reached, and the tortuous labor was all the more rewarding when a beautiful green valley was discovered. Here they encamped for the night.

On December 8, 1857, the command reached the banks of the Gunnison River, which Marcy called the Bunkara, near the site of modern Delta, Colorado. The deep, turbulent waters of the Gunnison were covered with jagged chunks of ice, which made the task of fording it extremely uncomfortable and difficult. Once the men and animals had crossed this barrier safely, they bivouacked near the ruins of another fur-trading post, Fort Robidoux, to dry their clothes and rest for the night. According to the commander's calculations, they had now traveled 160 miles and were within a short distance of the western base of the Rocky Mountains. This tremendous range, "the backbone of North America," could be seen to the east of the old post, "covered with ice and snow."

Near the site of the encampment they met another band of Ute Indians, whom Marcy described as a "ragged, villainous-looking set that subsisted chiefly upon rabbits, bugs, and crickets." Their women flocked around the Americans and attempted to steal everything that came in their way. When Captain Marcy tried to persuade the chief of the band to guide his party to Cochetopa Pass, he met with cool indifference, which even the tempting offer of valuables equivalent to three good horses would not change. Instead, the Ute only shook his head, pointed to the distant mountains, and shivered as with cold. No amount of talking could have been more expressive.

Despite the Indian's insistence, by sign language, that the travelers would surely die if they attempted to cross the mountains, Marcy brushed him aside and unhesitatingly ordered his men forward. His immediate concern now was to locate the headwaters of the Gunnison, for the guides had told him that the only practicable and known pass across the Great Divide in the present latitude was to be found near by. This pass was known to the mountain men and Indians as "Kutch-e-tope," and that is what Marcy named it in his journal and on his map. Today it is called Cochetopa Pass, or Pass of the Buffaloes.

The Gunnison has more tributaries than fingers on a giant hand, and every man in the party realized that failure to follow the right one could be disastrous, as indeed John Charles Frémont had discovered nine years before when his ill-fated expedition lost 120 mules and eleven men in an unsuccessful attempt to find the same Cochetopa Pass. Undoubtedly the knowledge of this catastrophe bore heavily upon the minds of Captain Marcy and his comrades when they began the ascent of the western slope of the Rockies on December 11, 1857.

As they approached the edge of the timber line, the snow gradually became so deep that it brought progress almost to a standstill, and the icy crust on the surface cut the legs of the animals until many of them refused to go on. Marcy realized that he was now at the crisis; he must either turn back or devise another order of march. Painful as it was, he had no alternative but to order the men in front in single file to tramp down the snow and break the trail so that the pack mules and horses could be led forward. The difficult work was equalized by having one man retain the lead position for a certain distance, then permitting him to turn out of the track, allowing the others to pass him. When the powdery snow became too deep for the lead man to walk upright, he continued on his hands and knees.

In spite of all these efforts to save the starving animals and conserve their strength, some still became too weak to walk and consequently died along the way. Even when loads were lightened and all surplus baggage discarded, losses continued to be heavy. "One day we lost five mules and another day as many as eight died out of our little stock. This gave me very serious uneasiness," Marcy wrote, "as our supply of provisions was becoming very small, and I knew after these were gone our only dependence for subsistence must be upon our famished animals. Our beef cattle were nearly all consumed, and our stock of bread was very limited."[3]

Several days before the summit of the Rockies was reached, the entire supply of rations was exhausted, making it necessary for the men to subsist solely upon the flesh of the starving mules and horses. The first animal to be killed was a small colt belonging to Tim Goodale's wife. The poor woman cried bitterly over the loss of her pet, but Marcy consoled her with the promise that he would buy her another as soon as they reached New Mexico. For the next several days the only food to be had was the less appretizing carcasses of the animals as they became too exhausted to be of further use.

There were other misfortunes, too, when twelve of the men had their feet frozen one night, so that they were unable to walk, thus placing an added burden upon the poor beasts that had to carry them. The commander even gave up his own horse to one of the crippled soldiers and took his turn blazing the trail. Despite the enormous quantities of mule meat that was consumed, appetites remained insatiable. The absence of salt left the meat tasteless until it was eventually discovered that by sprinkling a little gunpowder on the broiled steaks, a not too extensive imagination was required to fancy the presence of both salt and pepper.

New Year's day of 1858 was the most disheartening day yet experienced. The travelers, wallowing through five feet of snow, covered only two miles in ten hours, and from their bivouac that night they could see the smoldering fires of their last encampment.

[3] Marcy, *Army Life on the Border*, 232.

Everyone by now was so completely exhausted that Marcy doubted their ability to reach the pass; indeed, many of his men were practically barefooted. The commander cut so many pieces from his coat to protect his feet and legs that it hung on him in shreds, but mostly the men mended their clothing and shoes with green mule skin—a poor substitute indeed. To add to the miseries of cold and hunger, the blinding glare of the white landscape proved unbearable until the men blackened their faces with charcoal or gunpowder. Hardship followed upon hardship, but the most disconcerting one of all came when the supply of tobacco was exhausted. No substitute could be had, and those who were accustomed to use it suffered greatly.

Yet, through all the suffering, every man performed his duties without a murmur. "I feel for them from the bottom of my heart," Marcy recorded in his journal, "and I should be recreant to my duty as their commander if I neglected to give expression to my profound gratitude for the almost superhuman efforts put forth by them to extricate the party from our perilous position."

Days passed and the commander became even more troubled with the dread suspicion that he was following the wrong course. His chief guide, Jim Baker, likewise became less certain of his knowledge of the country and observed to Marcy that the landmarks were so obscured that it was impossible to determine the exact location. Fear mounted among the men as time went on. The commander was unable to sleep at night despite his weariness, and this lack of rest, plus inadequate food caused him to drop from 170 to 130 pounds in weight.

Finally, as matters progressed from bad to worse, a young Mexican packer, Miguel Alona, who heretofore had remained rather quiet, approached the Captain to offer his opinion that the command had long since taken the wrong route. Marcy studied Miguel's face carefully as he pointed toward a depression in the mountains at right angles to their course and declared that it was the Cochetopa Pass. Questioned further about his source of knowledge, the Mexican declared that he had traveled through the region before and had seen the pass from various angles. Marcy then offered Miguel the position as principal guide and promised him a handsome reward in addition to his regular salary if he could lead them to Fort Massachusetts. At the same time he informed the newly hired guide that if at any time he discovered he was taking them in the wrong direction, he would hang him to the nearest tree. Miguel took several minutes to think over the proposition and, figuring that he had nothing to lose but his life, finally replied in a confident voice, "I'll risk my neck on it, Captain." And so he did.

Nine more days passed, and somehow the travelers managed to keep struggling forward, but on the tenth day they were on the summit of a mountain which Miguel pronounced to be the crest of the long-sought Cochetopa Pass. "Although I was by no means certain he was right," the commander wrote, "yet I was much rejoiced, and I now felt in a great measure relieved from the burden of responsibility which had given me such anxiety and distress of mind during the last days and nights." The snow at the crest of the pass was not as deep as along the slopes recently traversed, and to the east could be seen a vast plain stretching for many miles. Miguel declared that they were gazing upon the valley of the Río del Norte, beyond which loomed a tremendous peak (Mount Blanca) which was barely visible to the naked eye. The peak was still some seventy-five snow-covered miles away, but somewhere close by was Fort Massachusetts—as everyone well knew.

Only three good mules were left of the original sixty-five that Marcy had started with from Camp Scott, and he now ordered Miguel and another Mexican packer to take them and ride to Fort Massachusetts and bring back supplies as rapidly as possible. He expected that the two would return in six or seven days, and after they took their leave, the main party pushed forward as rapidly as they could. Eleven days passed, and then late in the evening out of nowhere the two Mexicans rode joyously into camp on fresh horses, their revolvers ablaze in the air. Everyone joined in the celebration at once—some laughing, dancing, and screaming with delight, while others, including the commander, cried openly and unashamed, like children.

Miguel and his companion reported that three supply wagons were behind them, while from their pockets they produced several large plugs of tobacco and cast them among the delirious men like happy children feeding a flock of chickens. When the supply wagons arrived the next day, the commander was forced to post a guard over them to prevent the half-crazed men from seizing the food and gorging themselves to death. Then he ordered a fire built and a large kettle of soup put on to boil. Among the luxuries sent by the commander at Fort Massachusetts was a jug of brandy, and Marcy reasoned that the occasion was proper to indulge his men in a moderate toast while awaiting their first adequate food in over two weeks. The drink took immediate effect upon the starved soldiers and mountain men, and many became crazily drunk, but Marcy felt no inclination to censure them.

Each man was eventually rationed to coffee, butter, bread, and one cup of thick soup. Marcy sternly forbade them to eat any more for the time being because of possible harmful effects. Nevertheless, several men did manage to steal food and gorge themselves during the night, and their identity was revealed the next morning when all became violently ill. One of the men died a few hours later—ironically, the only fatality of the expedition.

On January 18, 1858, four days after obtaining the fresh supplies, the party reached Fort Massachusetts. This post was situated on the lowest branch of the Sierra Blanca Mountains in present San Luis Park. It had been established there in 1852, but a few months after Marcy's arrival in 1858, it was moved six miles farther south and renamed Fort Garland. The journey across the snow-covered mountains from Camp Scott to Fort Massachusetts had taken fifty-two days instead of the anticipated twenty-five. And what a sad picture the bearded and hollow-eyed men presented upon their arrival! More than half were without caps, none had shoes other than mule skins or blankets wrapped around their feet, and their trousers were worn out at the knees from crawling over the ice and snow. Yet the hospitality of the New Mexico garrison quickly dissipated all memories of the past two months.

From Fort Massachusetts, Marcy speedily marched his crew to Taos, New Mexico, where he paid off the civilian packers and bade them farewell. Remembering his promise to reward Miguel if he could lead them out of the mountains safely, Marcy now presented him with an additional five hundred dollars, which he believed would prove sufficient to supply all his wants for a long time. Imagine the Captain's surprise when Miguel approached him the next morning and asked for a loan of five dollars. The commander anxiously inquired if he had been robbed, to which

Miguel sheepishly answered, "No, but me lose him all at monte, messieur." Marcy did not approve of gambling, but he could not refuse the little hero's modest request; nevertheless, he gave him a stern lecture on the folly of his ways. Miguel thanked him for the money and advice and berated himself for being so foolish, but as he turned to walk away, he shrugged his shoulders and observed philosophically, "Maybe so sometime me win, messieur."[4]

Doubtless the Mexican actually said "*señor*," but Marcy, who knew more French than he did Spanish, set it down "*messieur.*"

As soon as Marcy had recovered from the ill effects of the journey, he wrote to Colonel Johnston at Camp Scott to inform him of his safe arrival in New Mexico, and Miguel agreed to take the dispatch back by a different route—along with another more detailed account of the venture, which ultimately was forwarded to General S. Cooper in Washington.[5] Two days later, on January 25, 1858, the commander took time to write Mary that he was well and safe. "It is now nearly five months since I have received a letter from you or Nelly and I have not the faintest idea where you are," he added. "I shall, however, direct this to Amherst as usual and send it by an ox train which travels at the rate of about twelve miles a day, so I suppose you may get it about 40 days from this time."

Marcy then observed that by the time he could return to Camp Scott, additional troops from Fort Leavenworth would probably have joined Johnston's forces there. "We shall then have enough men to whip all the Mormons in the United States, and if there was ever a holy war it is the one to be waged against them as they are the vilest and most debased people on earth. They are a set of murderous robbers and highwaymen and deserve to be annihilated. . . . We shall have about 450 men in our party [on the return to Fort Bridger] and if they come near us we shall most certainly fire upon them and destroy all we can."[6]

Marcy's recent exploits were not long in being reported by the press. "This daring and adventurous undertaking by Captain Marcy cannot fail to add fresh laurels to his already national repu-

[4] *Ibid.*, 249.
[5] Marcy to Cooper, January 23, 1858, Letters Received, File No. 72M-58, A. G. O.
[6] McClellan Papers, 2nd Series, I.

tation as a brave and skillful and determined officer," observed the *Santa Fé Weekly Gazette* on January 30, 1858. Indeed, the forty-six-year-old Marcy had again captured the admiration of the nation and was proclaimed "the hero of the Mormon War." Practically every large newspaper in the country, from New York to New Orleans and San Francisco, devoted several columns to a detailed account of the hazardous journey, and each praised the commander of the expedition for his unswerving devotion to duty.

When General Scott received official notice of the successful journey from Camp Scott to Fort Massachusetts, he wrote immediately to the Secretary of War, now John B. Floyd, and said, "In my opinion Captain Marcy has again richly earned, by gallantry and good conduct the rank of major by brevet."[7]

Marcy's intimate friend George B. McClellan read the story of the daring feat with much interest, and it provided an excellent excuse to write to Mary Ellen: "He has made the most difficult journey ever made by an army officer, and I do not see how they can avoid promoting him if new regiments are raised. What a contrast his conduct presents to that of Frémont. My Captain did not desert his men, but stood by them nobly and shared their hardships. . . . One of these days I shall have to tell you in strict confidence—if you care to listen—why I left the services; I fear you will laugh heartily at me."[8] The letter could not have been better timed, for Mary Ellen had recently and finally given up Lieutenant Hill for good. She answered McClellan's letter—her first message to him in three years.

Captain Marcy remained in New Mexico for several weeks, during which time he continued to write frequently to his wife and daughter the details of his visits to the principal settlements throughout New Mexico to purchase animals for the army. Ultimately, he assembled some 960 mules and 160 horses, and by the middle of March, 1858, he was ready to begin the long trek back to Camp Scott. Meanwhile, Colonel Johnston could do nothing about the Mormons until Marcy arrived with the animals.

"It is believed the army will commence operations against

[7] Scott to Floyd, May 29, 1858, Letters Received, File No. 17A–58, A. G. O.

[8] March 17, 1858, McClellan Papers, 2nd Series, V.

Salt Lake City by the 1st of May," remarked the *Santa Fé Gazette* on February 20, 1858, "and we presume will have it in their possession in a short time thereafter. It is not known what course the Mormons will pursue. If they fight as well as they boast, Colonel Johnston will have some trouble." A few weeks before (January 8, 1858) this same exuberant editor had written: "If the war proves to be a reality we wish to be counted in. We have an itching to see a live Mormon—one who can endure the chatter and melody of a dozen wives and twenty or thirty little musical boxes. What a luxury it must be to have one better-half to comb your hair, another to mix your toddy, another to do this and another to do that, the whole interspersed with an occasional solo from a dirty, squalling baby! Ah! Precious privilege! We certainly shall see some of the beauties and mysteries of Mormondom if we have half a chance."

By March 6, 1858, Marcy's work was almost done, and he wrote to Mary Ellen from Mora, New Mexico, that he would depart soon with a company of 250 men. "I shall have a very heavy responsibility in the charge of the large number of animals that I take back," he added, "but if I am fortunate in not losing many of them it will be much to my credit as they are of the utmost importance to the future movements of the army of Utah. I shall take wagons with me and a very fine carriage, which a gentleman has presented me here, so that I shall be very comfortable. I shall have tents and shall take sufficient provisions so that I will not be under the necessity of eating any more mules or horses. I shall probably be at Fort Bridger in about two months from the time I leave here."[9]

Within ten days after writing this letter, Marcy had assembled his cumbersome company of men and animals at Fort Union, New Mexico, in final preparation for departure. In addition to the thirty-nine soldiers who had survived the march across the mountains the previous winter, Marcy now had a party of 140 mountain men, teamsters, and camp followers. Despite such a heterogeneous crew, the party was well equipped and organized to travel swiftly. The route to be followed northward from Fort Union was along the Front Range of the Rockies by way of Raton

[9] All of Marcy's remaining letters to his wife and daughter of his stay in the West are to be found in the McClellan Papers, 2nd Series, V.

Pass and present Pueblo, Colorado. By March 27, the company had already moved about 250 miles, when Marcy received orders from the commander at Fort Union to halt immediately to await reinforcements. The express rider who brought these instructions also explained to the Captain that Colonel Johnston had learned from a soldier recently held prisoner by the Mormons that the enemy planned to organize a force and capture the horses and mules before they reached Johnston's army. Accordingly, the commander at Camp Scott rushed orders to the commander at Fort Union to send Marcy as many reinforcements as he could spare.

Even before Marcy received orders to await military reinforcements, Colonel W. W. Loring had already departed from Fort Union with a force of 194 troops. This officer, like Marcy, was an experienced traveler, and his adventures in some respects were to be even more extensive. In 1861, he resigned from the United States Army to become a brigadier general in the Confederate Army and fought through the Civil War. From 1865 to 1869, he lived in New York, and then entered the services of the Khedive of Egypt, assuming command of all Egyptian coastal defenses in 1870. He fought in the Abyssinian war in 1875–76, and eventually was elevated to the rank of pasha.

Colonel Loring did not arrive at Marcy's camp until April 30, 1858. Meanwhile, the Captain remained pleasantly situated on a tributary of the Arkansas within sight of Pikes Peak at a place called *Fontaine qui Bouille* (Boiling Springs) Creek, not far from present Colorado Springs. Although he was slightly disconcerted by the delay in reaching Camp Scott, Marcy as usual made good use of his leisure time, for the region was truly a hunter's paradise. Indeed, the great number of elk, mountain sheep, grizzly bear, black or white-tailed deer, and antelope were a joy to behold, and he could have supplied the whole camp with choice game solely by his own efforts. When not exploring the country or hunting big game, the Captain passed the long hours writing letters to his family.

At this time, Marcy took occasion to compose the first of many articles that were subsequently published in *Harper's Weekly* and the *New York Tribune*. The following excerpt from the first one seems to contain a prophetic touch: "My travels through an unsettled territory have been somewhat extended, yet I have never before met with so striking a natural curiosity [as the *Fontaine qui Bouille*]. The water issues from a solid sandstone rock, that has been worn out by attrition into the shape of a huge symmetrical bowl or reservoir. The column of water rushes up with great force but never to overflowing; and it resembles an artificial fountain more than a natural one. What the mineral constituents of the water are we have no means of determining. It had to my taste a great similarity to Congress water, but is more agreeably pungent and delicate; and I have no doubt if the locality was accessible to the people of the Eastern States it would soon become more popular than the Saratoga waters. Who knows but what this may some day become a rival watering place?"[10]

With the long delayed arrival of Colonel Loring's command on April 30, the various companies presented a formidable array of wagons, men, and animals, and en route the train stretched out more than two miles in length. According to official War Department records there were now 233 troops, with even more civilians. In a letter to Mary Ellen dated May 13, 1858, Marcy stated that the combined forces exceeded six hundred men and that they expected to reach Camp Scott in five or six weeks.

Near disaster struck the command during the first day after Loring's arrival when a sudden severe storm caught everyone unaware. Marcy later described it as the most violent freak of nature he had ever witnessed, and stated that the men and animals were compelled to flee to the nearest grove of trees to keep from being blown away. Some three hundred horses, mules, oxen, and sheep frantically stampeded and traveled more than fifty miles before they stopped. Three experienced mountain men were sent to recover the stock, but lost their way in the blinding snow. One of the men, when eventually found, was severely frostbitten and had been without food for four days. He was crawling about on his hands and knees in a state of hysteria. The second member of the party apparently became bewildered soon after leaving camp and wandered in a circle, for his body was recovered only two hundred yards away. Still another was found dead some three miles distant, where he had stopped to build a fire. The exhausted man probably had lain down in the snow and gone to sleep, for his body was almost entirely consumed by the fire.

[10] Scrapbook.

More than one hundred animals perished during the storm, but all the others were finally rounded up and brought back to camp. The expedition then set forth again, continuing northward until it struck Cherry Creek. The stream was followed to a point where it flows into the South Platte near the site of modern Denver, and here a halt was called while rafts were made to ferry the heavy supply wagons across the turbulent waters. During the delay on the banks of the South Platte, one of the civilian teamsters washed from the sands of Cherry Creek a small amount of gold dust. In relating the event several years later, Marcy observed that the man was ultimately discharged and returned to St. Louis, where he told of his discovery. "Within a short time the miners commenced to flock to the locality and eventually laid out the town of Denver. . . . I feel quite confident that the representations made by our discharged teamster in St. Louis and other places were the origin of the location and establishment of a new city and Territory."[11]

Apparently the employee referred to by Marcy was George S. Simpson, a trader who had been in the mountains for several years. In after years Simpson claimed such a discovery and emphasized its importance, but tradition has it that the man who started the Pikes Peak gold rush was William Green Russell, who arrived after Marcy had passed through.[12]

When the South Platte had finally been conquered on May 14, 1858, the caravan continued along its same well-marked route —the "Cherokee California Trail"—and skirted the grassy eastern slope of the Rockies until it reached the *Cache la Poudre* Creek three days later. Not far from present Greeley, Colorado, the road began to bear to the left and ascend into the mountains until it reached Medicine Bow Creek. Ten miles west of this stream the travelers struck a section of the trail then known as Bryan's Road and followed it to the North Platte. Once across this stream the expedition was only two hundred miles due west of Camp Scott, which it reached on June 10, 1858. According to the odometer attached to the wheel of one of the wagons, Marcy had completed 762.5 miles since leaving Fort Union eighty-six days before.

[11] Marcy, *Army Life on the Border*, 263.
[12] LeRoy R. Hafen (ed.), *Pikes Peak Gold Rush Guide Books of 1859*, *Southwest Historical Series*, IX, 47.

The Captain and all the company reached Camp Scott in good health, and with the exception of the severe hardships encountered on the initial journey, Marcy somehow escaped serious illness. By now his weight was back to its normal 170 pounds and he could boast that he had never felt better. Doubtless he could not say the same about his appearance. "I have a beard of two years growth some eight inches long," he wrote Mary Ellen on the day of his return, "and my wardrobe would not, I fancy, exactly conform to the present modes of Broadway—my laundress is a soldier who scorns the use of starch and smoothing irons, but he manages to scrape off some of the dirt and this is the main consideration."

Pleasing rewards awaited the gallant traveler at Camp Scott. There was a thick bundle of letters from Mary and Mary Ellen, the first word Marcy had had from either in more than seven months. Also, Brevet Brigadier General Johnston (recently promoted from colonel) informed him of a complimentary citation forwarded to the Secretary of War and subsequently published in newspapers throughout the country. Better still—as a special recognition for his recent services—General Johnston immediately appointed the Captain "Inspecting General of the Utah Army." "So you see that your Daddy is a man of no little consequence now," he remarked in a half-serious tone to Mary Ellen.

Meanwhile the war against the Mormons had already reached a climax. President Buchanan had issued a special proclamation on April 6, 1858, offering the inhabitants of Utah who submitted to federal laws "a full pardon for all treasons and seditions committed." A peace commission headed by Colonel T. L. Kane, an old friend of the Saints, subsequently had met with Brigham Young and a delegation of officials of the Church of Latter-day Saints. The Mormons agreed to the terms of the President's proclamation, thus bringing to an end the excitement of the past year.

On June 23, 1858, General Johnston and his staff, including Inspector General Randolph B. Marcy, of course, marched at the head of a column of some five thousand troops through the streets of the Mormon capital "with colors flying and bands playing." They passed on through the town without stopping and encamped in a church pasture on the west bank of the Jordon River, and the next day Marcy described the event to his beloved daughter: "We found a mass of houses without occupants. . . . There are very few Mormon men about here but not a single woman or child that I have seen. They must think we are barbarous if they suppose we would harm their women or children. They are rather shy and sulky and I presume they entertain no love for us Gentiles. . . . I have seen Brigham Young's harem where he kept his numerous wives and children. It is a very large and handsome building surrounded by a high stone wall, which very effectively excludes his family from the eyes of all inquisitive outsiders. He must have lived in considerable style."

The army remained encamped near Salt Lake City until July 6, 1858, at which time it was dispersed throughout the Utah Territory to build new military cantonments. Marcy spent most of his first few weeks assisting General Johnston in selecting the military sites and later participated in supervising their construction. By now he could write to his wife, without stuffiness, that he was "recognized as the hero of the Mormon War," and that "there seems to be a very general appreciation of my services and all congratulate me without jealousy." He also told Mary that he had received a letter from General Scott in which "the general-in-chief extended me the most complimentary notice I have ever seen."

Near the end of June, 1858, Salt Lake City had returned to near normal except for the presence of a few soldiers wandering aimlessly about its streets. Yet the Saints were still not happy, and on one occasion an Elder remarked to Marcy that if the army were allowed to mix with their people, every woman within the city would be pregnant within a few months. "If that is the case," he wrote to Mary on July 5, "they must indeed be a very virtuous community and they must entertain a very favorable opinion of military men. . . . If perchance he [Brigham Young] should take it into his head to invite me to tarry overnight with him, what would you advise me to do? I am afraid after being so long virtuous to trust myself among so many pretty women, as many of them must necessarily be in a very suffering condition, and it would be a very severe tax upon my virtue if any of them should make an attack upon it. I think therefore upon reflection that I should decline the invitation."

All soldiers after all wars, when the first fruits of victory have been tasted or the bitter gloom of defeat has worn away, want nothing so badly as to return home. Marcy was no exception, and he received with overwhelming delight on August 7, 1858, the news from General Johnston that he was to be granted a sixty day leave of absence.

The long journey across the continent in many respects marked another turning point in Marcy's adventurous life. Although his military career was far from ended, his pioneering work as an explorer, trail blazer, and map maker was now complete. Soon he would be playing a prominent role in the great conflict between the states, and like hundreds of his fellow officers, he would find himself pitted against former friends and intimate associates. Yet in the fall of 1858, as he rode eastward across the Great Plains to a river steamboat docked at boisterous St. Louis, Randolph B. Marcy had only one thought—his much beloved, much neglected family.

XV

"Destined to hold a high rank"

1858–1868

D URING THE FIRST PORTION of the long journey homeward Captain Marcy was accompanied by Colonel E. B. Alexander, who, it will be remembered, was in command of the Utah expedition until superseded by Albert Sidney Johnston. The two officers parted company at Fort Leavenworth, at which time Alexander presented Marcy with the following commendation: "As we are about to separate and as an act of justice to you: I take great pleasure in acknowledging the high services rendered by you to the army under my command in the latter part of our march last autumn. Which added to your achievements some years ago and during the last winter are well known and have added to your reputation for courage, sagacity, and devotion to the duties of your profession. No officer in the army is more entitled to the high considerations of the authorities in power."[1]

From Fort Leavenworth, Marcy continued by army ambulance with several officer companions to St. Louis, thence he pursued the familiar route by steamer to Pittsburgh, and from there by train to New York where he reported to army headquarters on October 5, 1858. From New York, Marcy must have gone immediately to his wife and two daughters at Hartford, but we do not hear from him again for three weeks. At that time (October 26, 1858), he wrote to the Adjutant General stating that his leave of absence had been extended for two months and that he would remain in Hartford for most of that period.[2]

[1] September 15, 1858. This document is now in the possession of Marcy's granddaughter, Mrs. M. J. Kernan, Clinton, New York.

[2] Marcy to Samuel Cooper, Letters Received, File No. 400M–58, A. G. O.

The Captain's return to the East brought a flurry of notices in the newspapers. Several laudatory articles appeared in the Hartford paper and subsequently were reprinted in Washington, Philadelphia, and New York newspapers. Marcy's record as a soldier and trail blazer was reviewed, and a detailed account given of his recent services in the Mormon war. One editor noted prophetically that "the indefatigable officer is destined to hold a high rank in our army."

On December 1, 1858, the officer's short leave of absence was interrupted when he was appointed by Adjutant General Samuel Cooper to "a court of inquiry to investigate the matter of a complaint of First Lieutenant James St. Clair Morton, Corps of Engineers, against Professor Dennis H. Mahan of the U. S. Military Academy."[3] The court assembled at West Point on December 15, 1858, and among the officers who constituted the board of inquiry was Marcy's former colleague at Ringgold Barracks and Fort Brown, Brevet Colonel Robert E. Lee, who had been visiting his family at Arlington. Another member of the court was Major Robert Anderson, soon to become the well-known Union commander of Fort Sumter.

The charges against Professor Mahan, father of the future naval officer and historian, Alfred Thayer Mahan, were shortly dismissed, and Marcy left for Washington in January, 1859. For several months he had contemplated writing a manual on the subject of campaigning and traveling in the West; he now proposed to Adjutant General Cooper that he be placed on special duty in New York to prepare the manuscript, stating that the firm of Harper and Brothers had already agreed to publish it. Cooper approved the plan and made the requested assignment without hesitation.

The book, which required some eight or nine months' labor on Marcy's part, appeared in October, 1859, under the title *The Prairie Traveler: A Handbook For Overland Expeditions*. A thousand copies, at one dollar each, were purchased immediately by the War Department and placed in the hands of various officers and government officials. Marcy's "literary work" received a number of laudatory and lengthy reviews, the following comment being more or less typical.

[3] Special Order No. 167, *Special Orders*, Vol. VI, War Department, December 1, 1858.

"This little volume, unpretentious and modest in its external appearance, is one of rare value, and comprehends within its small compass an amount of information concerning the routes to the Pacific which will be sought for in vain elsewhere. . . . Being written by one who has passed through every phase of life on the plains and been compelled to encounter and surmount every new difficulty and to contrive means for the accomplishment of a successful journey, it may be received as reliable and treated with the confidence reposed in the scouts between Missouri and the Pacific. . . . Travellers to Salt Lake, Oregon, New Mexico, Texas, Pikes Peak, and California ought not to think of starting without this book. It will answer a thousand questions—put one in the way of complete preparation for the journey, and be a pleasant companion during all the long and weary route."[4]

As soon as he had completed the writing project, Marcy again attempted to transfer from the infantry to some other department of the army where his work would be less strenuous. In a letter to Mary Ellen, whose whereabouts at this time are not quite clear, he stated on August 15, 1859, that he had applied for an appointment in the office of paymaster general but believed that his hopes "appeared dim." Surprisingly, however, his luck was beginning to change, and on August 22, 1858, he received notice of his promotion to major and also of his transfer to the Paymaster Department of the army. Thus, after thirty-one years in the service of a seemingly ungrateful country, the forty-seven-year-old officer at long last was getting the kind of recognition that he most appreciated. His base pay was increased from sixty to eighty dollars a month, with allowances for two servants, three horses, and four rations a day. His only other source of income was whatever he received from his book royalties, plus approximately five hundred dollars a year from investments made after the sale of his Wisconsin lands.[5] The Marcys were better off financially in 1859 than they had ever been before.

Marcy did not have long to wait to assume his new duties in the Paymaster Department. On August 27, 1859, Brigadier

[4] More than two dozen clippings of reviews, or summaries, of the *Prairie Traveller* are found in Marcy's Scrapbook. All of the clippings are undated.

[5] Marcy eventually received a total of five thousand dollars for the land which he acquired while stationed in Wisconsin twenty years previously. This sum was invested for him by a friend in Chicago at 10 per cent interest.

General Benjamin F. Larned, paymaster general, ordered him to report for duty at St. Paul, Minnesota, as quickly as possible. Since he would not be away from home for long periods at a time, Mary and Mary Ellen decided to accompany him and spend the winter in the frontier city. Arrangements were made to leave Fanny at Hartford to finish school, and the other three members of the family prepared to depart on October 10, 1859.

The news of Marcy's recent promotion and anticipated move to St. Paul soon reached his close friend George B. McClellan, now living in Chicago. McClellan hastened to extend his congratulations and to invite the Marcys to stop for a visit with him en route to their new home. "It will give us much pleasure to stay with you in Chicago," Marcy replied on September 16, 1859.[6] McClellan must have been delighted, for five long years had passed since he had last seen Mary Ellen Marcy—and it was she he was most concerned about seeing. During these lonely years, McClellan had remained faithful to her, and there is no evidence that he ever had any interest in any other woman. Indeed, he had held tenaciously to the hope that by some miracle he might win her yet. Mary Ellen, on the other hand, had "played the field" and apparently had already experienced a number of romances.

The Marcys arrived in Chicago by train on October 20, 1859. The meeting between Marcy and McClellan was the first since their expedition together in 1852 to the source of the Red River, but they had kept up a warm correspondence in the intervening seven years. McClellan proudly escorted his guests to his spacious home at Number 1 Park Row, on the shore of Lake Michigan and at the foot of Lake Park. Here he lived with his old West Point classmate, Ambrose E. Burnside, whom he had rescued from bankruptcy a few months before by obtaining a position for him with the Illinois Central Railroad Company. Mrs. Burnside added much to the attractiveness of the McClellan home, and the three seem to have gotten along famously.

By an ironic twist of fate, this intimate relationship would be severely strained by the fortunes of war in 1862, when Burnside, albeit reluctantly, relieved McClellan of the command of the Army of the Potomac after the Battle of Antietam.

McClellan's long-standing adoration for Mary Ellen at last

[6] McClellan Papers, 2nd Series, Vol. V.

kindled a glowing response. Mary Ellen had always liked him. Now, almost immediately, his skillful plans began to bear fruit. The advancing years had made him more mature, and his prominent position in business, his comfortable home on the lake, and his doglike devotion melted her resistance rapidly. Each passing hour brought the two closer together, and as the Marcys prepared to depart on October 24, McClellan asked if he might accompany them in his private railroad car on the long and uncomfortable journey to St. Paul. Randolph and Mary were delighted, and Mary Ellen was by no means averse to the idea. En route the following day, McClellan found his chance and proposed to Mary Ellen. This time he was not refused.

Thus the ardent and—until now—one-sided courtship had reached a climax, although for some reason Mary Ellen insisted that they keep the engagement a secret for several weeks. One of McClellan's biographers states that "seldom in history is found a more beautiful unity, more tender love and understanding, than made complete the happiness and domestic peace of George Mc-Clellan and Ellen Marcy. This is one of the greatest factors in all the remainder of his life, and the loving and devoted wife, after death suddenly had removed him, cherished his name and memory during the thirty years of her widowhood."[7]

McClellan remained in St. Paul until the Marcys had established themselves at a hotel. He was unable to return again until the Christmas holidays two months later, and at that time he wrote to his adoring mother in Philadelphia: "Having accidently found Major Marcy and his family staying here (much to my surprise) I have accepted their polite and unexpected invitation to pass a few days with them. As you suppose, I find them the same good friends as of old—the only drawback is that I have discovered that Miss Nelly is engaged—and you know these fiancées are never half as agreeable to outsiders—so that is the only thing that mars the pleasure of my visit. There is, however, one slightly mitigating circumstance which I neglected to mention—it is that I am the fortunate individual to whom Miss Nelly is engaged."[8]

One other letter found in the McClellan collection telling of

[7] William S. Myers, *General George Brinton McClellan* (New York, 1934), 147.
[8] McClellan Papers, 2nd Series, Vol. VI.

the engagement of George McClellan and Mary Ellen Marcy is even more interesting. Postmarked Hartford, Connecticut, January 10, 1860, it is addressed to "Nelly" and reads in part as follows: "I congratulate you, and I congratulate papa and mama, for they have wanted you to marry Captain McClellan for a long time."[9] The correspondence is signed "Fanny," who was then thirteen years of age and obviously not a stupid child.

The McClellans were married in New York City on May 22, 1860, in "a brilliant ceremony." According to a brief notice in the *Tribune,* distinguished guests at the wedding included "General Scott, Colonel Joseph E. Johnston, and Major Hill." Whether the latter was A. P. Hill, to whom Mary Ellen had once been engaged, is not known, but it is entirely probable that her old suitor, a gallant southern gentleman, was invited to the affair and did actually attend. This speculation is supported by the discovery of a letter in the McClellan collection written several years after the Civil War and signed "E. B. Hill": "I am a brother of General A. P. Hill, who was your old roommate at West Point, and your dear friend during his life. . . . I think you visited our home before the War." It continues with a pathetic reference to the sad fortune of the once proud Hill family and a request for McClellan's help in obtaining an appointment as "Assistant Door-keeper of the Ladies' Gallery of the United States Senate Chamber."[10]

If A. P. Hill did attend his former roommate's wedding, it is all the more ironic that a few months later the two should meet again at Seven Pines and at Antietam. In both instances Hill's troops effected a masterful attack upon McClellan's army and earned for their commander the reputation of being one of the ablest generals of the Civil War.

McClellan and his beautiful bride returned to Chicago early in June, 1860, where they settled down to several months of blissful domesticity. On June 23, Marcy wrote to them from St. Paul that he would soon be transferred to St. Joseph, Missouri. He also reported that Fanny, who had returned with them after the wedding in New York, had been seriously ill, and that she and her mother would visit them at the time of his departure for Missouri.

9 *Ibid.*
10 *Ibid.,* Vol. XXIX.

In September, 1860, McClellan became president of the eastern division of the Ohio and Mississippi Railroad Company and moved his home to Cincinnati. Mary and Fanny went to visit there a short time later. In December, Marcy wrote to his family from St. Joseph that he had been seriously ill for the past several weeks, but that he expected to join them soon.

Events in the early months of 1861 moved swiftly, as they inevitably do when war impends. In April, 1861, Marcy was transferred to Cincinnati to take charge of the pay district recently vacated by Major R. H. Chilton; in the same month his famous son-in-law resigned his position with the railroad to accept the rank of major general in the Ohio Volunteer Militia. "The Young Napoleon of the West," as McClellan soon became known, set about the task of organizing the Ohio regiments with a zeal and imagination that captured the attention of the entire North. On May 3, 1861, he was placed in command of the Department of Ohio, which consisted of the states of Ohio, Indiana, Illinois, and parts of Pennsylvania and Virginia. A few days later, May 14, he was appointed major general in the United States Volunteer Army.

McClellan quickly realized the need for experienced assistants in training and using large numbers of troops, and he made repeated attempts to obtain a staff of competent officers. He was thoroughly grounded in the art of war and knew firsthand how European armies were organized. The office of chief of staff was common in Europe, but had never been considered necessary in our small peacetime army of no more than eleven thousand troops. The functions of the office as previously exercised had been included in the Adjutant General Department, but this department in 1860 was so small that it was unable to perform the increasing demands made upon it.

As the ambitious General's repeated requests for a staff apparently were ignored by the befuddled military authorities in Washington, McClellan wrote directly to President Lincoln on June 1, 1861: "I wish to ask of you the appointment of Inspector General . . . Major R. B. Marcy of the Pay Department with the earnest request that he may be assigned to my command as the chief of my staff. . . . You will double my efficiency if you will find it possible to place Major Marcy in the position I refer to. . . . If Major Marcy cannot be made Inspector General, I hope that he may command a brigade of regulars under me."[11]

Meanwhile, before his appointment was officially approved, Marcy had already assumed the duties of chief of staff on May 21, 1861, at which time he joined his son-in-law at Grafton, Virginia— Mary, Fanny, and Mary Ellen remaining temporarily in Cincinnati. One cannot help but wonder if the brash McClellan now recalled a remark he had made eight years before, when in a letter to his brother John on April 14, 1853, he had expressed his displeasure with Marcy's official report of the Red River expedition, because he had not been given sufficient credit for his part in the venture. "I only hope that he may propose to me to go on another expedition with him," he remarked, "and I should in that case take occasion to decline with a plain expression of the reason why. . . . One of these days I may have that gentleman serving under me."[12] Much had happened since 1853 to change McClellan's attitude toward his former commander, and, indeed, few friendships were ever more affectionate than theirs.

From May to July, 1861, McClellan's campaign in western Virginia met with brilliant and decisive success, and he received the warm plaudits of General Scott, President Lincoln, and members of Congress, and, in fact, the unanimous approval of the supporters of the Union cause. His name soon became a household word, and on July 22, 1861, the day after the Union disaster at Bull Run, he was placed in command of the Army of the Potomac. McClellan's story from there until his removal on November 7, 1862, is too well known to be retold in detail here. As for Marcy, it was more or less inevitable that his military fortunes hinged upon those of his son-in-law. On August 9, 1861, he was promoted to the permanent rank of colonel in the regular army, and a short time later, September 23, he was transferred to the United States Volunteer Army and made a brigadier general, which rank he retained until March 4, 1863.[13]

During the whole time that McClellan remained at the head

[11] McClellan Papers, *Letter Book*, 1861.
[12] McClellan Papers, 2nd Series, I.
[13] The pay of a brigadier general in 1861 was $124 a month, twelve rations a day, three horses, and three servants.

of the Army of the Potomac, Marcy served as his chief of staff, and for several months after his removal, Marcy remained to assist him with his official report. Since the position of chief of staff was new to American military tradition in 1861–62, the duties of the officer were not yet clearly defined. An examination of the *Official Records of the War of Rebellion* reveals the general pattern of Marcy's activities during these two years. For the most part he seems to have been in charge of operations and to have acted in the combined capacities of an executive secretary, courier, public information officer, and liaison between McClellan and the officials of the War Department and the administration.

Also, the Chief of Staff spent considerable time in Washington in a ceaseless effort to obtain more troops and supplies for the Army of the Potomac, sometimes telegraphing the General at field headquarters two or three times daily. He also kept McClellan informed of the various machinations of his personal enemies in Washington—and they were many.

Throughout most of the major battles joined by the Army of the Potomac under McClellan in northern Virginia and Maryland, Marcy remained in the field. Yet in only one instance in McClellan's writing is there a reference to the fact that his father-in-law ever actually directed troops in combat. In reviewing the battle of South Mountain (September, 1862) several years later, McClellan observed: "Marcy met with him [Burnside] and remained there [Middletown] most of the day. I rather think that he really deserved most of the credit for directing the movement, but, with his usual modesty, he would say little about it."[14]

All during the campaigning, Marcy and McClellan shared the same tent and mess, and their relationship remained one of confidence and mutual admiration. In his *Report of the Organization and Campaigns of the Army of the Potomac*, McClellan wrote in 1865 that General Marcy had discharged his various and important duties with great "fidelity, industry, and ability."[15]

When Lincoln was finally forced to remove McClellan, there obviously was no place for McClellan's relative on the staff of the new commander. Marcy shortly became no less embittered than

[14] George B. McClellan, *McClellan's Own Story* (New York, 1887), 583.
[15] George B. McClellan, *Report of the Organization and Campaigns of the Army of the Potomac* (New York, 1865), 60.

McClellan against the administration, and particularly against Secretary of War Stanton, who, perhaps more than any other single individual, was responsible for McClellan's removal. In their vituperative attacks against McClellan's conduct and character, the enemies of the deposed General did not omit the charge of nepotism—in addition to his father-in-law, McClellan had appointed his brother, Arthur McClellan, to his staff.

Marcy never suffered as much abuse as McClellan did; nevertheless, he came in for a share. The radical Adam Gurowski wrote of him: "McClellan makes his father-in-law, a man of *very* secondary capacity, the chief of the staff of the army. It seems that McClellan ignores what a highly responsible position it is, and what a special and transcendent capacity must be that of a chief of staff—the more so when of an army of several hundreds of thousands. I do not look for a Bertheir, a Gneisenau, a Diebitsch, or Gortschakoff, but a Marcy will not do."[16]

Undoubtedly General McClellan's reputation as a soldier has suffered at the hands of zealous Lincoln scholars. In order to build up a man to the status of a demigod, as has been done with Lincoln, it becomes necessary to tear down his enemies. Such has happened in the case of McClellan, and likewise, to some extent, of the men around him.

How much of the blame for McClellan's failure as a commander in the field should be shared by his chief of staff, Marcy? The question is not easy to answer. Indeed, few students of the Civil War have even bothered to raise it. In the first place, McClellan delegated little responsibility to his subordinates, his father-in-law included. Also, at that time, the chief of staff was concerned with neither military strategy nor policy, as he is today, but was more or less an aide to the commanding general. He attended to details of administration and logistics that the commander did not have time to look after himself. Certainly Marcy was not the kind to give unsolicited advice freely, and McClellan was not one to seek the counsel of others.

When McClellan retired from active military service in 1863, Marcy had no alternative but to continue in the profession to which he had devoted his adult life. Sometime early in 1863, his

[16] Adam Gurowski, *Diary, from March 4, 1861, to November 12, 1862* (Boston, 1862), 94.

George B. McClellan

commission as a brigadier general in the United States Volunteers was revoked, and he again assumed the rank of colonel in the regular army. As long as Stanton remained secretary of war, Marcy could expect no favors from Washington officials (especially since the retirement of his old friend General Scott in 1861), and none did he get. In July, 1863, he was "exiled" to the western border and assigned the rather unexciting duty of inspecting militia troops, but he still had friends and supporters, as a clipping from a Washington newspaper reveals: "It will be heard with satisfaction by the country that General Marcy has been reappointed Inspector General by the President. The occasion of his non-confirmation by the Senate is attributed to the fact that he brought to this city a copy of the *Richmond Examiner,* which shows the monstrous losses of the rebels in the battle before Richmond, and therefore operated against the radicals in the great effort to supersede General McClellan."[17]

Marcy remained in the region of St. Louis for the most part until 1865. It is not certain whether Mary and Fanny were with him there, but the absence of correspondence with them during this period in the McClellan collection would indicate that they were. On the other hand, many reports are found in the National Archives (War Records Division) which Marcy made during 1864 to the Adjutant General's Office.

Somewhat typical of these reports is one dated April 6, 1864, in which Marcy reported that rebel bands of guerrillas were causing havoc to Union troops in southern Missouri and northern Alabama: "Troops have been stationed at frequent intervals in the district where these depredations have been committed, but they have been unable to put a stop to them, and but few of the Bushwhackers have thus far been captured. . . . A small number . . . are thus enabled to hold a large district of country in a continual state of alarm." He recommended that the various border states' militia be enlisted as volunteers in the United States service and reorganized. He observed that under the state laws officers were elected by vote of the enlisted men, and thus when they incurred the displeasure of their troops, they could not receive promotion.[18]

[17] Scrapbook.
[18] Marcy to Thomas, Letters Received, File No. 538M–64, A. G. O.

Politics at this stage of the war dictated that the states retain control of their militia, and Marcy's opinions were not shared by his superiors. There is no evidence that anyone even bothered to reply to his suggestions. Perhaps officials in Washington were too engrossed in the all-important campaigns in Virginia at this time, and if so, their lack of interest in the West is understandable.

Marcy soon found a friend who not only would answer his letters but would help him. It was the new supreme commander of the Union Armies, General U. S. Grant. On December 26, 1864, Grant wrote to McClellan that he had given endorsement to "a short leave of absence to Colonel Marcy so that he might go to New York to see his daughter before she sailed."[19] McClellan had been Lincoln's Democratic opponent in the presidential election of November, 1864, and after his overwhelming defeat, on January 25, 1865, he and his wife and infant daughter, Mary, left for an extended tour of Europe.

A short time after Marcy appealed directly to Grant for a leave of absence, he wrote again, on December 24, 1864, asking for his help in obtaining a promotion. "I have been twice nominated by President Lincoln," he remarked, "but in neither case did the Senate act upon it."[20] Grant promptly recommended Marcy's promotion, and this time it carried through Congress. According to Cullum's *Biographical Register*, Marcy was promoted to brevet brigadier general in the United States Army on March 13, 1865, "for gallant and meritorious services in the field during the Rebellion." Thus, a rank befitting his thirty-seven years of service finally came to Randolph B. Marcy.

Shortly after the close of the Civil War, Marcy was sent to New Orleans to inspect the various military establishments and occupation forces in the Gulf Coast District. During his stay in the South, Marcy found time to write several long letters to the McClellans in Europe.[21] These letters reveal a keen insight into the happenings of the day, particularly matters relating to the army, politics, and reconstruction.

19 McClellan Papers, 2nd Series, Vol. XIV.
20 Letters Received, File No. 201M–64, A. G. O.
21 For the most part these letters are found in the McClellan Papers, 2nd Series, Vols. XXIV–XXV.

On May 1, 1865, he wrote from New Orleans to Mary Ellen (in Rome) of his recent visit to Natchez, Mississippi: "Some of the people were still there at the time of my visit, but many of them had gone off into the heart of the Confederacy and were beggars." He then added a rather apt sentence about conditions in the once gay city of New Orleans: "Bailey Smith is here investigating frauds in the government, and I think he finds a rich field, for there has been a great amount of corruption and fraud perpetrated here ever since our troops took possession."

In a letter to McClellan in London a few weeks later, July 5, 1865, Marcy remarked that he had applied to General George Thomas for authority to go home to make his report of the tour of inspection of the Department of the Gulf, but thought it doubtful his request would be granted—"especially if Secretary of War Stanton is consulted." He then reviewed the public squabble involving General Sherman, Secretary Stanton, and General Halleck: "Sherman wrote a letter in which he scores them unmercifully, among other things he says it is very easy for those who have never been under fire to slander those who do the fighting. They remind him of camp followers who sneak in after the battle and rifle the dead. Sherman plays his cards boldly and does not appear to fear them. Sherman's enemies have an ardent champion in that very reputable individual, Mr. George Wilkes . . . who classes Sherman with you and the rest of the traitors of the country. He calls him the Pedestrian General who walked across Georgia and Alabama stealing chickens but without meeting any enemy (a part of which by the bye there is some truth in)."

Marcy also commented at the same time on the recent publication of General Robert E. Lee's report, observing that it contained many complimentary remarks about McClellan, but likewise many errors: "For instance, he says that we had greatly superior numbers on the east side of the Chickamauga at Gaines' Mill, when one of their own writers admits that they had 67,000 after Jackson came up, which [*sic*] we only had, if I remember right about 35,000. Lee admits that you fooled him by going to James River while his dispositions were all made to cut you off from a retreat by the White House. I was always sure of this. He further states that we left our wounded at Savage Station without medical supplies, when abundance of supplies of medicines and provisions were left for all our sick, but they were stolen by the local rebel soldiers when they came up. One of our surgeons who was left behind told me so himself. Lee was probably deceived about this, for I do not believe he would wilfully misrepresent the matter."

Regarding conditions in the South at this period, Marcy observed that everything had quieted down and that guerrilla operations seemed to have ceased almost entirely. "Many of the Confederate officers and men who have returned home are very bitter and far from satisfied with the manner in which the war has ended," he continued. "It is generally thought that the President will be disposed to treat them leniently. Buckner, Magruder, Beauregard, Bragg, and others were in New Orleans and looked very much cast down."

Six weeks later, on August 18, Marcy complained bitterly to McClellan about Stanton's refusal to grant him a leave of absence: "I have worked faithfully in the boiling sun of Louisiana for months, and when I arrived here [St. Louis] I applied for authority to go home and make my report. It was referred to Stanton and the answer as usual was 'No.' Grant is expected here in a few days, when I am going to see him and make a representation to him of my case and request authority from him to refer further applications to his decision. This will be fortified by Sherman, I think from what he has said to me."

General Grant arrived in St. Louis a short time thereafter and, in defiance of Secretary Stanton's orders, granted Marcy a well-earned leave of absence. It is presumed that the Inspector General left soon afterwards for New York, probably to see about the publication of his latest book and to be with Fanny and Mary prior to their departure for Europe early in 1866. His book, *Army Life on the Border,* was published in October, 1866, by Harper and Brothers, and perhaps it is Marcy's best-known work. The reviews were most favorable, and its reception by the general public exceeded the author's expectations. His droll sense of humor is never more apparent than in this volume, and his many anecdotes still make good reading.[22]

22 In addition to one other book, *Border Reminiscences,* published in 1871, Marcy's reports of his five western expeditions were published as government documents. Three of these were book-length narratives.

Not only did the book contain a collection of rare and humorous experiences, but it further established Marcy as one of the best serious writers about the western frontier a century ago. The *New York Times* made the following pertinent remark regarding Marcy and his latest work: "The writer has enjoyed an unusually extended experience on our frontier, on the Great Plains, and in the Rocky Mountains, and is not only a keen and accurate observer, but a good narrator of what he has seen.

"His description of the Indian tribes of the Plains; his account of explorations in new territories; the thrilling history of his trip across the mountains in winter, during the Utah War; his chapter on the habits of western game, and of the proper methods of hunting, together with the humorous incidents in frontier life, constitute a volume of extreme interest and of real instructiveness. The chapter on 'Unexplored Territory' contains much new and valuable information in regard to a portion of the Rocky Mountain range of which very little is known."[23]

Marcy's letters to McClellan throughout the latter's stay in Europe continued their pertinent comments: "The most interesting topic now [July 20, 1866] is the President's veto of the Nigger bill which was the pet scheme of the Sumner faction. It was vetoed and the reasons assigned were most cogent and conclusive, and such as to place the President [Johnson] in direct antagonism with the Radicals forever. It is a document that might have come from you or any other conservative Democrat. . . . If you had been elected President you would have had a sweet time with the radicals in Congress. They would have rode [*sic*] over you rough shod and defeated all you could have done for the benefit of the country, as they are now doing with Mr. Johnson. I think it far better that you were not elected."

General Marcy returned to the West in September, 1866, as inspector general of the District of Missouri. Meanwhile, his whole family was still in Europe, remaining there until sometime in 1866. If his previous years in the army resembled the life of a gypsy, they were nothing compared to the next decade and a half. These later years would be as strenuous and lonely as any Marcy had ever experienced, for he would be required to travel almost con-

[23] Scrapbook.

stantly, inspecting the more than eight military posts in the vast district which stretched as far south as Texas, west to the Rockies, and north to the Dakota Territory.

In the summer of 1868, Marcy's family returned from abroad; Fanny and Mary went to live at Orange, New Jersey, where Marcy had purchased a home on top of Orange Mountain, a few miles west of the city. A short distance away the McClellans ultimately constructed a large, beautiful mansion. These were to be, for both families, their final homes.

XVI

"For the good of the service"

1868–1887

AFTER THIRTY YEARS of married life, living in cold garrison quarters, drab hotels, crowded boardinghouses, and—worse yet—with friends or relatives, Mary Marcy attained the height of her desires, a simple but very beautiful and comfortable home. Unfortunately, the old soldier had little opportunity to share this long-awaited home with her, but even so, Marcy had a place to come back to occasionally.

As he began to slip past middle age into later life, Marcy retained his spritely disposition and love of the outdoors. Except for an increase in weight, he changed little in appearance from his earlier days as an explorer. The luxuriant crop of flowing whiskers gave him a patriarchal appearance, and long years of exposure to wind and sun had left their mark upon his bronzed, wrinkled face. He looked what he was, a true pioneer.

In December, 1868, Marcy was promoted from brevet to permanent brigadier general, a rank he held until his retirement in 1881, and he continued in the office of inspector general throughout the remainder of his career. During these years he traveled literally thousands of miles in the performance of his duties, riding in an army ambulance over long stretches of the West and Southwest from one military post to the other. Wherever he visited, he was duly honored by his fellow officers and old friends, and although he was frequently identified as the father-in-law of General McClellan, there was always the reminder that Marcy had achieved prominence in his own right as an explorer, map maker, writer, and authority on the western Indians.

On the rare occasions that Marcy obtained a leave of absence and returned to his Orange, New Jersey, home, he and Mary were the center of many social activities. The General's large Scrapbook contains clippings of many gatherings of social importance at which the Marcys were either the guests of honor or their presence carefully noted, along with that of other celebrities of the day.

In 1871, Marcy's last book, *Border Reminiscences*, appeared in print, first in serial form in *Harper's Weekly*, and later as a single volume. Although not as well put together as his *Army Life on the Border*, it seems to have had an even wider sale. The *New York Times* called it "by and large a very interesting work." It was largely a compilation of random sketches, "the results of long personal experience in a sphere of life that had heretofore found but few chroniclers." If nothing more, it helped maintain Marcy's position as an author, again bringing to the attention of the general public his standing as a western traveler and his many unique and exciting adventures on the frontier.

Later generations would literally be flooded with adventure stories relating to Indians, wagon trains, buffaloes, and the army on the frontier. Randolph B. Marcy was one of the pioneers on this boundless sea of western literature. His observations of the country and its inhabitants show a keen insight into human nature and a talent for accurate observation and reporting. Despite a limited classical education, he possessed a literary style, an extensive and fluent vocabulary, and—what is more important—an energy for writing.

Marcy's works on the West, particularly in regard to the Indians, likewise reflected a large and dignified point of view. Emerson Hough observed in 1918 that "no one who follows his [Marcy's] pages can close them with anything but respect and admiration. . . . He himself as an army officer looked at the . . . [Indians] philosophically, but his estimate of conditions was exact. Long ago as he wrote, his conclusions were such as might have been given forty years later."[1]

Although he played a prominent role in the Civil War as General McClellan's chief of staff, Marcy is primarily remembered as an explorer, map maker, and chronicler of the West. From

[1] Emerson Hough, *The Passing of the Frontier* (New Haven, 1918), 116–17.

1849 to 1858, he was engaged in five major exploring expeditions throughout the Southwest and the Rocky Mountain areas. His detailed maps, particularly of present Oklahoma, western Texas, and New Mexico, were in most instances the first accurate charts of a previously unexplored region. And his march across the mountains from Fort Bridger, Wyoming, to Fort Massachusetts, New Mexico, during the winter of 1857–58, will stand as one of the most daring feats ever recorded.

Perhaps more than any other man, Marcy deserves to be ranked alongside John Wesley Powell, explorer, writer, and geographer of the late nineteenth century. He was not brilliant in the sense of achieving high scholastic standing in school, but he was catholic in his interests and tireless in his devotion to duty. He gave names to streams and mountains, selected sites for frontier forts, blazed trails, and accumulated a great store of firsthand information about the Plains Indians. He explored the vast unknown region beyond the Cross Timbers more thoroughly than any man of his time, and his contribution to the geographical nomenclature of this region is unexcelled. He was the first Anglo-American to discover and chart the two principal sources of the Red River, the first to explore the headwaters of the Wichita, Colorado, and Brazos rivers, and the first to select a reservation site for the Plains Indians.

In addition, Marcy was the foremost among army officers writing extensively about the trans-Mississippi frontier during the nineteenth century; his observations were based upon personal experience and not upon stories told by others. He was known to a wide circle of friends and readers for his ability to relate droll and exciting anecdotes.

Marcy also was a serious observer of the West in all its various aspects of geography, climate, plant and animal life, and aborigines; even today he is cited by historians as the principal authority on the southern Plains Indians prior to the Civil War. His extensive journeys established him as an authority on travel upon the southern plains years before the coming of the stage lines and railroads.

Two significant events in the General's life occurred in 1878— the election of his son-in-law McClellan to the governorship of New Jersey and the death of his beloved wife, Mary. The last years of Mary Marcy's life were years of unalloyed pleasure, probably the happiest she had known. In her own home she frequently remarked that she had no more to wish for except to have "Ran" with her at all times. But during the winter of 1875–76, she experienced a severe attack of pneumonia and never entirely regained her former health and strength. In December, 1877, while walking down a street in Baltimore, she fell and fractured a leg and was confined to bed. A few weeks later, on January 27, 1878, congestion of the lungs set in and terminated her life after a few hours of unconsciousness. Her two daughters and son-in-law were with her at the time of her death, but General Marcy, who had been absent on duty in the West, returned just two hours too late. Mary was buried at Riverview Cemetery in Orange, New Jersey.

Among the many documents relating to General Marcy in the War Records Office of the National Archives is a brief but significant letter written by him on December 13, 1880. In it he states that he had served continuously in the army for forty-eight years and six months, and trusted that his request to be retired on February 1, 1881, would not be regarded by the President—Rutherford B. Hayes—as incompatible with the good of the service. The request to retire was granted, and the old soldier, now sixty-nine, was at last free to abandon the gypsy life he had lived so fully and so long.

He returned to his home on Orange Mountain to be near the McClellans and his two grandchildren.[2] Soon after the death of her mother in 1878, Fanny had married Dr. Edward H. Clark, a retired physician of New York, and Marcy also kept in close contact with her after his retirement. It is obvious that his attachment for her was as strong as it ever was for his elder and more famous daughter. He now took up the hobby of wood carving and proved extremely proficient in the art, according to Fanny's daughter, Mrs. M. J. Kernan, of Clinton, New York.

Each year until his death, Marcy and his personal physician, Dr. J. L. Seward, and a group of former army cronies went on a big-game hunt to the Rockies, for Marcy never lost his skill with the rifle or his love for hunting. In 1885, Marcy and McClellan

[2] Mary McClellan was born in 1862, and George Brinton McClellan in 1865.

made a seven-thousand-mile trip through the West, combining business with hunting and sight-seeing. They spent several days in Denver, a city that had grown from one settler in 1858, when Marcy camped at the mouth of Cherry Creek, to more than seventy thousand in 1885. From Denver they continued in a private railroad car to California, thence to Oregon and Washington, and ultimately back to New Jersey by way of St. Paul and Chicago. They were honored with special dinners and receptions in each of the large cities where they stopped, and prominent notice was always given to their visits in the local newspapers.

Soon after their return General McClellan suffered a severe heart attack and was forced to retire from active life. Within a few weeks he had another attack, and on October 29, 1885, he died at the age of fifty-nine. He was buried at the other end of the lot in Riverview Cemetery from Mary Marcy. His death was a shock to both his wife and General Marcy—who had loved and admired McClellan as few men are capable of loving another.

In 1885–86, Marcy made his last hunting expedition to the Rockies. Upon his return home he found himself much enfeebled, and he realized that his body, like an old machine, was beginning to wear out. Mary Ellen had recently gone to Europe, but he wrote to Fanny and asked her to come to him. On November 22, 1887, death came to the seventy-seven-year-old traveler. The next day he was buried by the side of Mary, thus ending their long and painful years of separation forever.[3]

Randolph B. Marcy admirably typifies the professional officer during the extended period of the nineteenth century when the United States Army was small and foreign enemies few. It was the era before the American people felt the need of military powers beyond the small forces to quell the Indians on the frontier. The day of narrow specialization and military technicians was still in the future. The army officer then was required to be a "jack-of-all-trades" and frequently was thrown upon his own resources. Military life was sometimes arduous, occasionally dangerous, and nearly always lonely. The uncertainties of future promotions, the

[3] Mary Ellen died in 1906, at the age of seventy-one and was buried by her husband and parents, but Fanny lived until 1920—spending the last twenty-five years of life in widowhood.

low pay, the numerous privations, and the absence of public appreciation made most men abandon the profession early. But in spite of all of this some did stay to make a career of the army, and to those important few we owe much for keeping alive a profession which was sometimes tolerated out of necessity.

Such a man was Randolph B. Marcy.

Bibliographical Note

RESEARCH MATERIALS for this study include principally four general sources: government documents, the Marcy family correspondence, newspapers, and secondary sources. Several thousand government documents were examined in the War Records Division, National Archives, in an effort to secure all of the available official correspondence relative to General Marcy's military career. For the most part this correspondence is filed in the Records of the Adjutant General's Office, 1828–81 under Letters Received and Copies of Letters Sent.

In addition to military correspondence, other government documents that yielded materials pertaining to Marcy's military career are these: Merit Rolls, United States Military Academy, 1828–32; Regimental Returns (Fifth Regiment), 1832–64; Post Returns, 1832–58; General Orders, War Department, 1832–81; Special Orders, War Department, 1832–81; *American State Papers, Military Affairs*, 1828–38. The original official reports of Marcy's five major exploring ventures are also deposited in the War Records Division, National Archives. Two of these reports—the Santa Fé expedition, 1849, and the Red River expedition, 1854—are printed as House and Senate executive documents, and a third report—the journey through Utah, Colorado, and New Mexico, 1857—is printed as a House document. The Inspector General Reports, 1864–81, are particularly rich in materials in Marcy's own handwriting. They comprise reports of the General's many tours of inspection to various western military establishments during the years cited. However, they yield little pertinent information about the man himself and therefore have been used rather sparingly in this study.

Hundreds of references to Marcy's activities during the Civil War are found in the voluminous *Records of the War of Rebellion.* The Cartographic Division, National Archives, also contains Marcy's original maps of the Southwest, as well as the original plans of various forts which he personally designed and other forts on the frontier at which he was stationed from time to time.

Approximately five hundred letters written to or by General Marcy, his wife, and two daughters are found in the Papers of General George Brinton McClellan, 1826–85, Manuscripts Division, Library of Congress. The McClellan collection is tremendous, and the Marcy family correspondence is scattered throughout the 153 bound volumes. This correspondence was indispensable to this study, for it constitutes the nucleus of the information relevant to Marcy's personal life. The Lincoln Papers, Manuscripts Division, Library of Congress, contain approximately two dozen letters from General Marcy to President Lincoln. The private library of the late George B. McClellan, Jr., Washington, D. C., likewise contains several Marcy letters. Also, General Marcy's, granddaughter, Mrs. M. J. Kernan, Clinton, New York, possesses more than thirty family letters which are pertinent to Marcy's biography.

All of the newspapers cited are in the Newspaper Collection, Library of Congress. The information relating to Marcy in the various newspapers examined pertains chiefly to his accomplishments as a recruiting officer, reviews and summaries of his published books, his various exploring expeditions, public lectures, and accounts of social activities of the Marcy family. General Marcy's personal scrapbook, now in the possession of Mrs. M. J. Kernan, contains hundreds of newspaper clippings relative to Marcy's activities and accomplishments from 1846 to 1887.

The three books written by General Marcy between 1859 and 1871—*Prairie Traveller, Thirty Years of Army Life on the Border,* and *Border Reminiscences*—are cited extensively. These works are largely autobiographical and contain much information of an anecdotal nature not found elsewhere. Other published sources consulted frequently are the journals of Marcy's expeditions in 1849

(Marcy and the Gold Seekers) and 1854 (*Adventure on Red River*), which have been edited by Grant Foreman and published by the University of Oklahoma Press in 1939 and 1937. Many works of a secondary nature—most of which are cited in full in the footnotes—yielded information either directly relating to Marcy's career or to the period and region to which he belongs.

Index

Index

259

Index

Democratic party: 6

Denison, Texas: 85

Dent, Captain Frederick T.: 60, 61n., 62, 97

Denver, Colorado: 229, 253

Detroit, Michigan: 11, 14, 17; description, 25, 28ff.; 30, 50

Dickinson, Edward: 6

Dictionary of American History: 7n, 69n.

Doña Ana, New Mexico: 76, 76n, 77, 78, 84, 89, 167, 180

Double Mountain Fork of Brazos River: 83, 84, 116, 178

Doxater, Polly: 21

Duncan, Oklahoma: 153

East Pascagoula, Mississippi: 45

Edwards, James: 61

Edwards' Trading Post: 61, 61n., 72

El Dorado: 56

Elm Fork (Red River): 138, 179

El Paso, Texas: 56, 76, 88, 89, 89n., 90, 101, 114, 116, 122, 123

Erie Canal: 29

Ewell, Benjamin S.: 9

Exploration of the Red River of Louisiana: 164

Federalist party: 6

Fifth Infantry: 13, 17, 21, 28, 33, 35, 40, 44, 45, 45n., 60, 95, 98, 99, 100, 114, 115, 124, 189, 203, 204, 207

Fillmore, Millard: 155, 208

First Dragoons: 60

Five Civilized Tribes, removal to Oklahoma: 47

Flat Top Mountain: 178

Flint, Lieutenant F. F.: 59n., 87n.

Florida: 28, 63, 203–206

Floyd, Secretary of War, John B.: 225, 225n.

Fontaine qui Bouille Creek: 227–28

Foreman, Grant: 58n., 77n., 100n., 132n., 141n.

Fort Arbuckle: 109n., 111, 113, 115, 122, 129, 147, 148, 150, 151, 153–54, 157, 158, 170–72

Fort Armstrong, Treaty of: 12, 17

Fort Belknap, Texas: 84, 89, 116–17, 122, 124, 129, 130, 147, 154, 158, 169, 170, 172–74, 184–86

Fort Bridger: 211, 213, 214, 216, 224, 226, 251

Fort Brown: 201, 203, 234

Fort Chadbourne: 122, 169

Fort Columbus, New York: 45

Fort Crawford: 16, 17, 22, 25

Fort David Crockett: 217

Fort Dearborn, Illinois: 24; *see also* Chicago, Illinois

Fort Garland: 223

Fort Gates: 123

Fort Gibson: 48, 95–99, 117

Fort Gratiot, Michigan: 25, 28ff., 52

Fort Grogan: 123

Fort Holmes: 63

Fort Howard: 13, 14ff., 16, 17ff., 28, 33

Fort Kearney: 209, 210

Fort Laramie: 210, 211

Fort Leavenworth, Kansas: 209, 232

Fort McIntosh: 192, 198, 199

Fort Marcy: 76, 76n., 77

Fort Martin Scott: 123

Fort Massachusetts, New Mexico: 215, 216, 221, 222, 223, 251

Fort Myers, Florida: 207

Fort Phantom Hill: 122, 123, 169

Fort Ringgold Barracks: 190n., 199, 200, 234

Fort Robidoux: 218

Fort Sill: 123, 147

Fort Smith, Arkansas: 46, 51, 52, 55, 57, 59, 60, 61, 62, 64, 73, 76, 77, 82, 87, 89, 92, 93, 94, 97, 99, 100, 101, 116, 122, 123, 126, 153, 157, 158, 167, 170, 171, 187

Fort Smith Company, The: 60ff.

Fort Smith Herald: 58, 158

Fort Snelling, Minnesota: 25

Fort Towson: 46; built in 1824, 48; 50, 51, 52, 53, 53n., 59, 61, 61n.,

Index

Harrisburg, Pennsylvania: 41, 42, 43ff., 105, 105n., 121, 155
Harrison, Benjamin: 66
Harrison, Lieutenant M. P.: 60, 65, 66; death of, 81–82; 85, 87
Harrison, William Henry: 65
Hartfort, Connecticut: 6n., 27, 28, 32, 48, 117, 118, 161, 163, 171, 190, 233, 234, 238
Haskell County, Texas: 178
Hayes, Rutherford B.: 252
Henshaw, Captain J. C.: 153, 154, 157
Hicks, John: 96n.
Highway 69, U. S.: 96
Highway 77, U. S.: 60
Hill, Lieutenant A. P.: 3, 192, 192n., 193ff., 202, 204, 206, 207, 207n., 238
Hill, E. B.: 238
Hitchcock, Doctor Edward: 131, 134, 145, 162
Hoffman, Colonel: 211
Holcomb, Victor: 28
Holdenville, Oklahoma: 61
Hollon, W. Eugene: 123n.
Holmes, Major: 120, 127
Hood, Lieutenant General John B.: 96
Horne, Fanny: 6
Horsehead Crossing: 89
Hough, Emerson: 250, 250n.
Houston, Sam: 189
Hubbard Creek: 117
Humboldt's map of New Spain: 123
Humboldt River: 56

Illinois: 10, 11, 14, 24, 239
Illinois Central Railroad: 205, 236
Independence, Missouri: 73
Indiana: 16, 239
Indianola, Texas: 161, 191
Indian Territory: 56, 77, 85, 95, 96, 97, 114, 115, 117, 129, 131, 136, 173, 200, 203
Irving, Washington: 59

Is-so-Kee (Wolf Shoulder): 70, 71, 72

Jackson, Andrew: 10
Jackson, T. J. (Stonewall): 3, 245
James River: 245
Jane, Negro servant: 50
JA Ranch: 143
Jay Treaty: 29n.
Jefferson Barracks, Missouri: 12, 207, 209
John, Mexican servant: 93, 98, 101, 104, 113, 129
Johnson, Andrew: 247
Johnson, W. Cass: 163, 163n.
Johnston, Colonel Albert Sidney: 3, 96, 199, 213; description of, 214, 214n.; 215, 224, 225, 226, 227, 230, 231, 232, 233
Johnston, General Joseph E.: 238
Joliet, Louis: 17
Jones, Adjutant General R.: 28n., 42, 101n., 118, 133
Jones County, Texas: 122
Jordon River: 250
Jornada del Muerto: 77
Journal of Army Life: 51n., 113n.

Kane, Colonel T. L.: 230
Katy Railroad: 96
Katy, the servant girl: 98
Kearny, Major General Stephen W.: 96
Ke-che-a-qui-ho-no: 142
Ketumsee, Chief: 112, 179, 180, 181, 184, 185
Kellog, Louise Phelps: 18n.
Kernan, Mrs. M. J.: 43n., 61n., 105n., 119n., 233n., 252
Keys, Erasmus D.: 8
Kickapoos: 83, 84, 100, 111, 153, 154
King, Captain Richard: 201
King Ranch: 201
Kingsbury, Mrs.: 53
Kiowa Peak: 177
Kiowas: 47, 67, 82, 84, 124, 150
Knox County, Texas: 176

Index

Pierce, Lieutenant N. B.: 172
Pikes Peak: 229, 229n., 235
Pike, Zebulon Montgomery: 66, 69, 123, 123n.
Pittsburgh, Pennsylvania: 30, 50, 124, 161, 170, 187, 233
Plains Indians: removal of, 47; 48, 59, 63, 67, 113, 116, 156, 165–66, 185, 188, 250
Platte River: 56
Plymouth: 33
Plymouth Rock: 156
Point Isabel, Texas: 37, 38, 39, 41
Polk, James L.: 33, 34, 42
Pope, Captain John: 168, 168n.
Portage City, Wisconsin: 16; *see also* Fort Winnebago
Porter, Major Giles: 200, 201, 203, 204
Port Huron: 31
Post Records: 53
Post Returns: 23, 30, 46n.
Potomac: Army of the: 236, 240, 241
Powell, John Wesley: 251
Prairie-dog-town River: 142
Prairie du Chien, Wisconsin: 16, 22, 24
Prairie Traveler, The: 234–35
Preston Road: 85
Preston, Texas: 85, 89, 116, 126, 127, 129, 173
Pueblo, Colorado: 227

Quartermaster Department: 214
Quatosett, Connecticut: 5; *see also* Woodstock, Connecticut

Raton Pass: 226–27
Records of the Marcy Family: 5n., 6n.
Red Patriot, The Story of the Seminoles: 204n., 206n.
Red River: 46, 48, 49, 76, 79, 80, 84, 88, 91, 109, 114, 115, 122, 123, 124, 126, 128, 129, 130, 131; expedition, 132ff.; 147, 153, 161, 164, 167, 170, 171, 173, 180, 240, 251

Red Springs, Texas: 178
Regimental Returns: 21, 22n., 31, 35, 35n., 44, 45, 45n., 100, 115
Report of the Organization and Campaigns of the Army of the Potomac: 241, 241n.
Resaca de la Palma, battle of: 40
Reynolds, Captain A. W.: 189
Rhode Island: 38
Richmond Examiner: 243
Río Chiquito: 73
Río del Norte: *see* Río Grande River
Río Grande City, Texas: 199
Río Grande River: 33, 34, 36, 37, 38, 40, 42, 62, 77, 88, 112, 222; *see also* Río del Norte
Riverview Cemetery: 253
Rock Island, Illinois: 10
Rock Roe, Arkansas: 158, 160
Rocky Mountains: 62, 168, 215, 218, 219, 247, 251, 253
Rogers, Doctor Julian: 59, 65
Rogers, John William: 85n.
Roxbury, Massachusetts: 5
Ruckesville, Oklahoma: 102
Ruggles, Major: 50
Ruggles, Mrs.: 110, 121
Rush Springs, Oklahoma: 150
Russell, William Green: 229
Ryan, Oklahoma: 130

Sac and Fox: 10, 12
Sackett, Lieutenant Delos B.: 77, 81, 82
Sagerton, Texas: 178
Salt Fork (Red River): 138, 142
Salt Lake City, Utah: 209, 214, 226, 231, 235
San Antonio, Texas: 34ff., 98, 152, 161
San Augustine Pass: 77
San Diego, California: 76n.
San Francisco, California: 89
Sangre de Cristo Range: 73
San Luis Park: 223
San Miguel, New Mexico: 72, 76
Santa Fé, New Mexico: 52, 55, 57,

Index

Tenth Infantry: 214

Texas: 33, 36, 49, 63, 79, 84, 88, 91, 98, 115, 122, 133, 147, 173, 235, 251

Texas and Pacific Railroad: 89–90

Texas Boundary Commission: 136, 137n.

Texas Gulf Coast: 33, 35, 189

Texas, History of: 9n.

Texas Land Commission: 181

Texas Legislature creates Indian reserves: 169ff.

Texas, Military Department of: 191, 199, 213

Texas Panhandle: 67, 122, 136

Texas, Republic of: 32, 85

Thirty Years of Army Life on the Border: *see Army Life on the Border*

Thomas, George H.: 96, 200, 243n., 245

Throckmorton, Texas: 179

Through Unexplored Texas: *see* W. B. Parker

Tierra incognita: 132

Tipton, Oklahoma: 135

Toledo, Ohio: 13

Tolland, Connecticut: 6

Tonkawas: 84, 184

Torrey, John: 134, 162

Towakonies: 184

Treaty of 1819 with Spain: 136

Trenton, New Jersey: 50

Trinity River: 84, 169

Tule Canyon: 143

Turner, W. W.: 135

Tyler, John: 32

Uinta Mountains: 216

Uncle Andrew, Negro servant: 93, 95, 98, 101, 104, 111, 113, 129

Union Pacific Railroad: 89

United States Army: 2, 7, 253

University of Oklahoma Press: 132

Updegraff, Lieutenant J.: 60, 62, 81, 98, 104, 113, 115, 130, 158

Utah, territory of: 208, 209, 216, 226, 230

Utah War: *see* Mormon War

Ute Indians: 217, 219

Van Buren, Arkansas: 57

Vial, Pedro: 132n.

Viameter: 66, 66n.

Vidaurri, General: 201

Virginia: 239, 241

Waco (Hueco) Mountains: 77, 78

Waco Indians: 78, 84, 150, 151, 184

Wagon: 127, 128

Waite, Colonel C. A.: 200

Walnut Creek: 64

War Department: 22, 44, 45, 80, 84, 100, 101, 114, 123, 124, 147, 157, 187, 191, 209, 241

War of 1812: 7, 12, 16, 26

War Records Office: 115, 243, 252; *see also* National Archives

Washington, D. C.: 14n., 33, 58, 124, 164, 234, 244

Washington Intelligencer: 166

Washington *Star*: 134

Washington, state of: 253

Washita Indians: 100

Washita River: 51, 154

Webster-Ashburton Treaty: 32

West Point, Military Academy: description of, 7ff.; 214, 234

West Texas Historical Association Year Book (1938): 122n.

Westward Expansion: 30n., 47n.

Whitall, Captain: 50

Whitall, Mrs.: 99, 110, 121

White House: 245

White River: 158, 161

Wichita Falls, Texas: 109, 130, 175

Wichita Mountains: 131, 132, 135, 137, 138, 147, 148, 153

Wichita River: 176, 178, 251

Wichitas: 47, 84, 135, 137, 148, 150, 151, 153

Wilbarger County, Texas: 175

Wild Cat, Chief: 112

Wild Horse Creek: 110, 113, 115, 153

269

Beyond the Cross Timbers
has been printed from type in the Caledonia face
designed by W. A. Dwiggins. The letter forms are
transitional in character, neither pure old style nor
sharp modern. As the name indicates, the face has
Scotch ancestry, but it is enlivened by the designer's
command of subtle variations.

UNIVERSITY OF OKLAHOMA PRESS

NORMAN